Dress in North America

VOLUME I

William Chamberlin, *Portrait of Benjamin Franklin,* 1762

Dress in North America

VOLUME I

The New World, 1492–1800

Diana de Marly

HM

HOLMES & MEIER

New York   London

Published in the United States of America 1990 by
Holmes & Meier Publishers, Inc.
30 Irving Place
New York, NY 10003

Book design by Marilyn Marcus

This book has been printed on acid-free paper.

Library of Congress Cataloging-in-Publication Data

De Marly, Diana.
    Dress in North America / Diana de Marly.
        p.   cm.
    Includes bibliographical references and index.
    Contents: v. 1. The New World, 1492–1800.
    ISBN 0-8419-1199-1 (cloth : acid-free paper)
    1. Costume—United States—History.   2. Costume—Canada—History.
3. United States—Social conditions—To 1865.   4. Canada—Social
conditions—To 1763.   I. Title.
    GT603.D4   1990
    391'.0097—dc20
                                                                    90-4905
                                                                    CIP

Manufactured in the United States of America

Contents

Illustrations vii

Chronology of Major Events xii

* 1 *

The Discovery of the Indians 1

* 2 *

New England in the Seventeenth Century 27

* 3 *

La Nouvelle France 61

* 4 *

The English Colonies, 1689–1774 85

* 5 *

The United States and Canada, 1775–1800 131

Glossary of Textiles 173

APPENDIX I

*English Cloth and Clothing Exports
to the American Colonies and Canada* 175

APPENDIX II

The Commencement of American Cloth Production 199

Notes 202   *Bibliography* 210   *Index* 216

Color Plates appear between pages 88 and 89.

Books by Diana de Marly

Christian Dior (1990)
Worth: Father of Haute Couture (second edition, 1990)
Fashion for Men (1985; 1989)
Louis XIV and Versailles (1987)
Working Dress (1987)
Costume on the Stage (1980)
The History of Haute Couture, 1850–1950 (1980)

Illustrations

Frontispiece:
Mason Chamberlin, *Portrait of Benjamin Franklin*, 1762
*(Philadelphia Museum of Art, the Mr. and Mrs. Wharton
Sinkler Collection)*

1 *Codex Mendoza (The Bodleian Library, Oxford)*
2 Christophe Weiditz, *Indian Man*, 1529 *(The British Library)*
3 Christophe Weiditz, *An Indian Woman*, 1529
(The British Library)
4 John White after Le Moyne, *A Florida Chief*, c. 1585 *(The
Trustees of the British Museum)*
5 John White after Le Moyne, *A Woman of Florida*, c. 1585
(The Trustees of the British Museum)
6 John White, *A Chief of Virginia*, c. 1585 *(The Trustees of the
British Museum)*
7 John White, *A Chiefe Herowans Wyfe of Pomeoc*, c. 1585 *(The
Trustees of the British Museum)*
8 John White, *The Aged Man in His Wynter Garment*, c. 1585
(The Trustees of the British Museum)
9 John White, *The Flyer or Conjuror*, 1585 *(The Trustees of the
British Museum)*
10 Robert Vaughan, *A Description of Part of the Adventures of
Captain Smith in Virginia* from Captain Smith's *General
History of Virginia*, 1624 *(The British Library)*
11 John White, *An Eskimo Man*, c. 1585 *(The Trustees of the
British Museum)*
12 John White, *An Eskimo Woman*, c. 1585 *(The Trustees of the
British Museum)*
13 Flemish School, *Still Life with Young Woman*, c. 1615 *(Musée
des Beaux Arts de Montréal)*
14 Robert Vaughan, *Matoaka or Rebecca Daughter of the Mighty
Prince Powhatan Emperor of Virginia aetatis suae 21 anno 1616*,
from Captain Smith's *General History of Virginia (The British
Library)*

CHAPTER 1

CHAPTER 2

15 Daniel Mytens, *Carolus magnae Britanniae Princeps, aetatis suae xxiii, anno domini 1624 (National Gallery of Canada, Ottawa)*

16 British School, *The Actor Manager Edward Alleyn, Founder of the College of God's Gift, Dulwich,* insr. 1626 *(The Governors of Dulwich Picture Gallery)*

17 British School, *Mrs. Dirge,* c. 1630 *(The Governors of Dulwich Picture Gallery)*

18 British School, *Edward Winslow,* c. 1645 *(The Pilgrim Society, Plymouth, Massachusetts)*

19 Bartholomeus van der Helst, *Portrait of a Gentleman, 1644 (Musée des Beaux Arts de Montréal)*

20 Wenceslaus Hollar, *Marchants Wife of London, 1642 (The British Museum)*

21 British School, *Mrs. Cartwright's Sister aetatis suae 65 anno domini 1644 (The Governors of Dulwich Picture Gallery)*

22 British School, *Catherine Davenant, Mrs. Thomas Lamplugh,* c. 1664 *(York City Art Gallery, Yorkshire)*

23 American School, *Elizabeth Eggington, 1664 (Wadsworth Atheneum, Gift of Mrs. Walter H. Clark)*

24 David Teniers II, *A Peasant Eating Mussels,* c. 1655 *(The Governors of Dulwich Picture Gallery)*

25 Jan Weenix, *Landscape with Shepherd Boy, 1664 (The Governors of Dulwich Picture Gallery)*

26 American School, *Elizabeth Paddy, Mrs. J. Wensley,* c. 1678 *(Pilgrim Society, Plymouth, Massachusetts)*

27 British School, *A Bagpiper and His Girl,* c. 1670 *(The Governors of Dulwich Picture Gallery)*

28 Egbert van Heemskerck, *The Quakers' Meeting, London,* c. 1685 *(The Trustees of the British Museum)*

29 John Riley, *Bridget Holmes aetatis suae 96 anni (By Gracious Permission of Her Majesty Queen Elizabeth II)*

CHAPTER 3   **30** French School, *The Vegetable Merchant,* c. 1630 *(Musée des Beaux Arts, Chambery, Savoy)*

31 Louise Moillon, *The Fruit and Vegetable Merchant,* s.d. 1631 *(Musée du Louvre, cliché des Musées Nationaux)*

32 Louis le Nain, *Peasant Family,* d. 1642 *(Musée du Louvre, cliché des Musées Nationaux)*

33 Jean Michelin, *The Bread-seller and the Water Carriers,* s.d. 1653 *(Musée du Louvre, cliché des Musées Nationaux)*

34 Michel Dessaillant, *Votive of Mme Reverin and Her Children,*
1703 *(The Basilica of Ste Anne de Beaupré, Québec, Les Pères
Rédemptoristes)*

35 French School, *A Rustic Meal,* c. 1740 *(Musée des Beaux
Arts, Cholet, Maine et Loire)*

36 Antoine Raspal, *A Couture Workroom in Arles,* s.d. 1760
(Archives photographiques des Musées d'Arles, Provence)

37 Matthijs Naiveu, *The Cloth Shop,* 1709 *(Stedelijk Museum de
Lakenhal* [Drapers' Hall], *Leiden, The Netherlands)*

38 Willem van Mieris, *Hurdy-Gurdy Player Asleep in a Tavern,*
d. 1690 *(Baron de Ferrière's Collection, Cheltenham Art Gallery
and Museum, Gloucestershire)*

39 Justus Kühn, *Eleanor Darnell,* c. 1710 *(Maryland Historical
Society, Baltimore)*

40 Anonymous, *Robert Sanders, Later Mayor of Albany, New
York,* c. 1714 *(Abby Aldrich Rockefeller Folk Art Center,
Williamsburg, Virginia)*

41 Anonymous, *Henrietta Maria Tilgham, Mrs. William
Goldsborough and Grandson Robins Chamberlain,* c. 1758
(Maryland Historical Society, Baltimore)

42 John Wollaston, *Family Group,* c. 1750 *(The Newark Museum,
New Jersey)*

43 George Knapton, *Lucy Ebberton,* c. 1755 *(The Governors of
Dulwich Picture Gallery)*

44 François Boucher, *Antoinette Poisson Marquise de Pompadour,*
1759 *(The Wallace Collection, London)*

45 John Singleton Copley, *Mary Mrs. Benjamin Pickman aged
19,* 1763 *(Yale University Art Gallery, Bequest of Edith Malvina
K. Wetmore)*

46 John Singleton Copley, *Isaac Smith,* 1759 *(Yale University
Art Gallery, gift of Maitland Fuller Griggs, 1869)*

47 Mason Chamberlin, *Portrait of Benjamin Franklin,* 1762
*(Philadelphia Museum of Art, the Mr. and Mrs. Wharton
Sinkler Collection)*

48 John Singleton Copley, *Mr. and Mrs. Thomas Mifflin,* c. 1768
(The Historical Society of Pennsylvania)

49 Augustin Brunais, *Free Natives of Dominica,* c. 1770 *(Yale
Center for British Art, Paul Mellon Collection)*

50 Augustin Brunais, *A Planter and His Wife Attended by a
Servant,* c. 1780 *(Yale Center for British Art, Paul Mellon
Collection)*

CHAPTER 4

51 Anonymous, *Israel Israel*, c. 1775 *(Abby Aldrich Rockefeller Folk Art Center, Williamsburg, Virginia)*

52 Anonymous, *Hannah Erwin, Mrs. Israel*, c. 1775 *(Abby Aldrich Rockefeller Folk Art Center, Williamsburg, Virginia)*

53 Antoine Raspal, *Madame de Privat and Her Daughters*, c. 1775 *(Museon Arlaten, Musées d'Arles, Archives Photographiques, Provence)*

54 Ralph Earl, *Representative Roger Sherman*, c. 1770 *(Yale University Art Gallery, gift of Roger Sherman White)*

CHAPTER 5   **55** The Beardsley Limner, *Harmony Mrs. Oliver Wight*, c. 1786 *(Abby Aldrich Rockefeller Folk Art Center, Williamsburg, Virginia)*

56 The Beardsley Limner, *Mr. Oliver Wight*, c. 1786 *(Abby Aldrich Rockefeller Folk Art Center, Williamsburg, Virginia)*

57 Benjamin West, *Benjamin Franklin Drawing Electricity from the Sky*, c. 1805 *(Philadelphia Museum of Art, the Mr. and Mrs. Wharton Sinkler Collection)*

58 Le Clerc, *Creole Dress in Louisiana*, from *La Galérie des Modes*, 1779

59 Le Clerc, *The Queen's Chemise Dress*, from *La Galérie des Modes*, 1784

60 Watteau fils, *Dress in the English Style*, from *La Galérie des Modes*, 1784

61 Pine and Savage, *Congress Voting for Independence* *(The Historical Society of Pennsylvania)*

62 Anonymous, *John Mix*, c. 1788 *(Abby Aldrich Rockefeller Folk Art Center, Williamsburg, Virginia)*

63 Anonymous, *Ruth Stanley, Mrs. Mix*, c. 1788 *(Abby Aldrich Rockefeller Folk Art Center, Williamsburg, Virginia)*

64 The Beardsley Limner, *Young Boy in a Green Suit*, c. 1790 *(Abby Aldrich Rockefeller Folk Art Center, Williamsburg, Virginia)*

65 Edward Savage, *The Washington Family*, c. 1796 *(National Gallery of Art, Washington; Andrew W. Mellon Collection)*

66 François Beaucourt, *Eustache-Ignace Trottier*, 1793 *(The Musée du Québec)*

67 François Beaucourt, *Marguerite Mailhot*, 1793 *(The Musée du Québec)*

68 Benjamin West, *Colonel Guy Johnson with Joseph Brant*, 1776 *(National Gallery of Art, Washington; Andrew W. Mellon Collection)*

69 William Berczy, *Portrait of Joseph Brant*, c. 1807 *(National Gallery of Canada, Ottawa)*

70 Ralph Earl, *Mrs. William Moseley and Her Son Charles*, 1791 *(Yale University Art Gallery; Bequest of Mrs. Katherine Rankin Wolcott Verplanck)*

71 Benjamin Latrobe, *Billiards at a Country Tavern, Virginia*, 1796 *(The British Library)*

72 Benjamin Latrobe, *Travel on Horseback in Virginia*, 1796 *(The British Library)*

73 Benjamin Latrobe, *Sketch of a Classic Group at Mount Vernon*, 1796 *(The British Library)*

74 Benjamin Latrobe, *Another Classic Group at Mount Vernon*, 1796 *(The British Library)*

75 Anonymous, *Deborah Richmond*, c. 1797 *(Abby Aldrich Rockefeller Folk Art Center, Williamsburg, Virginia)*

76 William Hogarth, *Trade Card for His Sisters Mary and Ann Hogarth*, c. 1730 *(The Trustees of the British Museum)*

APPENDIX I

Color Plates

I Jacques Le Moyne, *French Explorer René de Laudonnière with Chief Athore . . . at the Mouth of the St. Johns River*, 1564 *(Print Collection, Miriam & Ira D. Wallach Division of Arts, Prints and Photographs, The New York Public Library; Astor, Lenox, and Tilden Foundations)*

II Pieter Angillis, *Covent Garden*, London, c. 1726 *(Yale Center for British Art, Paul Mellon Collection)*

III Anonymous, *Deborah Glen*, c. 1739 *(Abby Aldrich Rockefeller Folk Art Center, Williamsburg, Virginia)*

IV William Dering (attrib.), *George Booth of Belleville, Virginia*, c. 1748 *(Colonial Williamsburg Foundation)*

V William Williams, *Deborah Hall*, 1766 *(The Brooklyn Museum, Dick S. Ramsay Fund)*

VI Ralph Earl, *Elijah Boardman*, 1789 *(The Metropolitan Museum of Art, Bequest of Susan W. Tyler, 1979)*

VII Gilbert Stuart, *George Washington*, c. 1797 *(The National Portrait Gallery, Smithsonian Institution)*

VIII Anonymous, *Baby in a Red Chair*, c. 1800 *(Abby Aldrich Rockefeller Folk Art Center, Williamsburg, Virginia)*

Chronology of Major Events

1492	Columbus discovers the Bahamas.
1497	John Cabot discovers Newfoundland.
1519	Cortés lands in Mexico. The Indian quilted tunic is adopted by the Spanish.
1540	Vásquez de Coronado explores Arizona and Kansas, and wears Indian cloaks.
1542	The first French settlement in Canada fails.
1580	Francis Drake claims the California coast for Britain.
1585–90	The first English settlement in Virginia fails.
1607	Jamestown is founded.
1608	Québec is founded.
1620	The Pilgrim fathers land at New Plymouth.
1625	The Dutch build New Amsterdam on Manhattan Island.
1634	Boston enacts the first sumptuary law against slashed clothing, gold, and silver.
1638	Boston enacts the second sumptuary law against costly apparel.
1642	Montréal is founded for the fur trade.
1660	English cloth exports to Virginia become regular.
1666	The English three-piece suit for men is established.
1672–73	The mantua gown becomes the uniform for women.
1686–1713	The towering commode headdress becomes the fashion for women.
1698	A great supply of English ready-made clothing becomes available for the American colonies.
1708	England revives hoops, and the fashion for both sexes grows wider.

1709	Textile production starts in New England.
1750	Mme de Pompadour gains fame as a fashion setter.
1755	The English country look influences the French and Americans.
1763	Canada and Florida become British; Louisiana is transferred to Spain.
1767	Boston starts the homespun movement.
1775	The American colonies revolt against Britain, who imposes a trade embargo. Benjamin Franklin gives up wigs.
1783	Britain recognizes the independence of the United States of America. Marie Antoinette introduces the revolutionary chemise dress.
1789	The French Revolution causes many French to cross the Atlantic.
1792	Captain Vancouver reclaims the Pacific coast for Britain.
1795	A new trade treaty is signed between the United States and Britain.
1795–1800	The neoclassical style is established in the United States.

Dress in
North America

VOLUME I

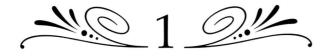

The Discovery of the Indians

The Voyage of Columbus

"Thirty-three days after my departure from Cádiz I reached the Indian Sea, where I discovered many islands, thickly peopled, of which I took possession without resistance, in the name of our most Illustrious Monarch."[1] Thus wrote Cristoforo Colombo, or Columbus, in 1492 to Lord Raphael Sánchez, Treasurer to the joint sovereigns of Spain, Ferdinand of Aragon and Isabella of Castile. The letter was printed in Latin to notify the educated world of the discovery of the Indies, but editors point out that the journey had taken 35 rather than 33 days, so a printer seems to have mistaken xxxv for xxxiii. That Spain, one of the poorest states in Europe, should have backed this expedition was surprising at the time. Other kings had turned down Columbus's project, and Spain had just defeated the last Moorish king on her territory; in April 1491 began the seige of Granada, and on 2 January 1492 the Christian cross was erected in the Alhambra. With the end of the crusade to drive the Moors from Christian Spain, the Spanish crusaders had nowhere else to fight. It was Queen Isabella who saw the possibilities in Columbus's proposals, to sail due west to reach the riches of the Indies. Spain

needed gold to rebuild following the defeat of the Moors, and
Isabella was doubtless impressed by the way neighboring Portugal was exploring the Gold Coast of Africa, returning with
gold and spices. Columbus thought that he could reach the East
by sailing west. Although most educated people agreed that the
world was round, nobody had yet tried to sail around it. But
Columbus's demands for the voyage were not modest: he
wanted three ships, the rank of admiral, a title if he succeeded,
and the post of viceroy in any lands discovered, along with a 10
percent commission on all trade. After two refusals, Isabella
influenced Ferdinand to agree to these demands. Columbus
sailed with the *Niña*, the *Pinta*, and the *Santa Maria*.

Columbus was in origin an Italian from Genoa, and com-
manding Spaniards was not easy. On Friday, 12 October, his
ships reached the Bahamas, and Columbus named the first
island on which he landed San Salvador. The Arawak Indians
received them kindly, and Columbus noted in his journal that
the natives were naked except for some leaves, or a branch or
apron, to cover their private parts. The hair of the Arawaks
looked like horses' tails, hanging down straight, with a deep
fringe over the eyes. They painted themselves in black, red, and
white; and though Columbus did not think to ask if this represented anything, rank in naked societies is indicated by body
paint and patterns. Gold was his chief reason for coming, and
he did not fail to notice the gold pins in their noses. Columbus
called the natives Indians, thinking he was in India, and he
presented them with red hats and glass beads, and received
from them skeins of Indian cotton. At the island of Española,
the chief gave Columbus a wampum girdle of white fishbones,
sewn with colored cottons, with a beaten gold mask at the front.
The Indians told him of a mainland 70 leagues to the west,
where the people wore more clothing, but he did not locate it.[2]
Columbus established a fort and garrison on Hispaniola, then
sailed through stormy seas to Spain, which he reached on 15
March 1493.

The king and queen of Spain created Columbus Count of
Barcelona and organized a second expedition of seventeen
ships, loaded with missionaries, settlers, horses, and cattle.
Sailing on 25 September 1493 Columbus reached the Leeward
Islands in November. His fort he found deserted, for the garrison had left its safety in their quest for gold. On this visit huge
gold nuggets were discovered, which wrecked the idea of an

agricultural settlement because none of the Spanish would plant crops when there was gold to be found. Columbus sent the nuggets back to Spain, with twenty-five Indians, and in 1495 shipped 500 Indians to be sold in the slave market in Seville, thus initiating the transatlantic trade in slaves. He returned to Spain in 1496, but had to wait two years before the monarch would finance another fleet. Columbus still thought he had discovered the route to India, for he wrote to the sovereigns: "Most serene and most exalted and powerful Princes, the King and Queen, our Sovreigns: The Blessed Trinity moved your Highnesses to the encouragement of this enterprise to the Indies."[3]

On his third voyage, he reached Jamaica and thought it paradise. The Indians were fairer here, and wore their hair long and straight like the Spanish. They wore scarves over their private parts, and their heads were bound with colored cotton, reminding Columbus of Moorish headdresses back in Spain. All the Indians wore some decoration on the breast or arm, such as gold or pearls. Columbus then landed in Venezuela, the first European to set foot in South America. His Spanish settlers proved a rebellious bunch, and the monarchs replaced Columbus with another governor. Thereafter, his fortunes rapidly declined. He was granted a fourth voyage in 1502, when he touched Panama, but he was marooned on Jamaica for nine months before the other Spaniards would help him. With the death of Queen Isabella came the end of Ferdinand's patronage. Columbus died disappointed. He had not found the emperor of China or Japan, and Spain was proving ungrateful despite all the new gold he sent her.

The Discovery of North America

Another Italian, John Cabot, discovered North America. Cabot was sent by Henry VII of England in 1497 to find a northern route to the Indies, and landed at Newfoundland. When he returned to England he brought back some natives, who were described by Fabian the historian:

> This yeere also were brought unto the king (Henry VII) thre men taken in the New found Island. These were clothed in beastes skinnes and eate raw fleshe, and spake such speech that no man

could understand them, and in their demeanour like to bruite beastes, whom the king kept a time after. Of the which upon two yeeres past after, I saw two apparelled after the manner of Englishmen in Westminster pallace, which at that time I could not discerne from Englishmen, till I was learned what they were.[4]

Cabot was awarded £10 out of the Privy Purse on 10 August 1497 for finding the new island. Although the fact of his second voyage in 1498 is the subject of dispute, it aroused enough interest to incite the king of Portugal to imitate it. Fifty Indians were taken back to Lisbon, where Alberto Cantino wrote about them to Ercole d'Este, Duke of Ferrara, on 17 October 1501:

Beginning with their size, I say they are bigger than our people, with well-formed limbs to correspond. The hair of the men is long, as we wear it, letting it hang in plaited rings. They have the face marked with great signs like those of the Indians. Their eyes incline to be green, and when they look from them it gives a great fierceness to the whole countenance. The woman has small breasts and a very beautiful body. She has a very gentle countenance, and its colour may be said to be more white than any other tint, but that of the men is much darker. *In fine,* except for the fierce look of the men, they are very like ourselves. They are naked except for a small covering made of deerskin.

The appearance of these Newfoundland, or coastal North American, Indians continued to fascinate European commentators, such as Pietro Pasqualigo, who saw them in Lisbon in 1501:

These are like gipsies in figure, stature and appearance, and are dressed in the skins of divers animals but chiefly otters. In summer they turn the skin inside, and in winter the other way. These skins are not sewn together in any way, nor tanned, but are thrown over the shoulders and arms just as they are taken from the animals. The loins are fastened with some cord made of the very strong sinews of a fish. Although they appear to be wild men, yet they are modest and gentle, and their arms, shoulders and legs are so well proportioned that I cannot describe. Their faces are marked in the fashion of the Indians, some with six, some with eight, some with no lines.[5]

Jacques Cartier described the coastal Indians he encountered after he sailed from St. Mâlo in 1534 to claim North America for France:

> They go altogither naked, saving their privities, which are covered
> with a little skinne, and certaine olde skinnes that they cast upon
> them. Their heads be altogither shaven, except one bush of haire,
> they suffer to grow upon the tope of their crowne, as long as a
> horses taile, and then with certaine leather strings binde it in a knot
> upon their heades.[6]

The women were in hiding when Cartier arrived, but they later
emerged to touch and rub him as their way of greeting. The
tribe ate raw flesh and lived in boats, and were probably the
same as those Cabot had taken back to London. Deerskin and
otterskin coverings differentiated northern Indians from the
Caribs and Arawaks in the south, who covered themselves with
leaves or cotton loincloth.

The Conquest of Mexico

Eventually the Spanish encountered the strongest Indian state
in the region, Mexico, which was ruled by the Aztecs. Cortés
landed in Mexico in 1519, and Prescott described the splendor
that awaited him:

> The dress of the higher warriors was picturesque, and often mag-
> nificent. Their bodies were covered with a close vest of quilted
> cotton, so thick as to be impenetrable to the light missiles of Indian
> warfare. This garment was so light and serviceable that it was
> adopted by the Spaniards. The wealthier chiefs sometimes wore,
> instead of this cotton mail, a cuirass made of thin plates of gold, or
> silver. Over it was thrown a surcoat of the gorgeous feather work in
> which they excelled. Their helmets were sometimes of wood, fash-
> ioned like the heads of wild animals, and sometimes of silver, on
> the top of which waved a *panache* of variegated feathers, sprinkled
> with precious stones, and ornaments of gold. They wore also
> collars, bracelets and earrings, of the same materials.[7]

Prescott writes that Cortés's own troops were wearing Indian
quilted cotton jackets when they attacked Tabasco on 25 March
1519; this was the first Indian garment adopted by Europeans in
the New World.

An Aztec chief, Teuhtile, greeted Cortés with gifts of cotton,
featherwork garments, and a basket of gold ornaments. Cortés
gave him a richly carved armchair for his emperor Montezuma,
along with a cap of crimson cloth embroidered with gold of St.

George defeating the dragon (of paganism). Cortés also presented many cut-glass ornaments, which the Aztecs took for jewels. The chief asked for a gilt helmet, because it was similar to that worn by their god Quetzalcoatl, and Cortés agreed to the request. The Spaniard was amazed to discover one of the chief's staff busily engaged in drawing him and his company, with their clothes and armor, to show later to the emperor. Montezuma ordered the Spanish not to approach his capital, and sent another embassy with gifts. One hundred Indian slaves of the Aztecs carried shields, helmets, and cuirasses of embossed gold, with collars and bracelets of the same, along with fans and crests of feathers. There were cotton robes almost as fine as silk in a variety of bright colors, decorated with featherwork. Thirty loads of cotton cloth were followed by gold and silver animals, and lastly, what looked to European eyes like two carriage wheels of gold and silver, circular plates representing the sun and the Aztec calendar. All this only whetted the Spaniards' gold lust even further.

Body paint was used by the Indian armies, as Cortés discovered when he met the Tlascalan troops: "The common file wore no covering except a girdle round the loins. Their bodies were painted with the appropriate colours of the chieftain whose banner they followed. The feather-mail of the higher class of warriors exhibited, also, a similar selection of colours . . ."[8] Prescott wrongly thought this coloring was similar to that of Scottish clan tartans. However, such tartans are an invention of the Romantic period; the Scots had worn several plaids at once or else stripes.

There was some simple heraldry in Mexico, with the heron on the rock representing the house of Xicotencatl and the golden eagle the republic of Tlascala. But these symbols were different in function from European heraldry. The Aztecs used pictures for writing, and employed the same images on their battle standards to identify a city group. The fact that chiefs painted their followers in their own colors was similar to the practice of wearing livery colors by the retainers of a count or baron in Europe, although this did not refer to the coats-of-arms of European liveries. Both kinds of heraldry evolved out of the needs of battle, as, for example, the Roman legions were identified by their eagle standards in antiquity. From a simple format under the Normans the heraldic system evolved into a sophisti-

FACING PAGE

1 • *Codex Mendoza.* The foundation of Tenochtitlan in 1325 as the Aztec capital is depicted in this manuscript painting. In the upper portion Chief Tenochtli and his warriors all wear mantles. The bottom depicts the Aztecs attacking and enslaving Colhuacan and Tenayuca. The two soldiers wear the quilted cotton tunics that were the first Indian garment to be adopted by the Spanish conquistadores. Slavery existed in the Aztec empire before any European set foot in the region. *(The Bodleian Library, Oxford)*

cated hereditary form in the twelfth century, with a College of Heralds to register grants of arms to nobles, knights, cities, and universities. Because most citizens could not read and write, the visual symbol was important in both the Old World and the New.

Cortés defeated the Tlascalan army, which later joined his allies; many Indian tribes hated their Aztec imperial masters and helped Cortés to defeat them. Later, Montezuma sent more gifts in an attempt to persuade Cortés to go away. Two hundred slaves arrived with 3,000 ounces of gold, several hundred cloaks, dresses of embroidered cotton, and examples of feather garments and work; the invasion force must have looked like an itinerant clothing outfitters. Since the cloaks would have been useful at night, the Spanish may have adopted them. There was

2 • Christophe Weiditz, *Indian Man,* 1529. Weiditz saw these Mexicans in Spain, where they had been carried as slaves and curiosities. The wearing of jewels in holes in the face horrified Europeans, but the feathered mantles were much admired for their workmanship. A skirt of feathers completes the ensemble. *(The British Library)*

one Indian woman on Cortés's staff, the famous Marina, but what she would have done with the dresses in such quantity remains a mystery, unless she exchanged them for food or gave them to the allies' women.

Montezuma himself is described when first encountered as dressed in his imperial robes:

> The *tlimatli,* his mantle of white and blue, flowed over his shoulders, held together by its rich clasp of the green *chalchivitl.* The same precious gem, with emeralds of uncommon size, set in gold, profusely ornamented other parts of his dress. His feet were shod with the golden sandals, and his brows covered by the *copilli,* or Mexican diadem, resembling in form the pontifical tiara.[9]

The Aztec priests who conducted human sacrifices wore black robes, stained with blood. Driven out of the capital, Cortés attempted to reach the coast, but found the way blocked by all the forces the Aztecs could muster. Their white-cotton quilted jackets covered the plain like snow. In order to break through this horde Cortés sought out the Aztec commander, depicted in images of feathers, gold, and precious stones:

> He was covered with a rich surcoat of feather-work; and a panache of beautiful plumes, gorgeously set in gold and precious stones, floated above his head. Rising above this, and attached to his back, between the shoulders, was a short staff bearing a golden net for a banner, the singular, but customary, symbol of authority for an Aztec commander. The cacique, whose name was Cihuaca, was borne on a litter, and a body of young warriors, whose gay and ornamented dresses showed them to be the flower of the Indian nobles.[10]

Clearly, in Aztec society rank was displayed by the wearing of feathers on the head and on the robes, as well as by bright colors, and the wearing of gold and jewels. The ordinary ranks wore only a loincloth, and the women a simple cotton dress down to the ankles. The German artist Weiditz copied some Mexican manuscripts sent back to Spain in 1529; and in 1520 an exhibition of Indian artifacts was held in Brussels, showing the gifts sent to the king, Charles V, the grandson of Ferdinand and Isabella, who was also Holy Roman Emperor in Germany and Austria, and whose territories included Brussels and the Netherlands. The artist Dürer went to see the artifacts:

August 27, 1520. I saw the things which have been brought back to the King from the new golden land, a sun all of gold a whole fathom broad, and a moon of silver of the same size, also two rooms full of the armour of the people there, and all manner of wondrous weapons of theirs, harness and darts, wonderful shields, strange clothing, bedspreads, and all kinds of wonderful objects of various uses, much more beautiful to behold than prodigies. These things were all so precious that they have been valued at one hundred, thousand gold florins. All the days of my life I have seen nothing that has gladdened my heart so much as these things, for I saw amongst them wonderful works of art, and I marvelled at the subtle *ingenia* of men in foreign lands. Indeed, I cannot express all that I thought there.[11]

Most of the gold and silver was melted down for the imperial coffers, but some of the feathered headdresses and shields

3 • Christophe Weiditz, *An Indian Woman*, 1529. The woman wears two mantles, although the Codex Mendoza (figure 1) also shows Mexican women wearing tunics and skirts. Her hair is bound with a cotton scarf, which to the Spanish looked Moorish. The Mexican Indians were exhibited throughout Spain, where the males gave demonstrations of their games, but most of them died of European diseases against which they had no immunity. *(The British Library)*

survive in the Hapsburg collection in the Ethnographical Museum in Vienna.

Cortés overthrew the Aztec empire, and after reporting to Emperor Charles V when he was made a marquess, he returned to Mexico to settle with a new bride and his mother. The general had an interest in developing the region. For example, he planted mulberry trees and imported silkworms, and planted flax and hemp as well, thus laying the groundwork for future textiles. He also introduced merino sheep to start up wool production.

Expeditions Northward

It was from Mexico that an expedition was sent out to explore northward from Arizona to Kansas in 1540. The Captain General was Francisco Vásquez de Coronado, who took twenty-two or twenty-three horses for himself and a few sets of horse armor. Other men took about thirteen horses each, to cover the long journey ahead, and some men had only a single horse. They wore the usual buckskin doublets when not wearing armor, and they also took with them chainmail coats, cuirasses, and helmets. The company consisted of 225 mounted men and 62 infantry. By the time they reached the Rio Grande in Pueblo country, their clothes were looking the worse for wear, so Vásquez told a local chief that he wanted some 300 pieces of cloth. The chief told him it was impossible for one village to supply that much; he would have to ask twelve villages. The Spaniards could not be bothered with that, so they took the blankets and cloaks off the Indian backs, ignoring native ranks. Similarly, when the Spaniards reached the Eastern Apaches, they took the buffalo skins, to the distress of the women who were preparing and decorating them. Most of the Apache women were painted, and one was painted white like a Castilian lady. White-lead face paint was used in Spain before the rest of Europe followed the fashion. By the time the expedition returned to Mexico, its members were wearing Indian buffalo-skin cloaks or blankets, to add to the Indian quilted cotton jackets and cotton cloaks that European men already had adopted in the New Land.[12]

On 18 May 1539, 600 Spaniards under Hernando de Soto left Havana, Cuba, to explore Florida. At Toalli, they found that the

Indians wore mantles made from the inner bark of trees, and also from a linen-like fabric made by treading grass-like nettles to extract the inner layers, as one did with flax. The Indian women wore two such mantles, one over the left shoulder in a manner similar to European gypsies, and one around the waist. The men wore a mantle around the shoulders, and a piece of

4 • John White after Le Moyne, *A Florida Chief,* c. 1585. In Florida, the hair was coated with mud into a cone, to which a tail was attached. As it was hotter than Virginia only a loincloth is worn by the men. Tattooing is more total than in the north, doubtless because more body was on show. The wristguard is similar to European types, but more fringed. The chief is decked with discs at his knees and elbows and with a large disc on a thong around his neck. *(Reproduced by courtesy of the Trustees of the British Museum)*

deerskin over their "privities," as the period termed that area. The deerskins were better dressed in Florida than further up the coast, and could have passed for fine broadcloth of the English type. Skins for wearing were usually vermilion, probably obtained from some berries as the dye, and skins for shoes, stockings, or long hose were usually dyed black. As in Mexico,

Of Florida.

5 • John White after Le Moyne, *A Woman of Florida*, c. 1585. The woman wears a mantle of blue hanging moss, which was found on trees in Florida. She is as highly tattooed as the man, but her hair is worn straight and hanging down. She wears two earplugs, probably of wood, and a coral necklace that might be European in origin. *(Reproduced by courtesy of the Trustees of the British Museum)*

the local Indians wore mantles of feathers—multicolored, white, gray, vermilion, and yellow. They also used body paint, as, for example, the forces of the chief Aquixo were painted ochre, probably his heraldic tone. Their helmets were decorated with feathers and their shields with feather patterns.[13] The French also visited Florida, and attempted to set up a colony there, but it was massacred by the Spanish, who regarded Terra Florida as their zone. In 1562 Jean Ribault described the local Indians as follows:

> The most part of them cover their raines and privities with faire harts skinnes, painted most commonly with sundrie colours; and the fore part of their body and armes bee painted with pretie devised workes, of Azure, red, and black, so well and so properly as the best painter of Europe could not amende it. The women have their bodies painted with a certaine herbe like unto Mosse, whereof the Cedar trees, and all other trees are always covered. The men for pleasure doe always trimme them selves therewith, after sundrie fashions. They bee of tawny colour, hawke nosed, of a pleasant countenance. The women are well favoured and will not suffer one dishonestly to approach too neare them.[14]

The naked breasts of the Indian women would have intrigued the Spanish and French, for they could not see such sights in Europe. There was a sexual element in the wish to explore, the hope of finding beauty not easily available back home.

The Virginia Settlement

It was Sir Walter Raleigh who decided that an English settlement in Virginia would provide an excellent base for raiding Spanish treasure fleets. Thus he sent a squadron to explore the coast in 1584, and in 1585 sent Sir Richard Grenville with 7 ships to settle the land they named Virginia, in honor of their Virgin Queen, Elizabeth I. When Sir Francis Drake called at Roanoke Island in 1586 he found the colonists unhappy and shipped all but two back home to England. In 1586 Grenville returned to leave 15 settlers, and in 1587 Raleigh sent John White as the first governor. He sailed from Portsmouth, England, on 26 April, with ninety-one men, seventeen women, and five children, leaving from the Sally Port, where a plaque to them is set now in the town wall. In Virginia they built Raleigh Cittie on Roanoke

Island, and the first English birth in North America was recorded, Governor White's granddaughter Virginia Dare on 18 August 1587. John White was an artist and he has left the first paintings of Indian types. In 1588 White sailed for more supplies, but the arrival of the Spanish Armada, when every English ship was called to defend the country, held him up for a

6 • Governor John White, *A Chief of Virginia*, c. 1585. The first governor of Virginia, John White, wrote "The manner of their attire and painting them selves when they goe to their generall huntings or at theire Solemne feasts." A fringed deerskin surrounds the chief's waist, but the long tail looks too long to be from one bison, and may be assembled from several. A small cockscomb starts at the forehead and reaches back to the nape. *(Reproduced by courtesy of the Trustees of the British Museum)*

year, and when he returned to Raleigh Cittie in 1590 the site was deserted, and the people taken by the Indians.

The chiefs, or lords, as White called them, of the Indians of Secota wore their hair long and bound up in knots over the ears, but the top was cut like a cockscomb, where they sported a long feather. Short feathers were set in the knots over the ears. Their

7 • John White, *A Chiefe Herowans Wyfe of Pomeoc,* c. 1585. The wife wears a fringed deerskin similar to the chief's, and her body paint probably includes some tattooing. Her hair is long and caught up in a roll at the back. Her daughter of eight or ten wears a collar and a thong, and carries the first English fashion doll to be depicted in Virginia. It is possible that the Spanish and French explorers brought similar dolls to show what European women looked like. *(Reproduced by courtesy of the Trustees of the British Museum)*

earrings were of pearl or an animal's or bird's claw. All the chiefs shaved their faces. They painted the body and were tattooed, but in a different way from the Florida Indians, although White did not detail the distinction. Around the waist these lords wore finely dressed skins, so arranged that the tail fell down behind. Beads and bracelets of copper were much prized by this group.

The aged man in his wynter garment.

8 • John White, *The Aged Man in His Wynter Garment*, c. 1585. White wrote that the elderly liked large mantles of deerskin to wrap themselves in, and there is an obvious seam down the side. The cockscomb is worn higher, perhaps to denote seniority, and the pigtail is bound up at the back of the neck. *(Reproduced by courtesy of the Trustees of the British Museum)*

The chiefs identified their own men by cutting marks, such as stripes, into their backs, which showed who belonged to the chiefs of Roanoke, Secota, Pomeeioc, and Aquascyoc.[15] The wives of these chiefs wore a deerskin round the waist, with the ends fringed. They were tattooed on the neck, arms, breasts, and legs. Their hair was cut short over the eyes, and hung down at the sides and back to the shoulder, bound with a wreath.

The flyer.

9 • John White, *The Flyer or Conjuror,* c. 1585. The magician's badge of office was the small black bird attached to the side of his head. His loincloth is the skin of a small animal with the face still attached. The highly fringed bag at his waist contains his magical bits and pieces. *(Reproduced by courtesy of the Trustees of the British Museum)*

Each dignitary in the Indian tribe had his own distinctive uniform, which is expressed by the hairstyle, garments, and paint. The priests of the tribes cut their hair short, apart from the cockscomb on top, and a standing fringe of hair from ear to ear, above the forehead, which reminded Governor White of a periwig, then meaning a postiche or hairpiece, not a whole wig. This was the distinctive style for priests only. They wore short cloaks of hares' skin, but mostly they went naked. Aged men or elders wore two mantles, a large deerskin over the left shoulder to leave the right arm free, and another piece of skin about the middle (see figure 8). For cold weather they would put on a fur mantle with the fur on the outside, and lined with other fur on the inside. Elders retained the crest or cockscomb style of hair-dressing, but no longer sported the ear knots. Instead, they wore the back of the hair long and tied up. Clearly the ear knots were reserved for active leaders. The tribal magician or shaman wore the same crest as other Virginia Indians, but his badge of office or trade was a small black bird fastened to one side of his head (see figure 9). He used only a light piece of deer or hareskin to cover his privities.

White observed how the locals, not having iron, burned down trees when they wanted to fell timber by lighting bonfires around their base. Maize was the principal diet, but they also smoked fish and flesh, or stewed it in a pot with fruit and meat, all boiled together in what the English then called a *gal-liemanfrye.*

The Jamestown Colony

The first successful English colony in North America was planted at Jamestown in 1607 by the Virginia Company, which was set up in 1606 as a commercial enterprise. Captain John Smith joined the expedition and was captured by the Indians when he was saved from death by the intervention of princess Pocahontas; so he knew the natives very well. He depicts them as follows:

> For their apparell they are sometimes covered with the skinnes of wild beasts, which in Winter are dressed with the hayre, but in Summer without. The better sort weare large mantels of Deere-skins, not much differing in fashion from the Irish mantels. Some

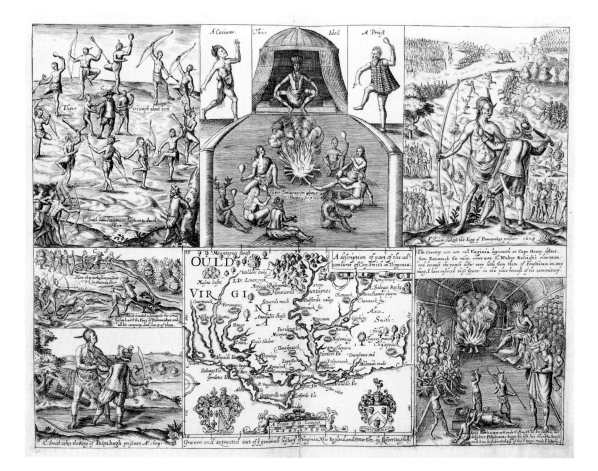

10 • Robert Vaughan, *A Description of Part of the Adventures of Captain Smith in Virginia* from Smith's *General History of Virginia,* 1624. In 1608 and 1609 Captain Smith captured two Indian kings in Virginia, usually grabbing hold of their pigtails. He himself was captured but was saved by Princess Pocahontas (bottom right-hand corner). The Indians resemble John White's studies, but Captain Smith was an English officer in a military doublet with vestigial hanging sleeves and knee-breeches. He was obviously shorter than the Indians. *(The British Library)*

imbroidered with white beads, some with Copper, others painted after their manner. But the common sort have scarce to cover their nakedness but with grasse, the leaves of trees or such like. We have seen some use mantels made of Turky feathers, so prettily wrought and woven with threads that nothing could be discerned but the feathers. That was exceeding warm and handsome. But the women were always covered about their middles with a skin and are very shame faced to be see seene bare. They adorne themselves most with copper beads and painting. The women, some have their legs, hands, breasts and face cunningly imbroidered with divers workes, as beasts, serpents, artificially wrought into their flesh with black spots. In each eare commonly they have three great holes whereat they hang chains, bracelets or copper. Some of the men weare in these holes a small greene and yellow coloured snake, neare half a yarde in length, which crawling and lapping herself about his necke oftentimes familiarly would kisse his lips.[16]

While some Indian men threaded snakes through the holes in their earlobes, other warriors preferred dead rats or birds' wings as earrings, or else in the hair, with snake rattles, or copper, or even a whole hawk with the wings outspread. Some would sport the hand of a dead enemy as a hair ornament. The women cut all the hair, using shells to scrape it way from the scalp. Smith and White both show that Indian society had its ranks, its rich and its poor. Captain Smith evidently tried out a turkey-feather mantle, for he said it was exceedingly warm, but whether he wore it outside of Indian society we do not know. If not worn, then it could have made a good bedspread.

New England

Martin Pring visited the coast of what is now Massachusetts in 1603, near the future Plymouth plantation, and described the local population:

These people in colour are inclined to be swart, tawnie, or chestnut colour, not by nature but accidentally (i.e., artificially) and doe weare their haire brayded in foure parts, and trussed up about their heads with a small knot behind; in which haire of theirs they stick many feathers and toyes for braverie and pleasure. They cover their privities only with pieces of leather drawne betwixt their twists and fastened to their Girdles behind and before, whereunto they hang their bags of Tobacco. They seeme to be somewhat jealous of their women for we saw not past two of them, who weare Aprons of leather before them downe to the knees, and a Beavers skinne like an Irish Mantle over one shoulder. The men are of stature somewhat taller than our ordinary people, strong, swift, well proportioned, and given to treacherie, as in the end we perceived.[17]

Further north, paint is replaced by oiling the skin, which may have begun as a method of protecting the skin against extremes in temperature. Irish mantles and gypsy mantles were the most obvious European garment to compare to the Indians' use of shoulder mantles, but they were worn widely in England, too, in this period.

The Pilgrim Fathers (and Mothers) encountered Indians when they founded New Plymouth in 1620. The first one they saw ran away, but on 16 March 1621 one man strolled into the settlement and addressed them in English. This was Samoset, who had picked up the language from the English fishing boats that had visited the coast ever since John Cabot discovered cod off Newfoundland in 1497. Edward Winslow depicts Samoset in his journal of the plantation: ". . . the wind was beginning to rise a little, we cast a horsemans coat about him, for he was starke naked, onely a leather about his wast, with a fringe about a span long, or little more. . . . he was a tall, straight man, the haire of his head blacke, long behind, onely short before, none on his face at all." Samoset asked for some English beer, and the next day returned with five other braves.

> They had every man a Deeres skin on him, and the principall of them had a wild Cats skin, or such like on the one arme, they had most of them long hosen up to their groynes, close made, and about their groynes to their wast another leather, they were altogether like the Irish trousers; they are of complexion like our English gipsies, no haire or very little on their faces, on their heads long haire to their shoulders, onely cut before, some trussed up before with a feather, broad wise like a fanne, and another a fox tail hanging out.

The group departed, but Samoset stayed for a day and was given a present of a pair of stockings, some shoes, a shirt, and a piece of cloth to tie about his middle. A meeting with the local chief or king was arranged and he came to visit the plantation:

> In his Attyre little or nothing was different from the rest of his followers, only a greate Chaine of white bone Beades about his necke, and at it behind his necke, hangs a little bag of Tobacco, which he dranke and gave us to drinke, his face was paynted with a sad red like murrey and oyled both heade and face, that he looked greasily. All his followers likewise wore in their faces in part or in whole paynted some blacke, some red, some yellow and

some white, some with crosses, and other Antick workes, some had skins on them, and some naked, all strong, tall, all men in appearance.[18]

Winslow wrote a sequel, *Good Newes from New England*, in 1624, in which he describes the appearance of Indian women. He mentions a custom for Indian brides, "when a maide is taken in marriage she first cutteth her haire, and after weareth a covering on her head till her hayre be growne out." He also portrays her general attire, mostly deerskin:

> As for their apparel, they weare breeches and stockings in one like some *Irish*, which is made of Deare skinnes, and have shoes of the same leather. They weare also a Deers skin loose about them like a cloak, which they will turn to the weather side. In this habit they travell, but when they are at home or come to their journeys end, presently they pull off their breeches, stockins, shooes, wring the water out of them if they bee wet, and dry them and rub and chase the same. Though they be off, yet they have another small garment that covereth their secrets. The men weare also when they go abroad in cold weather an otter or Foxe skin on their right arm, but only their bracer on the left. Women and all of that sexe weare strings about their legs, which the men never doe.[19]

The first study on the Indians by a New Englander appeared in 1643, when Roger Williams of Providence published in London his dictionary of Indian languages and customs. In Chapter 20 he comments on "their nakednesse and clothing." "They have a twofold nakednesse," he wrote:

> First, ordinary and constant, when although they have a Beasts skin, or an English mantle on yet that covers ordinarily but their hinder parts, and all the foreparts from top to toe (except their secret parts, covered with a little Apron, after the patterne of their and our first Parents) I say all else open and naked.
> The male children goe starke naked and have no Apron on till they come to ten or twelve yeeres of Age, their Female they, in a modest blush, cover with a little Apron on an hand breadth from their very birth.
> Their second nakednesse is when their men often abroad and both men and women within doores, leave off their beasts skin or English cloth, and so (excepting their little Apron) are wholly naked, yet but a few of the women will keepe their skin or cloth (though loose) as neare to them ready to gather it up about them.

Thus the women showed modesty about being seen naked since they kept their cloth or skins nearby in case of unexpected visitors. Of the Indians' painting, Williams wrote in Chapter 30: "They paint their Garments &c. The men paint their faces in Warre. Both men and women for pride etc. Their red painting which they most delight in, and is both the barke of the Pine, and also a red Earth.[20]

Williams shows that Indians in the New England area had started to wear English wool cloth as mantles, which were

11 • John White, *An Eskimo Man,* c. 1585. Sealskin was the chief covering in the American north, for seals were easier to catch than polar bears. The patches would be used for reinforcement since they are regular. A form of trouser was tucked in boots of seal-pup fur with the skin outside. *(Reproduced by courtesy of the Trustees of the British Museum)*

either gifts or else traded in exchange for beaver skins. The Irish-type trousers noted by Winslow were simply the old-fashioned long hose surviving from the fifteenth century. Fashionable men in Europe had begun to wear various types of knee-breeches during the 1580s, but by 1620 this change had not yet reached the outer reaches of Ireland, although knee-breeches could be found in Dublin. Both the Indian and the Irish trousers were tight-fitting; looser trousers were worn by sailors, be they English, Dutch, or Spanish, so the concept of

12 • John White, *An Eskimo Woman*, c. 1585. The woman's tunic is cut higher at the sides, and has a center front opening for breastfeeding the infant, who can be seen tucked inside the mother's hood. Her patches look more decorative since they are not located at pressure points. She is wearing two leg-warmers as well as trousers and boots. Her tunic dips to a tail at the back. Canadians quickly adopted snowshoes and hooded tunics for winter. *(Reproduced by courtesy of the Trustees of the British Museum)*

wider trousers, suitably trimmed with long fringes in the Indian custom, was probably copied by the Indians from European sailors who visited their shores long before the settlers arrived.

Obviously the coastal Indians were the first affected by the advent of European settlers, and some clothing exchanges took place. Woolen blankets would have been an improvement on deerskin, so they became a desirable object for trade. At least one Indian chief wanted to go all the way and become completely European. On 13 April 1631 Chief Chickatabot called on the deputy governor in Boston, John Winthrop, to ask for some English clothes for himself. Winthrop called for his tailor and ordered a suit for the chief. Chickatabot returned on the 15th to collect it, and paid two large beaver skins in exchange.[21]

The extent to which Europeans adopted Indian dress varied with circumstances. Explorers and hunters of necessity would have to wear buckskin and deerskin once they were away from towns importing cloth from England. But, in the settlements, it was important to keep national styles of dress as a means of maintaining a European identity in a strange, untamed land. The English and Dutch settlers were under contract to trading companies at home, so they expected the regular delivery of supplies and clothing in exchange for the beaver skins they collected. Thus they were under no compulsion to adopt Indian-style clothing. It was not until England appointed officers for Indian affairs that we find the English administrator adopting Indian dress, in part as a conscious effort to make his clients trust him by appearing as one of them. In the southern settlements, the Spanish had adopted the native quilted cotton tunics; and cotton garments would be important in that hot region. Therefore, although the degree of adoption varied, the discovery of the native Americans led to new attire for both the explorers and conquerors, and for the natives.

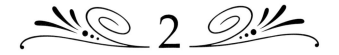

New England in the Seventeenth Century

The Puritan Settlers

When the Puritan fathers and mothers decided to escape from England in 1607–8 they had no thought of going to America; they settled at first in Leyden, in the Dutch Netherlands, where they had fled persecution at home. Spain had still not recognized the independence of her former Dutch territories; but *de facto* the Dutch states were an independent federation, and allowed religious freedom for nonconformists and Puritans. The Pilgrims lived contentedly in Leyden, where many worked as weavers; Bradford was with a silk firm, Brewster was a printer, and their leader, the Reverend Robinson, lectured at Leyden University. It was the start of the Thirty Years' War in 1618 that obliged the Pilgrims to leave the Netherlands. When the Spanish army in the Spanish Netherlands, now Belgium, began to attack the Dutch, and the Catholic Hapsburgs declared that they were going to destroy the Protestant revolution in northern Europe, the continent was no longer a safe haven.

After many difficult negotiations with the Virginia Company to back their settlement, the contract was signed on 1 July 1620. The very terms of the contract, for example, were to have major

implications for dress in the New World. For example, para-
graph 10 stated: "That all such persons as are of this colonie, are
to have their meate, drink, apparell, and all provisions out of
the common stock & goods of the said colonie."[1] This provision
explained the prominence of the brown, russet, gray, and black
colors conventionally associated with Puritan dress. Contrary to
popular belief, not all Puritan dress was black, which was an
expensive dye. The middle-class Puritans wore black, but the
artisans and farmhands wore the traditional colors instituted for
them by Edward III in 1362, when carters, ploughmen, ox-
herds, cowherds, swineherds, shepherds and dairymen, and
their wives, were restricted to undyed blanket cloth and russet.
Such colors were still worn by countryfolk on their smocks and
corduroys well into this century. Consequently the common
stock for the majority of the settlers consisted of brown or russet
clothes, and the undyed or natural cream of linen would have
been found in aprons, shirts, shifts, caps, smocks, and the
undyed woolen blankets. The same standards of dress associated with rank prevailed also in the Netherlands, with the
prosperous merchants wearing black and the countryfolk
browns and grays; so after living for twelve years in that country the Puritans dressed much as they did in England.

The first boat chartered at Delftshaven, the *Speedwell*, was
small, so families had to be divided and some left behind. They
met up with the *Mayflower* at Southampton in July 1620. They
were delayed by the Virginia Company increasing its demands
for returns on investment, and this delay forced them to sell £60
of butter, oil, shoe leather, swords, muskets and armor, to cover
living costs. The two vessels set sail on 5 August on what was
the first of three attempts to sail. The *Speedwell* sprung a leak off
Dartmouth, and had to be examined and repaired. She leaked
again on 27 August, and both ships had to return to Plymouth.
William Bradford decided the crew were causing the leaks themselves, since they wanted to avoid the voyage to America.
Eventually they decided to leave the *Speedwell* behind, and
some of the Pilgrims disembarked to wait for another opportunity. The *Mayflower* sailed alone on 6 September 1620 with one
hundred settlers on board. They reached Cape Cod on 9 November, after nine weeks at sea. They had arrived in the midst
of winter, and in the wrong place, not Virginia, where they had
intended to settle. Landing at Plymouth, the Pilgrims drew up

the Mayflower Compact on 11 November to establish their own government and laws in the name of James I and James VI. On the 13th and 14th of November the women went ashore to wash clothes, since it had been too stormy on the Atlantic to do that aboard ship. It was not until 20 December that they agreed on a site and began to build New Plymouth. While they had promised to repay the Virginia Company with fish and beaver skins, none of the settlers were fishermen, they had brought no fish hooks, and none were trappers. Half of the pilgrims died in the new year through a combination of poor diet, scurvy, and pneumonia from the cold. The first storehouse to hold their clothes burned down, and another had to be started on 17 January 1621. Their Indian friend Samoset brought along another English-speaking Indian, Squanto, who had visited England in 1619 with the fishing captain Dermer, who had taken him to Plymouth to show the merchants what an Indian looked like. Squanto organized a peace treaty with the local king, and told the settlers of the notorious Captain Hunt, who used to capture Indians to sell in the Spanish slave markets; the Spanish had continued the Moorish custom of having slaves, both African and Indian at this time. It was Squanto who trained the surviving pilgrims to set fish traps, to trap beaver, and to plant Indian corn. The harvest proved good in September 1621 when the first Thanksgiving feast with the Indians was held. To reward Squanto, they gave him an English suit of doublet and knee-breeches, and a horseman's coat, or overcoat.[2] Given the scarcity of clothing, this gift of a suit of clothes was not trivial but a token of great value.

Another ship, the *Fortune,* arrived with thirty-six settlers late in 1621, but the thoughtless voyagers brought no supplies with them, no clothes, no bedding, no pots or pans. Luckily the captain had some "bucking lane suits" on board, bought in the secondhand market in London, at Birchours Lane, so the settlers bought some off him. In 1623 the *Anne* brought a supply of coarse cloth, and the women were able to make some clothes for themselves. Bradford notes that the Indians loved English blankets to wear and sleep in, and glass beads, knives, and hatchets for which they would trade beaver skins. In 1626 a ship, possibly the *Sparrow Hawk,* was wrecked down the coast; it proved to have cloth, mixed cloths called perpetuanes, stockings, and shoes, all of which the pilgrims were much in need of.

In 1627 the colony leaders William Bradford, Captain Myles Standish, and Isaac Allerton agreed to trade beavers and Indian corn with England for six years in exchange for £50 worth of stockings and shoes a year; evidently those were the most difficult articles to acquire in the new land. In 1628, the pilgrims began to trade with the Dutch colonists. In 1609 the Dutch had asked Sir Henry Hudson to explore the American coast for them; he entered New York Bay and sailed up the river, the Hudson, which now bears his name. When Hudson returned home, King James ordered him to serve the Dutch no longer, but on his information the Dutch first built a fort at Nassau (Albany), and in 1621 set up the West India Company to encourage settlers. Dutch colonists settled up the Hudson and Delaware rivers, and in 1625–26 built New Amsterdam on Manhattan Island, for which they paid the Indians 60 guilders. In 1628 they made contact with New Plymouth, and brought the Pilgrim settlers coats, shirts, rugs, and blankets, which they traded for tobacco. Since these garments were male, the women probably demanded something for themselves, for the Dutch returned later that year, with linen, Holland—a fine linen—and lengths of coarse cloth, from which the women could make shifts, drawers, and caps from the linen, and plain dresses from the rough cloth.

In 1629 more settlers reached New Plymouth, bringing 125 yards of kersey cloth, 125 ells of linen, and 66 pairs of shoes, which were all welcome. A New England merchant's inventory for 1634 states that the Indians liked long coats and would take them if they had the chance, thus leaving the settlers with only short doublets. He stressed that neither the English or the Indians liked rough coverlets, and that his supply of hats were useless without hatbands. The shirts, stockings, and shoes were satisfactory, but the last would shrink in the snow. By the 1630s the colony started to receive regular visits from fishing boats and from merchants, so a regular supply of clothes from England was now available. Mr. Winter of Richmond Island wrote in June 1634 that the rate of exchange was as follows: coats for 2 pounds of beaver skins; Irish stockings for 2 pounds of beaver skin per dozen; shirts and waistcoats for half a pound of beaver skin each. Since he does not mention women's garments, we may assume once again that they would have to make their own from cloth, although they could wear men's coats, hats, and stockings if there was a surplus.[3]

Nineteenth-century paintings of the Pilgrims found at Pilgrim Hall dress them too late for their arrival in 1620, and they apply Victorian principles of modesty that distort the past, covering up the women's ankles when working women in the past wore their hems at the ankle, and fishwives at the knee for wading. The Puritan look in dress in 1620, in both the Netherlands and England, was for men to wear a very tight doublet, with a high waist and narrow sleeves. The knee-breeches were very full and padded out like melons, and they reached from the rib-cage down to above the knee. Women had similar tight bodices and sleeves, but the wealthy wore their skirts wide and padded out; the look for working women was slimmer in outline, although echoing the fullness by the number of petticoats. Ruffs were going through a transition in style. The upper classes were starting to wear wide collars, although the middle classes in England still wore ruffs into the 1630s and, in Holland, into the 1660s. In New Amsterdam,

13 • Flemish School, *Still Life with Young Woman*, c. 1615. This maidservant wears the basic uniform of European peasant women, with the jacket and skirt, which lasted from the sixteenth century to the twentieth. In winter it was in cloth, but in summer light linen versions were worn as shown here. The missing sleeve suggests that the jacket has been handed down from her mistress, as does the neckerchief in which some of the lace trim has frayed. Dutch and Flemish caps gripped the head by a wire spring that marked the cheeks at the side, as here. This costume was very common in Dutch New York and New England. The collection in Colonial Williamsburg includes some of these jackets. (*Musée des Beaux Arts de Montréal*)

therefore, ruffs would have been common, and would have continued to be worn in New Plymouth, especially by the senior citizens, who would have felt undressed without them. Hats became lower and wider for both sexes during the 1620s and '30s, and tall Puritan hats do not become fashionable until later, during the 1660s.

On 30 April 1629 the Company of Massachusetts Bay was established in London to replace an earlier scheme, and its first fleet of six vessels sailed from the Isle of Wight in May, with 300 men, 80 women, 26 children, 140 cattle, and 40 goats. They set their plantation at Boston and at Charlestown, Massachusetts. The future governor John Winthrop arrived with four shiploads in 1630 and settled at Charlton Bay, Charlestown. Regular meetings were held to discuss local problems, including issues of dress, as on 7 March 1634 the subject of women's veils, as worn in church and for mourning, was raised: "At the lecture at Boston a question was propounded about veils. Mr. Cotton concluded that where (by the custom of the place) they were not

14 • Robert Vaughan, *Matoaka or Rebecca Daughter of the Mighty Prince Powhatan Emperor of Virginia, aetatis suae 21 anno 1616,* from Captain Smith's *General History of Virginia.* Rebecca (alias Pocahontas) was converted to Christianity and married Mr. John Rolfe who became a tobacco exporter to London. She wears the height of English fashion for 1616, with the high hat, the standing collar held up by a piccadillie, and an open gown over a buttoned waistcoat. The fabric is probably silk. Such tight clothes must have felt strange after loose Indian mantles. She was probably forced into corsets as well. *(The British Library)*

15 • Daniel Mytens, *Carolus magnae Britanniae Princeps, aetatis suae xxiii, anno domini 1624.* Charles, Prince of Wales, painted the year before he became Charles I. He was the sovereign of the new English colonies from 1625. His fashionable suit is decorated with cuts, pinking, and with braid. The sloping shoulder line is emphasized by the shoulder wings. Waists are high but plunge to a *V* in front. The cloak-bag breeches end above the knee. Ornate rosettes are tied below the knee, and the shoes are tied with ribbon. A falling ruff surrounds the neck, and the hair is worn just below the ear. While the Pilgrim fathers would not have worn such a decorated style, their basic silhouette, especially among the leaders, would have imitated the line. *(National Gallery of Canada, Ottawa)*

16 • British School, *The Actor Manager Edward Alleyn, Founder of the College of God's Gift, Dulwich*, insr. 1626. Black was worn widely among the middle classes in England, for the dye was too expensive for the lower classes, who wore gray and browns. While Alleyn was rich enough to own two playhouses, and staged Marlowe's plays, he dresses with true Protestant sobriety, in a black suit and hose, with only his ruff and cuffs in white. His laced gown is that of a headmaster of his college, and would have long hanging sleeves. Hats grew wide in the 1620s. This was the ideal image for the Puritans, but all settlers did not share that opinion. *(By permission of the Governors of Dulwich Picture Gallery)*

a sign of women's subjection, they were not commanded by the apostle. Mr. Endecott opposed, and did maintain it by the general arguments brought by the apostle. After some debate, the governor, perceiving it grow to some earnestness, interposed, and so it brake off."[4]

The summer of 1638 was the peak of emigration to Boston, when 20 ships brought about 3,000 settlers. On 21 September a ship from Barnstaple, Devon, brought 80 West Country folk. They must have brought their local style with them, for as Celia Fiennes found on a visit to Taunton, England, in 1698, the West Country had its own look:

> you meete all sorts of country women wrapp'd up in the manteles called West Country rockets, a large mantle doubled together of a sort of serge, some are linseywolsey, and deep fringe or fag at the lower end; these hang downe some to their feete, some only just below the wast, in the summer they are in white garments of this sort, in the winter they are in red ones; I call them garments because they never go out without them and this is the universal fashion in Somerset, and Devonshire and Cornwall.[5]

Doubtless some west-country rockets now appeared in Boston and also in Charlestown, showing that Edward III's law was being honored three hundred years later as a tradition, with undyed and russet cloth still being worn by country people.

Dress and Social Order

In the early seventeenth century, the idea that clothing was an expression of one's rank in life was challenged by the prosperous middle-class merchants who wished to dress above the style allotted to them by law. The Boston Court, on 18 September 1634, had passed its first *sumptuary law* "against fashions and costly apparel," in which it banned the wearing of apparel such as gold, silver, lace, slashed clothing, cutwork, embroidered needlework caps, and hair bands. Another sumptuary law was passed on 25 September 1638:

> The Court, taking into consideration the great disorder general through the country in costliness of apparel, and following new fashions, sent for the elders of the churches, and conferred with them about it, and laid it upon them, as belonging to them to

redress it, by urging it upon the consciences of their people, which they promised to do. But little was done about it, for divers of the elders' wives etc. were in some measure partners in the general disorder.[6]

The colony thus imitated the Old World in its regulations, even though the colonial wives would not comply.

In New England, in particular, which thought of itself as a religious society ordered on God's word, disorder in dress was taken to reflect disorder in people's relationships to each other and to God, as noted by the reference twice to the word "disorder" in the excerpt above. The sumptuary laws were intended to enforce a modest and conservative style of dress among all inhabitants of the colony; for example, low necklines and short

17 • British School, *Mrs Dirge*, c. 1630. Cartwheel ruffs continued to be worn among the middle rank into the 1630s in England, and into the 1660s in Holland. Mrs. Dirge has put her shift collar over her ruff, so perhaps she found the starched ruff uncomfortable, but the fashionable would have scorned such behavior. She wears the same sort of wide hat as Alleyn, on top of her bonnet or cap, which has an edging of lace. Her black gown is decked with braid, but there are none of the slashes or pinking of court style, and the fabric is plain wool and linen. *(By permission of the Governors of Dulwich Picture Gallery)*

sleeves were specifically condemned, and they also aimed to ensure that clothing would indicate social rank. For example, the Massachusetts law of 1651 distinguished between people of low estate, which was defined as less than £200, and people of higher status, which included not only people with property valued more than £200 but also magistrates and other public officers. Gentlemen and their families were allowed to wear luxurious apparel such as gold braid and silk hoods, and the lower class was not. Sumptuary legislation was enacted in New England as late as 1676 in Connecticut and persisted here longer than in England, where the last sumptuary clothing law was decreed by Charles I in 1643.

Nevertheless, the general disorder in fashions that annoyed

18 • British School, *Edward Winslow,* c. 1645. The governor of New Plymouth, and first historian of the colonies, returned to England to serve the Commonwealth regime. While his dress is as black as a Puritan, his gold buttons denote the sort of luxury that was enfuriating the Pilgrim fathers. Winslow has grown his hair longer, and even sports a cavalier moustache. Collars grew smaller in the 1640s, particularly among Puritans and the military. *(The Pilgrim Society, Plymouth, Massachusetts)*

the Court of Boston only multiplied in variety and changeability. The Puritan William Prynne thundered in 1628 in England:

> Infinite, and many are the sinfull, strange and monstrous vanities, which this Unconstant, Vaine, Fantastique, Idle, Proud, Effeminate, and wanton Age of ours hath hatched and Produced in all parts and corners of the World; but especially, in this our *English* climate, which like another *Affricke,* is always bringing foorth *some New, some Strange, Mishapen, or Prodigious formes* and Fashion euery moment.[7]

This diversity of style affected the Puritans through the influence of the adventurer Thomas Morton, who set up an anti-Puritan estate called Merry Mount, complete with a maypole, dancing, and Indian women, and recruited some younger men to his side. Bad farmers, the Merry Mount settlers obtained food from the tribes by selling them guns, which made the colony even more furious. Eventually, Captain Myles Standish led an attack on the estate, and Morton and his acolytes were shipped back to England. But the more settlers who arrived, the more new styles increased in variety and the greater the refusal to heed the Puritan authorities. Back in England, Morton published an attack on the New Englanders for being dictators, which illustrates the basic moral problem: Should the nonconformists who placed so much importance on individual conscience dictate to others how to dress and behave? This struggle would continue in the colonies, between the conservative Puritans and the liberal rebels, between those who wanted a constant costume and those who wanted to follow the changing varieties of modern style.

The Influence of Protectionist Trade Laws

The civil war between the king and Parliament in England cut the overflow of settlers to New England. Edward Winslow (see figure 18), three times governor of New Plymouth, sailed back home to serve Cromwell's government and died in its service in 1655. The 1651 Navigation Act enacted by Cromwell's Parliament affected the colonies by requiring all trade to be carried in English ships. But with the restoration of the monarchy in 1660 the legislation of the Interregnum became invalid, and new laws had to be issued. The *Anno duodecimo Caroli II caput xviii*, An Act for Encouraging of Shipping and Navigation, was published in 1660, and stated:

> That from and after the first of Day of December 1660 and from thenceforward no goods or commodities whatsoever shall be imported into or exported out of any lands, islands, plantations or territories to his Majesty belonging or in the possession of his Majesty, his heirs and successors, in *Asia*, *Africa* or *America*, in any other ship or ships, vessel or vessels whatsoever, but in such ships

19 • Bartholomeus van der Helst, *Portrait of a Gentleman*, 1644. Satin was the most fashionable silk in the 1630s and '40s, so wealthy Calvinists in Holland wore black satin, edged with black braid and black lace in sober luxury. The general line of the 1640s was narrow, with straight sleeves and breeches. Hats grew smaller and slightly higher. Waists remained high in the early part of the decade, but would grow lower. Knee rosettes are still worn, but the style is now for clusters of ribbon to deck the knee. The glimpse of the shirt at the waist and the slits in the sleeves to reveal the shirt sleeves would explode in the 1650s and '60s to reveal whole areas of linen. Shoes are growing more square-toed. Each wave of settlers in New England brought something of such changes with them, be it only a hat, a shoe, or narrower sleeve. (*Musée des Beaux Arts de Montréal*)

or vessels as do truly and without fraud belong only to the people of *England* or *Ireland*, dominion of *Wales* or the town of *Berwick-upon-Tweed*, or are of the built of and belonging to the said lands, islands, plantations and territories as the proprietors and right owners thereof, and wherof the master and three quarters of the mariners at least are *English*."

At the same time an act blandly entitled "A Subsidy granted to the King of tonnage and poundage and other sums of money payable upon merchandize exported or imported," the *Anno duodecimo Caroli II caput iv*, was issued. It stated that indigo from the West Indies carried an import tax of 1/8d. per pound, but indigo from the New England plantations was taxed at only 12 pence a pound. The regulations fill forty pages, but a selection shows the following impact on American exports to England as well as articles exported from England to North America. "Garments or wearing apparel of all sorts to go free," the statute decreed, so clothes were free of tax, but some clothing materials and accessories were affected.

Buttons, hair, per gross (12 dozen) had an export tax of 6d.
Calve skins, dressed or undressed, per dozen £2.10s.
Cottons of Manchester, Taunton and Wales, per 100 goads, £2.
    [*a goad was 4½ feet*]
Freezes per yard, 6d.
Fustians English free
Garters worsted, per gross 2/6
Girdles leather, men's per gross 2/8
    Children's per gross 10/–
Gloves, plain, sheep, kid, lamb, per dozen pairs 4/–
    Fringed with silk, per dozen pairs 6/8
    Furred with coney wool (rabbit) per dozen pairs 6/8
    Buck leather per dozen pairs £1
Hatbands of crewel per gross 5/–
Hats, Beaver or demicastors English per dozen £2
    Felt and other types 10/–
Irish mantles 3/4. each
Lace, gold and silver per pound £1.6s.
    Velvet lace, free
    Statute silks see silks
Linnen of hemp or flax, fine or coarse, English, to 40 ells, 10/–
Lists of cloth, many types, per thousand yards, £1.10s.
English silks per pound 3/4
Other silks per pound 1/8
Stockings, Irish, per dozen were taxed on export at 5/–
    Kersey, long, per pair, 1/3

Kersey, short, per dozen pairs, 3/9
Woollen for children per dozen, 1/8
Worsted for children, per dozen 3/4
Woollen for men, per dozen, 12/6
Worsted for men per dozen, 6/8
Lower ends of worsted stockings, per dozen, 6/8
Stuffs, perpetuanas and serges, in regard of their coarseness, per lb. 1/8
All other cloths, of wool mixed with hair or thread, per lb. 1/4
Waistcoats, of cotton, kersey, flannel, worsted and wadmoll [a coarse wool
from the Orkneys & Shetlands], free
Worsted, English, per piece, 15s. when narrow
Broad, English per piece, £1

Therefore, although garments might be exported from England to the colonies free of tax, linen and woolen cloth, buttons, belts, stockings, and hats were still being taxed. Many kinds of skins were taxed on export, from coney to wolf, otter, and squirrels (£2.10 per thousand), although New England had its own wolves and beavers in plenty. Concerning American exports to England, beaver skin is not included, but buckskin carried an import tax of 2/6 each; beaver hats faced a tax of £10 per dozen. While garments were generally free, felt cloaks carried a tax of £2 each and silk petticoats, £3 each. Thus a Neapolitan silk, imported into England for export to the plantations, would have carried two taxes, for entry and departure, making silks very expensive in New England.[8]

The Influence of Europe

The variety of fashions was bewildering, but it was fueled by the fierce competition between the courts of France, Spain, and England for leadership in style, in politics as well as dress. By 1625 the high waist was ousted by a plunging "V" waist for both sexes, and tight sleeves started to expand at the upper arm by being padded out. In the 1630s both parts of the sleeve were padded, to produce a bulbous look which was decked with panes (slashes) and braid. Men's breeches subsided from the cloak-bag breeches with padding to a less full knee-breech in the late 1620s, which became even slimmer and longer in the 1630s. Lacing the breeches to the doublet was made a feature in the 1620s, with the laces being tied in bows; but in 1630 John Aubrey wrote that hooks and eyes replaced lacing, which led to a simpler, clearer line. Waists began to rise again by 1632, and returned to the normal level after 1638. Generally fashions had a life of six years for the social elite; of course, they lingered for the bottom of society. As ruffs collapsed, wide lace collars took their place—in plain linen for Puritans and expensive lace for the court. A sloping neckline displayed these collars to advantage, and hair grew longer. By the 1630s and '40s the line

Marchants wife of London

20 • Wenceslaus Hollar, *Marchants Wife of London*, 1642. The Latin text refers to the wife of a London citizen of better quality. This is shown by her petticoat trimmed with lace of gold or silver. She follows the Dutch fashion of holding up the skirt to show the finery beneath. This became a permanent style among working women, for hitched-up skirts could be used to hold produce, piglets, or eggs. The lady has the typical narrow sleeve of the 1640s, but with a memory of the elbow-length sleeve of the 1630s still in evidence as a double sleeve at that point. Front-lacing the bodice returned to favor from 1638 onward. The neckerchief is trimmed with lace and even has a little sleeve attached. Her hat is less wide than those worn during the 1630s. *(The British Museum, photo John Freeman & Co.)*

became simpler, so the lower ranks in society were able to echo it in their rough fabrics, although the court wore its simpler style in hugely expensive satins and laces. A more tubular look emerged in the 1640s, sleeves became straight, and knee-breeches, tubes to the knees. Cavaliers started wearing riding boots indoors, so by the mid-1630s boots were given more ornamentation and began to expand at the top, into bucket-top boots with wide flaps, which formed an excellent platform for display of lace-decorated stockings. The wider the boots grew, the more difficult they were to walk in but young men persisted, having to swing their legs out in order to walk. Thus, bucket-top boots imposed the Baroque way of walking—in curves, so to speak.

21 • British School, *Mrs. Cartwright's Sister aetatis suae 65 anno domini 1644.* This lady shows how the English cap was flared out at the sides, and was worn without clips, unlike figure 13. She wears a broad felt hat and a plain black gown, with her white neckerchief as the white contrast. She is dressed in sober, middle-class style, and her pure white linen was the mark of a non-laboring person. The farm worker and settler out in the fields were not able to keep their clothes so clean. *(Reproduced by permission of the Governors of Dulwich Picture Gallery)*

For women, the biggest change in styles during the seventeenth century was from the Elizabethan and Jacobean open kirtle and petticoat to the closed gown of the 1630s, where the front of the skirt was seamed together and no petticoat could be seen. Such simple two-piece dresses with a bodice and a skirt were much copied by the artisan classes, although of course their hemlines were at the ankle, not down to the ground, as with fine ladies. After a few years fashion moved on, and open skirts displaying petticoats returned in the 1640s; but below high fashion the simple closed dress persisted, and was found particularly on urban women, who doubtless carried it to New England and Massachusetts.

22 • British School, *Catherine Davenant, Mrs. Thomas Lamplugh,* c. 1664. Despite the Puritans' dislike of bishops, Puritan dress was worn by bishops' families. Catherine was niece of the Bishop of Salisbury, and her husband, after being Professor of Divinity at Oxford University, was appointed Archdeacon of London in 1664, and later Bishop of Exeter and Archbishop of York. Catherine wears the new huge hat of the 1660s, the sugarloaf, so termed because it resembled a sugar cone. The hat survived in farming communities throughout the eighteenth century. She wears a black cape trimmed with gray, and a black hood, which became very fashionable in the 1630s. She reflects current style in the fullness of her sleeves that stop at the elbow. She has no lace, but there is a linen frill on her shift sleeve. Exposing the wrists, as in the 1630s, made long gloves necessary in cool weather. *(York City Art Gallery, Yorkshire)*

The wearing of gold and silver embroidery with quantities of colored ribbons became more marked as Louis XIV attained manhood.[9] He was determined to overthrow the more austere Spanish dress, as well as Spanish power; and a theatrical, extravagant style became compulsory at the court of this theatrical ruler. Such luxury drew the attention of the founder of the Quaker movement, George Fox, who condemned the fashion of wearing jeweled ornament, ribbons, laces, and patches as too worldly and extravagant. Fox himself was known as the man in leather breeches, for he traveled around England in leather doublet and knee-breeches, which made a very durable water-repellant suit. In 1655 he delivered a lecture on the subject:

> They must be in the fashion of the world, else they are not in esteem, else they shall not be respected, if they have not gold or silver upon their backs, or if the hair be not powdered. But if he have store of ribands hanging about his waist, and at his knees, and in his hat, or divers colours, red, white, black, or yellow, and his hair is powdered, then he is a brave man; then he is accepted, he is no Quaker, because he has ribands on his back, front, and knees, and his hair powdered. This is the array of the world. But is not this from the lust of the eye, the lust of the flesh, or the pride of life?
>
> Likewise, the women having their gold, their patches on their faces, noses, cheeks, foreheads, having their rings on their fingers, wearing gold, having their cuffs double, under and above, like unto a butcher with his white sleeves; having their ribands, tied about their hands, and their gold laces about their clothes; this is no Quaker say they. The attire pleaseth for the world; and if they cannot get these things, they are discontented.

Fox returned to the matter of women's dress in 1685, basing himself upon the apostles:

> The apostle Peter saith (in 1 Pet. iii) of the women's adorning: Let it not be that outward adorning of plaiting the hair, and of wearing gold, or putting on of apparel. . . . And the apostle saith (1 Tim. ii 9, 10) in like manner also, that women adorn themselves in modest apparel, with shamefacedness and sobriety, not with broidered hair, or gold, or pearls, or costly array, but (which becometh women professing godliness) with good works.

The Quakers were not welcomed in New England, the Puritans acting against them as harshly or worse than had the Church of England. Fox was much incensed to learn in 1661 from the colonies that "the government there had made a law to banish the Quakers out of the colonies, upon pain of death, in case they returned, and that several Friends having been so banished and returning were taken and actually hung; and that many more were in prison in danger of the like sentence being executed."[10] Fox asked Edward Burrough to take up the matter with Charles II, and the king did order the execution of Quakers in New England to cease. Fox also tackled Governor Winthrop from Boston, when the governor visited London. Thereafter Quakers could settle across the Atlantic in safety.

The first Quaker to settle on the west side of the Delaware River was Robert Wade in 1675. Swedes and Dutch were already

23 • American School, *Elizabeth Eggington*, 1664. Despite Puritan attempts to control dress, their own wives undermined the legislation. Elizabeth, painted some thirty years later, shows that the regulation had failed. She wears an elaborate necklace of pearls and wire, and a pearl-enclosed miniature portrait possibly of her husband. Her black dress seems patterned, and she echoes fashion in her short sleeves caught with bows. Unfortunately she has not shortened her shift sleeves enough to match the gown sleeves, which is a sign of provincialism. She is showy enough to fix a pearl drop at her hood bow, and to sport a feathered fan, but her taste is not perfect. The edging to her neckerchief may be knitted bonelace. *(Wadsworth Atheneum, Hartford, Gift of Mrs. Walter H. Clark. © Wadsworth Atheneum.)*

in the area. On 17 March 1675 an agreement was made with the Indian chief Sacetores to acquire land for four Quaker families in exchange for four match coats, which were made from match cloth and were an English product the Indians wore as a mantle. Another four match coats were added to the list, along with two pairs of stockings. Such exchanges were continued by the founder of Pennsylvania, William Penn, when he arrived in 1682. On 12 April 1682 he delivered 20 white blankets, 20 coats, 40 shirts, 40 pairs of stockings, as well as knives, scissors, and needles to the Indians, worth the value of 300 guilders, Dutch currency being common in the area. On July 15, at Delaware Falls, Penn exchanged for land in Bucks County 40 white blankets, 40 kersey coats, 60 shirts, 40 pairs of stockings, 20 mounteare caps, and 20 pairs of shoes, as well as knives, axes, powder, and such. The Delaware Indians were now wearing English suits and mantles in some quantity. And the undyed blanket cloth could double its role as a mantle and bedcover, which is how the Indians used their deerskin mantles. Penn also observed of the Indian upbringing of children, that in order to toughen them, they "Plunge them in the Rivers to harden and embolden them, then Having wrapt them in a Clout, they lay them upon a straight, thin Board, a little more than the length and breadth of the Board, to make it straight; whereof all Indians have flat heads."[11] Similar distortions caused by swaddling and head binding could be found in European babies, and will be discussed more fully in Chapter 3, on New France, since the French continued the custom longer than did the English.

Pennsylvania was not, of course, the first new colony to be founded after Virginia and Massachusetts. Maryland had been founded in 1632 by Lord Baltimore who intended it as a refuge for Catholics. The Dutch in New Amsterdam destroyed the Swedish attempt to found a New Sweden on the Delaware, only to be defeated themselves by the English, who in 1664 turned New Amsterdam into New York, in honor of the Lord High Admiral James Duke of York. New Jersey was established as an English entity at the same time. Settlers from Virginia began to move into North Carolina in the 1650s, and it received legal status in 1663, when South Carolina was also established by a charter. Massachusetts settlers founded New Hampshire, which received its charter in 1692. The last in the line of colonies along the Atlantic shore was Georgia, which was established in

1732 as a buffer state against Spanish Florida. The Spaniards regarded Florida as vital for control of the Bahama Channel through which the Spanish treasure fleets sailed for Spain; and they watched English and French attempts to expand in the Americas very closely. The Spanish suffered a major revolt of Pueblo Indians in New Mexico in 1680, but managed to reconquer the region. They already owned lower California, and did not settle upper California until 1769. Thus, Spain was the only power with colonies on both the Atlantic and Pacific coasts.

24 • David Teniers II, *A Peasant Eating Mussels,* c. 1655. Peasants wore brown and grays, and the men either knee-breeches or trousers. A lot of trousers were worn below high society, by sailors and peasants, so some must have been taken across to the new colonies. Both men have doublets, which roughly approximate the modish shape but are devoid of any decoration. The mussel eater's flat hat is Tudor period in ancestry, for peasants maintained styles a century or more after the court had discarded them. The thatched cottages were copied in wood in New England and New Amsterdam. *(Reproduced by permission of the Governors of Dulwich Picture Gallery)*

France was looking for a way to restrict English settlement on the eastern coast, and claimed the interior Great Lakes and Mississippi for France, establishing a colony above New Orleans in 1699. The seeds for future struggle between England, Spain, and France had been sown.

The expansionist wars in Europe, in which Louis XIV attacked the Dutch and Germans, increased the number of European settlers eager to settle in New England. The Quaker founder George Fox also sent copies of his publications into

25 • Jan Weenix, *Landscape with Shepherd Boy,* 1664. A patched pair of trousers is worn in this Italianate landscape. The shepherd boy also wears a new long coat that entered fashion in the 1650s and '60s. It looks quite worn and patched so it is probably secondhand. Few peasants adopted long coats for they got in the way of their work. The fullness of the boy's shirt imitates current style as do his long locks. His high hat is typical of the 1660s. He has his water bottle and crook, and may be filing the puppy's claws. *(Reproduced by permission of the Governors of Dulwich Picture Gallery)*

Germany, with the result that in 1683 a number of German Quakers, with some Baptists, Mennonites, and Dunkers, arrived in Pennsylvania where they built Germantown. They consisted of a doctor, a French captain, a Dutch cake baker, an apothecary, a mason, a smith, a wheelwright, a cabinet maker, a hatter, a cobbler, a tailor, a gardener, and several farmers and seamstresses.

When Louis XIV revoked the Edict of Nantes in 1685 and thereby deprived French Protestants, the Huguenots, of their freedom of religion, some of them found their way to South Carolina. A petition of 1697 lists fifty-nine Huguenots in the colony, among whom were twelve planters, twelve weavers, eleven merchants, four shipwrights, three coopers, three smiths, two goldsmiths, two gunsmiths, two joiners, two leather workers, an apothecary, a blockmaker, a brazier, a doctor, a gardener, a saddle maker, a sailmaker, a silk throwster, a watchmaker, and a wheelwright. By the end of the seventeenth century, New England possessed sufficient skilled crafts people to satisfy an elegant society.[12]

Fashion and Class

This demand for elegant fashion arose first among the tobacco plantation owners of Virginia, which became the leading center for fashion in the colonies. In 1614 John Rolfe, who married the Indian princess Pocahontas (see figure 14), sold some tobacco in London, which established a demand for the product. As a result, in 1617 planting tobacco on a large scale was started in Jamestown in Virginia. The plantation owners sold their products to London, Glasgow, and Bristol, and some became very rich, expecting to live like English country gentlemen with nice houses, servants, carriages, and eventually family portraits, the earliest of which date from 1670. Since the plantations were very hot in summer, with lots of mosquitoes, these planters preferred to move to the coast for coolness, and Charlestown became a fashionable spa, with bookshops, assemblies, dances, and racing. The city attracted mantua makers, milliners, and tailors, as well as hatters, glovers, and jewelers to cater for this market, and a replica of English fashionable society was established. Indeed, the wealthier planters sent their sons to England to complete their education, and even to find English wives, so high society was very English in its ways. The Dutch, Swedish, and French settlements were different, as were the Puritan centers, which all shared a tradition of sobriety and modesty in attire and conduct. However, the Virginians flattered themselves that they were the most stylish Americans, and regarded New Englanders in the north as dowdy.

26 • American School, *Elizabeth Paddy, Mrs. J. Wensley*, c. 1678. A lean line returned in the 1670s with a very low waist. Mrs. Wensley is wearing her best for her portrait. Her gown, with the typical cap sleeves of that decade, is silk with the pattern of stripes and flowers, which preceded the vogue for all stripes in the 1680s. A silver petticoat gleams beneath the fashionable fan. Elizabeth wears an English cap under her white hood, and a pearl necklace and earrings. Luxurious style had crossed the Atlantic and the Puritans could not stop it. The artist was probably Dutch in origin since he has included a still life of flowers. *(Pilgrim Society, Plymouth, Massachusetts)*

Fashion became increasingly divisive when periwigs and English suits became the vogue. Since they were both too impractical for working men, a demarcation of occupation by dress became glaringly obvious. The addition of long coats to the suit began in the 1650s in the Netherlands, and Louis XIV of France adopted the coats to wear over his full petticoat breeches. The English court found this style too fussy, so in 1666 Charles II introduced his version of the suit, a long coat to the knee, over an equally long vest or waistcoat and narrow knee-breeches. The English three-piece suit had been born, although it was not until the late 1670s before the French could bring themselves to wear it. Thus the English suit began its triumphant establishment. However, it was too long for the workers, and the distinction between the laboring classes and the professionals and merchants was given a new illustration. Whereas the wealthy men wore wigs and long suits, the manual workers had to remain in their doublets, knee-breeches, and their own hair for practical reasons. The suit revolutionized male fashion thereafter, for style would no longer be set by the introduction of new garments, but simply by modification of the suit as the standard costume for fashionable men; the male uniform had arrived. But there was no equivalent ensemble in the female wardrobe apart from the riding habits that were based exactly upon the masculine suit, right down to the periwig. The riding habits were the only items in the clothes chest that buttoned; otherwise women were laced or hooked into their corsets and bodices. Men had always worn buttons more than women, since the introduction of buttonholes in the 1200s, and buttons and loops were even older.

A revolution in fashionable information began in the 1670s. Louis XIV was the first monarch to have a permanent propaganda committee, the Petite Académie; and in that decade it licensed the publication of scores of engravings of French fashions as well as the leaders of the French court, as part of the king's campaign to display the superiority of his court and culture. Artists like Callot and Hollar had produced occasional sets of fashion plates earlier in the century, but the French introduced a regular production line, with engravings by St. Jean, Le Clerc, and the Bonnarts appearing every year. Some of these French prints were collected by Samuel Pepys in London, and some were carried to Virginia. Although width had returned to favor in the 1650s and '60s, the look in the 1670s was lean with a low waist at the hips, and it was this style that received the greatest publicity. Stripes became the vogue in the 1680s, and were again shown to the educated world in French engravings. For women, the *manteau*, or *manto gown*, entered their wardrobe in 1673 and became an institution. It arose from the loose *mantua* gowns, similar to dressing gowns in construction, that needed to be worn with a belt to hold them together. The pleats that were formed in front and at the back as a result of this gathering were subsequently sewn into the garment as a permanent feature. Since the manto covered the shoulders, unlike the low-cut gowns required at court, women welcomed them. The skirts could be altered according to the width or narrowness of the current style, but the construction remained constant, with lacing in front. They became the nearest equivalent to a female uniform for 120 years, up to the French Revolution.

Below fashion were the peasants and laborers, who could cross the Atlantic as indentured staff to work on the plantations. For the men, doublets and knee-breeches were standard, but

27 • British School, *A Bagpiper and His Girl*, c. 1670. Although the panel is very dirty, this is a rare portrayal of the English farm woman's summer uniform, when she discarded jackets, to work in her shift, corset, petticoat, and apron. The corset has two shoulder straps, but it looks homemade since it lacks the fierce boning of a corsetier. Such corsets were still worn in the nineteenth century. The broad straw hat protects the complexion from the sun, while the wearing of a rose in the hat was a folk tradition to show a couple were pledged. The Scotsman playing bagpipes is the girl's intended, but the artist has dressed him in sixteenth-century style to give his picture an antique air. The old man in a fur hat and overall (greatcoat) is trying to intrude. *(Reproduced by permission of the Governors of Dulwich Picture Gallery)*

some peasants preferred trousers, so they would have some trousers with them. All countries prohibited the lower classes from wearing any finery, and the browns and beiges worn by European peasants were little different from the russets and undyed cloth of English farm workers. Their womenfolk wore jackets to the hip, also called mantelets, which were similar to doublets in construction, and fastened down the front with laces or hooks. A plain skirt accompanied the jacket, reaching to the ankle or just above. Thick stockings and stout shoes completed the outfit. Underneath were a shift and a corset. In summer the jacket could be kept off, and the corset, which had two shoulder straps, could be worn alone. Straw hats were common for both sexes in hot weather, and felt hats in winter. All women at this level wore linen caps indoors and out, which were long enough to reach the neck at the sides and back, but middle-class women wore them shorter, to the bottom of the ear. To what extent the peasant was aware of fashion depended on whether they lived within a hundred miles of a metropolitan center, noted Roger North M.P. on his legal tours in 1680; for London style spread as far as Wiltshire, and one had to reach Dorset to find any difference in style. This was true of farmers in any region, and it applied to the colonies as well. Farming folk miles away from Boston or Charlestown would know nothing of changes in style in the cities, but those within a day or two's journey would know what was going on there, and might sport some fashion detail such as a wider collar or a frillier cap to show that they were more modern than their country cousins.

Since the first sumptuary law in Boston was attempted in 1634, only fourteen years after the arrival of the Pilgrims, it was obvious that the Puritan ideal was being ignored almost from the beginning. Foreigners visiting England and the London area were amazed at how the lower classes tried to follow upper-class fashion, even wearing second- or third-hand versions of court style, instead of trying to maintain a special uniform of their own as did continental European peasants. This bold attitude of not being content to look like one's lot was carried across the Atlantic, and an insistence on keeping up with fashionable developments was rooted in the English settlers, to the shock of the Puritan authorities. A people who had already decapitated a king were not going to be told how to dress.[13] This independent attitude gradually impressed the English gov-

28 • Egbert van Heemskerck, *The Quakers' Meeting, London,* c. 1685. The difference between Quaker simplicity and the mode is shown by the contrast with the two visitors on the right. They sport periwigs, cravats, cocked hats, and stylish suits. The Quakers wore plain round hats for men, and hoods and sugarloaf hats for women. Most of the Quaker men have the long-coated suit, but without the full pleats in the skirt that the visitors wear; and they have plain collars, not cravats. The women mostly wear neckerchiefs, but one has a small cape instead. The woman sitting with her back to the spectator has her petticoat pulled right back, imitating fashion but without the decoration. Aprons in white and color were worn with plain gowns. All the Quakers wore cloaks. *(Reproduced by courtesy of the Trustees of the British Museum)*

ernment, and the last sumptuary law (except for grave clothes) was Charles I's of 1643 banning the wearing of gold and silver. Charles II made declarations about dress, but his only acts, in 1666–67 and 1677–80, were those for burying the dead in woolen shrouds. Thereafter, the government dropped the subject, although sumptuary laws continued to be enforced on the continent. The colonists, therefore, as well as English citizens at home, could claim the right to wear what they liked, if they could afford it.[14]

Political problems increased when James II, an open Catholic, succeeded to the throne. The Duke of Monmouth's revolt in 1685 resulted in some 800 West Country rebels being transported to America as white slaves for the plantations. In 1688 James II was ousted in the Glorious Revolution, and replaced by his daughter Mary II and her Dutch husband and cousin William III. William and Mary assented to the Bill of Rights that reduced royal powers, and in 1690 approved the Toleration Act that allowed freedom of worship to nonconformists from Quakers to Puritans, although Catholics were still restricted. The writings of John Locke, the political philosopher who interpreted these events, were to have an enormous impact on France and the American colonies. Locke argued that a king entered into a contract with his peoples, and could be replaced if he broke that contract. The American colonies would find such arguments very attractive, having inherited both the English attitudes toward dress and toward rights.

The Scarcity of Clothing

In 1652 the Dutch allowed fifty-four English Calvinists from New England to settle in the New Netherlands at Middleburgh in New York. The court cases for Middleburgh and Newton show just how simple life was in New Netherlands. An inventory of the goods of the deceased small farmer Thomas Cornish, taken on 12 August 1662, showed that he owned just one suit and a hat, valued at two guineas. It was normal among the poor to have only one outfit. No mention is made of shirts, drawers, or stockings and shoes, which may have been too worn to have any value. Some barter was used in this small society, for the court was informed on 1 November 1671 that James Lawrence gave John Mills a cowhide in partial payment for two pairs of shoes. At the same time, a dispute about holes burned in a blanket resulted in a fine of 10s. In 1668 a dispute was recorded between Mr. W. Croft and Mr. Wandell about a buff coat, scarf, and belt. For settlers, the military buff coat of stout oxhide leather, treated with oil, and light yellow to beige in color, was an important garment. It was much cheaper than plate armor, and provided good protection against Indian arrows. In February 1677–78 the court heard a case in which Isaac Grey was charged by Mr. Wandell with wearing a scarf that his cousin had lost. Such arguments about clothing show just how scarce and important garments were to the colonists. Every garment had to be looked after carefully, for one did not know when the next supply of clothes from England or the Netherlands would arrive.[15]

This dependence on the home countries for clothing would continue into the eighteenth century. It was not easy to set up a cloth industry in the colonies, where large numbers of wolves still were devouring the sheep. In England, on the other hand, the wolf had almost been hunted into extinction, and sheep could flourish in peace, producing the long fleece that weavers worshiped. Since the settlers had to be prepared to make their own clothes, or else import them ready-made or secondhand from England, clothing became a precious and expensive commodity. This state of affairs is illustrated by some examples from the different colonies.

Carolina, for example, was owned by English noblemen and royal office-holders who had received a charter from Charles II. These Lords Proprietors—the Lord Chancellor Edward Earl of Clarendon, Anthony Lord Ashley Chancellor of the Exchequer, George Duke of Albemarle the Master of the Horse, William Earl Craven and John Lord Berkeley with some knights—ran Carolina until 1728. The extent to which clothing was scarce in the colony is reflected in the publicity pamphlet written by Samuel Wilson in 1682 to attract settlers to Carolina: "The merchandize which sells best in Carolina are Linnen and Woollen and all other stuffs to make Clothes of; with Thread, Sewing Silk, Buttons, Ribbons, Hats, Stockings, Shoes &c. which they sell at very good Rates."[16] Wilson noted that the colony had large numbers of mulberry trees, enabling it to start a silk industry, and that the soil was excellent for growing cotton, indigo, flax, and hemp. Passage to Carolina was offered for £5, and applicants told to report to the Lords Proprietors, who would be at the Carolina Coffee House, Burching Lane, London, every Tuesday (right at the center of the secondhand clothing trade, where emigrants could obtain cheap clothing).

The same problem of clothing scarcity also confronted the Swedes who settled along the Delaware before William Penn arrived, as their descendants told the Swedish professor Pehr Kalm in 1750:

> Before the English came to settle here the Swedes could not get as many clothes as they needed, and were therefore obliged to get along as best they could. The men wore waistcoats and breeches of skins. Hats were not in fashion and they made little caps, provided with flaps; some made fur caps. They had worsted stockings. Their shoes were of their own making. . . . At that time, they likewise sewed flax here and wove linen cloth. Hemp was not to be had, and they made use of linen and wild hemp for fishing tackle. The women were dressed in jackets and petticoats of skins. Their beds, excepting the sheets, were skins of various animals, such as bears, wolves etc.[17]

Once the English Quakers settled in the area, English ships began to call and a supply of English clothes became available. Under the Navigation Acts, English clothes were the only ones to be imported, so Swedes, Dutch, Germans, Finns, and French Huguenots had no choice but to dress in the English manner, although they could modify the style of caps and dye garments in different colors if they wished. Fortunately, the modest approach of the English to clothes, under the impact of the Protestant Clothing Ethic, ensured that plain attire was the main import. Finery for Virginian society had to be ordered specially from relations or tailors in England.

This situation applied also to the West Indies. Christopher Jeaffreson from Cambridgeshire inherited an estate on St. Kitts where he took a fancy to a local belle, so he wrote to London on 25 July 1681 that he wanted a new hat, broadcloth, and bright lining material for a fashionable coat, a lace cravat, lace cuffs, a swordbelt, and silk stockings. Evidently there was a tailor on the island who could make up the suit. Plainer wear was ordered for Barbadoes in 1638 by Thomas Verney, who was sent out to manage an estate. It was usual on English estates to give laborers some clothing, since they were classified with the servants, and this custom was transferred to the colonies. Verney wrote home that he would need twenty men, including a weaver and a tailor, and asked for "twelve dozen of drawers, twelve dozen of shirts, and twelve dozen of shoes, six dozen of cours neckcloths, six dozen of cour linnen stockins, large

enough or els they will not be seruiceable, six dozen cours munmouth caps."[18] Thomas Verney's bulk order shows the sort of large supply of clothing that English merchants could furnish. He ordered mostly underwear since workers in hot climates worked in their shirts and doubtless used more of them.

It was not simply individual families who sent to England for clothes, but entire plantations. Bulk orders predate the Industrial Revolution. Thus the export of clothing from England to North America gradually became a major business enterprise from the 1630s onward, and the majority of the population was dressed in English ready-made clothing, which was the sole supply. Remote settlements might have to try to make their own clothing and shoes; but the major settlements were situated along the coast where they could receive regular visits from the English merchant fleet, so there was no need for them to start up a ready-made clothing industry themselves. Indeed, the English government would have prevented it. Since the colonies were a tied market for English goods, bound by protectionist tariffs and regulations, colonial manufacture was not permitted. During this period the concept of American dress as an independent entity simply did not exist.

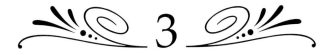

3

La Nouvelle France

The French Explorers

Along with other European states, France wanted to find a route to the riches of the East, which at that time was thought to be reached by sailing west. Following John Cabot's discovery of Newfoundland in North America, Jean Denis explored the mouth of the St. Lawrence River in 1506. In 1524 François I sent his Florentine navigator Verrazzano to look for land on which to establish a new France, and was very disappointed when he returned without finding gold. In 1534 Jacques Cartier from St. Mâlo made his first voyage. He reached Newfoundland on 10 May 1534 and described the first Canadians he saw:

> There are men of an indifferent stature and bigness, but wild and unruly; they wear their hair tied on the top like a wreath of hay, and put a wooden pin within it, or any other such thing instead of nails, and with them they bind certain birds' feathers. They are clothed with beasts skins, as well the men as women, but the women go somewhat straighter and closer in their garments than the men do, with their waists girded: they paint themselves with certain roan colors.[1]

Cartier encountered a French fishing boat from La Rochelle which was lost. Cabot's reports of the great amounts of cod in these waters had encouraged Basque, Dutch, English, French, and Spanish fishing boats to visit the shores of North America, long before settlers arrived. At Cape Royal, Cartier's crew caught 100 codfish in one hour, which proved Cabot's report. In July the local Indians started bringing skins to trade for iron goods. Other Indians were fishing for mackerel with nets, and were described as follows by Cartier: "They go altogether naked saving the privities which are covered with a little skin, and certain old skins which they cast upon them . . . their heads be altogether shaven, except one bush of hair which they suffer to grow on the top of the crown, as long as a horse's tail, and then with certain leather strings bind it in a knot upon their heads."[2]

On 24 July, Cartier erected a large cross as a landmark. When the local Indian chief objected, the French gave him two shirts, two colored coats and red hats, and a copper chain to pacify him. Cartier made a second voyage in 1535, when the Indians offered bundles of beaver and seawolf skins in exchange for iron axes. The Indian king of Canada, Dounakona, expressed a wish to visit the king of France, and Cartier took him back to France, where the old man died. In 1540 François I licensed Cartier to make another voyage. Sailing from Honfleur, laden with a cargo of crop seeds to test in the new land, he built a fort and founded a small settlement.

In 1542 the king appointed Jean François de la Roche, Lord Roberval, as lieutenant general in Canada. He took along 200 settlers and built a fort at France Roy, although during the first winter, 50 of the settlers and many of his crew died. Roberval's journals reflect a European fascination with the strange natives as well as an ignorance of their customs. For example, he believed that they painted themselves as a precaution against sunburn and heat, and considered they would be as white as the French if they wore clothing. He also depicted their attire and appearance as follows:

> Instead of apparel they wear skins upon them like mantles, and they have a small pair of breeches wherewith they cover their privities, as well men as women. They have hosen and shoes of leather excellently made and they have no shirts, neither cover they the head, but their hair is trussed up above the crown of their heads, and plaited or braided.[3]

None of these early French voyages discovered a route to China. And as the religious disputes of the Reformation began to claim their attention, the French kings eventually lost interest in northern exploration. But in the middle of the sixteenth century, the French did attempt to break into the Spanish monopoly by settling further south in the Americas. First French Huguenots, or Protestants, under Admiral Villegaignon tried to set up a colony in Rio de Janeiro in 1555, but were expelled by the Portuguese. In 1563 René de la Laudonnière (see Plate I) set up Huguenot colonies in Florida, but as mentioned earlier, they were massacred by Spain.

Early French Settlements

It was not until the seventeenth century that a new French drive into Canada recommenced under the Dieppe shipbuilder Samuel Champlain. In 1608, on 3 July, Champlain founded Québec, taking a name of the Algonquin Indians for the narrowing of the waters. Québec was established from the start as a trading base, where the Huron and Algonquin Indians brought furs in exchange for goods, there being an abundance of beaver, bear, deer, roe, otter, seals, martens, and lynxes in the area. Champlain notes that the Indians wore snow shoes, two or three times larger than European shoes, one of the Indian items that the settlers soon adopted for winter travel. In 1610 and 1611 Champlain brought over some artisans from Honfleur in Normandy to become the first settlers in Québec. However, as a result of the war between England and France, Captain David Kirk sailed up the St. Lawrence in 1628 and captured the town, along with Samuel Champlain, although both were restored to France under the peace treaty of 1632. In 1633 Champlain sailed back to France to return with Jesuits who began to convert the Indians. And in 1639, the nursing nuns of Dieppe sent over a team to found the first hospital in Québec, the Hôtel Dieu, with money provided by the Duchesse Daiguillon.[4]

Fur trading was the basis of the new colony at Québec, and the Company of Canada was established in 1627 to manage the enterprise. In 1663 Louis XIV required the company to change its name to the Company of New France, granting it exclusive rights to the fur trade. When the king was informed that this monopoly was being challenged by fur trappers who explored deep into Indian territory, Louis XIV commanded a fine of 2,000 livres to be imposed in 1676. These trappers were accused of selling their furs to people they met on their travels, such as the English in the Hudson's Bay, in northwest Québec. The English settlement was named after its discoverer, Henry Hudson, who had been seeking a route through the ice to the East in 1609 when he was abandoned, along with his sick sailors, to die at the bay. Despite the French claiming exclusive rights to all furs in Canada, in 1670 the English founded the Hudson's Bay Company under Prince Rupert of the Rhine, a cousin of Charles II. This company now also claimed the right to furs in Canada, and New France faced a competitor in the frozen north.[5]

The settlements founded by Cartier and Roberval failed because they were ill prepared for the severe winters and Indian attacks. The first permanent Norman settlement that is still inhabited is at the mouth of the St. Lawrence River, where Pierre Chauvin of Honfleur founded a fur-trading post, called Tadoussac, in 1599–1600. Samuel Champlain visited the trading post in 1603, and learning that it was often attacked by the Iroquois Indians, he equipped Québec with cannon, which enabled it to survive. The fur traders who lived there copied the Indian style of wearing furs, and probably made themselves fur hats, fur coats, fur trousers, and leggings, to wear with Indian snow shoes, as they learned how to adapt to the climate. In 1615 some Franciscan Recollect missionaries arrived in Tadoussac to begin converting the natives, and Jesuits followed in 1641. The economy in Québec was entirely fur-based at first. The first farmer, Louis Hébert, did not arrive until 1617, and his daughter was to be the first Norman bride in Canada. Neither did the English keep away for long, founding a settlement in Newfoundland in 1610, and one in Nova Scotia, where a French post had been established in 1605.

On 18 May 1642, Ville Marie de Montréal was founded by the young French officer Paul de Chomédy, Sieur de Maisonneuve, who brought twenty-three colonists with him from Normandy. Despite Iroquois attacks, the island site proved an excellent base for the fur trade, and the population increased rapidly from seventy-two people in 1642 to 760 in 1667. However, the Indian assaults continued, the Iroquois attacked the Huron Indians and drove them out of the territory, and they murdered the Jesuit missionaries in 1649. But, in spite of the great danger, Franciscans, Jesuits, and Ursuline sisters based themselves in Montréal, which resulted in increasing conflict with the fur traders of the Company of New France concerning the role of the Church. Following the bishop's complaints to King Louis XIV, the king took control of Canada as a royal province. A royal intendant was installed, along with the feudal system that still survived in France. The land was divided into estates, with manor houses for the lords; and peasants were brought to work the land, paying the lord a percentage of their produce and supplying labor for the lord on his personal farm.

New France was therefore a totally different colony from New England. The former was governed by the French crown and the established Catholic Church, the latter by Protestant nonconformists and commercial companies. New France was settled by feudal peasants, New England by independent farmers. The monopoly of the Company of New France further restricted development in New France, for the Company would not allow other industries to challenge its position. Consequently, commerce consisted only of fur trading, farming, and fishing, with no mineral produce. To increase the population, King Louis XIV sent over 4,000 Norman peasants. When they

30 • French School, *The Vegetable Merchant*, c. 1630. In the French provinces women wore a sixteenth-century type of cap with a long neckpiece called the *bavolet*, which gave good protection against the sun. This merchant has a plain gown fastened in front with hooks and eyes, for the poor had to dress themselves, and could not be laced up by servants. She has the wide collar typical of the 1630s, but in plain linen. The customer by his apron must be another stallholder, and wears a buff leather doublet, faintly echoing a shoulder wing in the way the shoulder overhangs the sleeve. He must have seen some gentry for he has imitated their moustaches and goatee beards; but his round hat looks local Savoyard. His companion wears a more fashionable size of hat, but not in the proper way. His greasy cloak illustrates the waxing and greasing of clothes for protection against rain. (*Musée des Beaux Arts, Chambery, Savoy*)

complained about the Iroquois attacks, the king dispatched 1,000 troops in 1665, and then decided to send over 1,000 young women for the troops to marry. After the troops were given two weeks to make their choice of a bride, they were married in several wedding ceremonies supervised by the first royal intendant, Jean Talon. The military governor, Frontenac, who was in charge of countering Indian attacks, in 1690 defeated an attempt by Governor Sir William Phipps of Massachusetts to seize Québec for a second time, the English having occupied the town in 1628. Québec was only 500 kilometers from Boston, and there would be many clashes to come. Although the French were attempting to restrict the New England settlement to the coastal fringe, the English were determined to expand.[6]

Dress and Social Class

As a royal province, Canada came under the jurisdiction of French sumptuary laws and protective tariffs. Already in existence was Louis XIV's declaration of 30 June 1661 requiring his subjects to wear only French-made lace and trimmings. Men might wear trimming or lace bands only around the collar, on the hem of a cloak, down the length of breeches or canons, and around the sleeve head, the sleeve seam, the center back seam, center front, and around the buttons placed there, and the basques of his doublet. Women might have lace or trimming only around the hem and down the front of gowns and petticoats, and around the bodices and basques; such trimmings should not be more than two fingers high, or cost more than 40 sols. A merchant who sold foreign trimmings would be fined 1,500 livres. On 23 November 1667 the importation of foreign lace and trimming was banned. Louis XIV's minister Colbert was trying to build up the French textile industry and erected barriers against importing all foreign textiles. At first European competitors were prohibited by high tariffs from selling to France, but by 1686 the French East India Company, modeled on the English and Dutch East India companies, was importing such quantities of painted and printed Indian calico, and Indian and Chinese silks flowered with gold and silver, that the government slapped a ban on these oriental imports, with a fine of 3,000 livres. Consequently New France was required to import only French fabrics, just as New England had to import only English cloth in English ships.[7]

The peasantry, of course, were too poor to be affected by sumptuary and protectionist laws, but the rising fur traders could face a fine if they dressed too grandly when in Québec or Montréal. Weddings were one event where striving to dress

31 • Louise Moillon, *The Fruit and Vegetable Merchant*, s.d. 1631. Louise was a Parisian artist, and her painting shows that in a city shop the long cap could be replaced by a short cap. It is obviously summer, for the shop–keeper has discarded her jacket to work in her shift, corset, apron, and petticoat, as in England. The customer shows the French obsession with fashion by dressing up in the height of style just to do the shopping. Her bodice sleeves are paned (slashed), and she has front lacing. The gauze collar is starched and wired, and sets off the pearl necklace. Wearing a flower at the breast was an old custom, practiced by Elizabeth I in the previous century. (*Musée du Louvre, cliché des Musées Nationaux*)

above one's rank in society was usual, so the participants had to be careful; the priests as well as the intendant were watching. The dominant colors of French peasant dress were brown and gray, to such an extent that country girls were called *grisettes*, from *gris*—gray. Another term for country women was *ba-*

32 • Louis le Nain, *Peasant Family*, d. 1642. The grandmother wears the basic peasant uniform with the jacket, skirt, and apron. In the region around Paris peasant women may have abandoned long neckpieces on their caps, but the *bavolets* survived from Normandy to Savoy. The elongation of grandmother's cap shows the effect of head binding. The grandchild is swaddled in a bed, but his head is much too covered to notice any binding. The mother has a front-laced gown for nursing, with a long apron. The father displays the absence of buttons among the poor, for a pin holds his doublet together. Such garments were copied in Canada in homespun drugget. (*Musée du Louvre, cliché des Musées Nationaux*)

volettes, because they wore a *bavolet*, the long neckpiece at the back of the linen cap, which was fifteenth century in origin. In Paris, shopgirls were discarding *bavolets* in the 1630s, but country women continued wearing them into the eighteenth and nineteenth centuries. As most of the population in New France were peasants, they arrived with gray and brown clothes, and the women with *bavolets* on their caps. And since the neckpiece served a real function, protecting the neck from the sun when the women were working in the fields, country women retained it in their costume.

The woman's basic wardrobe was similar to that of other European peasants. It began with a linen shift and the corset or stays, but the working woman's corset was not the heavily boned creation of a professional corsetier, but a homemade article often with wooden stays instead of bones sewn into a piece of canvas. Over that corset went the jacket-like bodice with basques to the hips, and the plain skirt to the ankles. The linen cap would be covered with a straw or felt hat out in the fields, and a linen neckerchief would be tucked in round the neck and into the bodice. In hot weather, the bodice could be left off, and the woman worked in the corset and shift. The men still wore doublets to the hip, which were usually laced together or else held together by a belt, as buttons were costly. Below, knee-breeches or trousers were worn according to preference. Drawers were usually knee-length, with strings at the bottom that were tied to fit into the knee-breeches neatly. Stockings for both sexes were tied on with garters, though in bad weather gaiters of straw or leather could be added. Whereas men had worn coifs in the Middle Ages, this custom had died out over the sixteenth and seventeenth centuries, and the only head cover for men were straw or felt hats. To cope with the Canadian winter, it became important for the women to wear several shifts and petticoats with thick woolen stockings along with long cloaks with hoods. The men would wear several full shirts, or half shirts, which were unseamed up the sides; and leggings and trousers gained in value. At the 1665 weddings, when the nuns had sorted the girls into virgins and others, the soldiers had felt that the fattest girls would survive the winter best, but this was not the case. Once married, the couples were given eleven crowns, a bull, a cow, a hog and a sow, a cock and a chicken, and two barrels of salt meat, and ordered to begin farming. According to the officer Baron Lahontan, who wrote

33 • Jean Michelin, *The Bread-seller and the Water Carriers,* s.d. 1653. For outdoor workers the *bavolet* neckpiece continued to be important outside Paris. Michelin hailed from Langres, so this may be a local scene. The water-women retain *bavolets* and wear wide linen collars fifteen years after they had gone out of fashion. Their wearing of dresses shows them to be townees rather than peasants. The girl's clothes are too big, but she had to wear what the family possessed. The boy's doublet has a few buttons, which show that it is second- or third-hand, but even so he fastens it with a string. The stockings are made of cloth, worsted being the most common fabric. The bread-seller has a fine cloak of better quality than the rest of his attire. There are no buttons on his doublet, which is probably buff leather for durability, and his knee-breeches are straight like tubes. Hats grew wide again in the 1650s. (*Musée du Louvre, cliché des Musées Nationaux*)

from Québec at this time, the peasants were better off there than in France, although he conceded that farming in Canada was more difficult; but they were excused the terrible *taille* tax per head, which was an enormous burden on peasants back home, and they had the right to fish and hunt, which no peasant possessed in France.[8]

Swaddling and Head Binding

One custom the French and Norman settlers would have taken with them was the common European tradition of baby swaddling and head binding, which dates back to antiquity. The English were beginning to have doubts about this practice, but the French maintained the custom. Dr. Charles Guillemeau, surgeon to Louis XIII, wrote in 1620 that the arms should be bound inside the swaddling for the first three weeks, at which time they could be allowed outside; but the baby had to start wearing a corset, male or female, to keep it straight.[9] The whole procedure was explained by Dr. François Mauriçeau in his *Traité des Maladies des Femmes*, which Charles II's physician, Hugh Chamberlen, translated in 1673. The midwife should "let her begin to swaddle it in its Swathing Cloaths, beginning first to cover the head with a small linnen Biggen [cap]," Chamberlen wrote, noting that this was a French fashion and continuing to describe the procedure:

> putting a Woolen Cap upon it, having first put upon the Mould of the Head a fine Linnen rag, three or four double, and four Fingers broad; which that it may not stir, pin to the Biggen with a small Pin on the outside that it may not prick the Child, this double Rag serves to defend the Child's Brain (which is not as yet covered over in this place with a Bone), as well as from the cold and other injuries: Let her put small Rags behind the Ears to dry up the filth which usually is there ingendred: that done, let her put other rags as well upon the Breast, as in the folds of the Armpits and Groynes, and so swathe it.[10]

At this point the doctor assumes that every woman born knew how to swaddle by instinct, but he did stress the avoidance of tight swaddling since it could cause breathing difficulties or the vomiting up of milk. The basic garment in swaddling was the bed, a linen sack:

> let his Arms and Legs be wrapped in his bed, and stretched strait out and swathed to keep them so, viz. his Arms along his sides, and his Legs equally both together, with a little of the bed between

them so that they may not be galled by rubbing one another: after all this, the Head must be kept steady and strait with a stay fastened on each side the Blanket, and wrap the Child up in a Mantle or Blanket, to keep it warm. He must thus be swaddled to give his little body a strait Figure, which is most decent and convenient for a Man, and to accustom him to keep upon the Feet, else he would go on all fours, as most other Animals do.

Since some children's heads did not close until they were three, the doctors recommended that head binding continue until then. Some women swore by scarlet cloth to strengthen the head, but Chamberlen noted that any cloth would suffice.

In France, however, head binding continued into adulthood and throughout life, and this practice was taken to Canada. It had the effect of causing baldness in front, which produced an elongated head with a high forehead, very fashionable in the Middle Ages. In France, particularly in Normandy, Gascony-Toulouse, central France, and Burgundy, the peasants continued the tradition down to the nineteenth century. The Musée de l'Homme in Paris has photographs from the late nineteenth century showing the long heads produced by this practice.[11]

Some English thinkers began to express doubts about swaddling in the seventeenth century. John Bulwer protested in 1650:

We in *England* are noted to have a perverse custome of Swathing Children and streightening their Breasts, which narrownesse of Breast occasioned by hard and strict swaddling them, is the cause of many inconveniences and dangerous consequences.[12]

In 1693 John Locke expressed similar concern. In rearing children, he stressed, never forget "that your Sons Cloaths be *never* made *strait*, especially about the Breast. Let Nature have scope to fashion the Body as she thinks best: she works of herself a great deal better, than we can direct her." Yet ignorant midwives and nurses, bodice and staymakers, would interfere, binding chests and forcing little girls into corsets when they were babies. "I have seen so many Instances of Children receiving great harm from *strait lacing*," wrote Locke of the "Narrow Breasts, short and stinking Breath, ill Lungs and Crookednesse, are the Natural and almost constant Effects of *hard Bodice* and *cloths that pinch*.[13]

Locke's advice to trust Nature was well in advance of Rousseau's call to go "back to Nature" in the next century. Fortunately the English swaddled babies only for about three months, in contrast to the French. In 1707 Louis XIV's second wife, Madame de Maintenon, declared the English system was better:

> If I were not so old, I would have tried raising children as one does in England, where they are almost all tall and well made, like we have seen them brought up at St. Germain [where the exiled James II was living]. When babies are two or three months old they are given a looser dress, and under their robe they have a wrapper and a nappy without any swaddling bands, which are changed as soon as the baby has made the least mess, so that the children never remain, as ours do, tightly swaddled in their excrement, which is what spares them from crying fits, bad moods and often mal-formed legs.[14]

The Indians in Canada also swaddled babies. Baron Lahon-tan recorded that "they swathe them down upon little Boards or Planks stuffed with Cotton, when they lye upon the Back."[15] The boards had strings attached so that the squaw would hang the papoose in a tree when she was gathering food. In the west the Flathead Indians went even further, having not only a board at the back that flattened the skull from behind, but also a board in front to flatten the forehead, producing a cone-shaped skull. John Bulwer had criticized a similar habit in England: "The English commonly love a broad or high forehead, and the Midwives and Nurses use much art and endeavour by stroking up their foreheads, and binding them hard with filets, to make children to have them faire and high ones."[16]

The English custom of head binding was also taken to the Americas, and the high foreheads in portraits show it persisting into the eighteenth century. The English began to give up swaddling and head binding during this period, although it took Rousseau in France to make the educated classes take notice. Even so, the first medical attack on the custom in France did not appear until 1772 in Paris, when Dr. Alphonse Leroy of the Faculty of Medicine published his *Récherches sur les habille-ments des femmes et des enfans*. Tracing the swaddling practice back to ancient Egypt, he described it as a curse for babies, yet the richer the baby's family, the more the infant was laden with swaddling and additional finery in silk, muslin, and lace, so that only its eyes and nose were visible. French high society began to take such advice in the eighteenth century, but the peasants could not read or buy medical books, and they continued in the customary way.

Once children were toddlers they were given petticoats, that is, a small coat for the boys and a dress for the girls. The boys usually had adult slashes—sleeves cut into strips so that the shirt or undersleeve could be seen—and collars and hats to denote their masculinity, as well as toy guns and horses, while the girls wore miniature dresses, with caps and aprons, and were given dolls to baby. Protective aids were available, such as puddings, as the padded head rolls toddlers wore were called, and the walking frames that prevented them from falling over.

Development of Colonial Textiles and Fashions

34 • Michel Dessaillant, *Votive of Mme Reverin and Her Children*, 1703. The wife of a merchant in Montréal, Mme Reverin wears the height of fashion at the frontier. Her gown is the manto, pulled back to show the petticoat, and on her head she wears the commode lace headdress in two tiers, with long lappets behind. The children are dressed as adults, the son in a coat and a cravat, with long hair like a periwig. The daughters are in mantos like maman, and the eldest has a commode cap as well. The younger girls have no lappets on their caps, and the baby wears an apron. *(Courtesy of the Basilica of Ste Anne de Beaupré, Québec, Les Pères Rédemptoristes)*

Although Québec's first royal intendant, Jean Talon, wanted to set out to conquer New York State, the king's minister Colbert urged him to first strengthen the French colony. Talon applied himself vigorously to building the economy. For example, thinking that all women should be trained to weave, he distributed looms throughout the settlements. Gradually this led to a small supply of rough cloth becoming available for carpets, druggets, serges, and bunting. Talon also established a leather tannery to produce the colony's shoes, and in 1671 he was able to write to Louis XIV that "I have sufficient Canadian products to clothe me from head to foot." Therefore, his suit, cloak, stockings, and shoes could all be homemade, and possibly his linen too; in quality, of course, the cloth could not equal the shaved velvety surface of English broadcloth.[17]

Québec was a capital city with a bishop, and Baron Lahontan was amazed by the elegant fashion he observed when he was posted there in 1685. On 2 October he wrote:

> The Gentlemen that have Charge of Children, especially Daughters, are oblig'd to be good Husbands, in order to bear the expense of the magnificent Cloaths with which they are set off; for Pride, Vanity, and Luxury reign as much in *New France* as in *Old France*, In

my opinion 't would do well if the King would prohibit the selling of Gold and Silver Brocadoes, Fringes, and Ribands, as well as Points and rich Laces.[18]

But a simple style of dress was not to be. Louis XIV made luxury the height of fashion. To appear at Versailles required cloth of gold and silver with diamonds, and this extravagant style was reflected by the officials in Québec. Suits in silk and brocade, embroidered with gold or decked with gold lace, contrasted enormously with the dress of the fur traders upon whom the riches of the colony depended.

Lahontan went to Montréal to observe how the Indians delivered the furs and was surprised at the quantities. Each

canoe carried 40 packs of furs weighing 50 pounds each, and each pack was worth 50 crowns. A lot of money was being made, and some officials made a bit on the side by allowing the Indians to sell furs to the English, who paid more and gave more items to the Indians in exchange. After the sales at Montréal were concluded, the Indian braves went shopping, as Lahontan writes: "Tis a comical sight to see 'em running from Shop to Shop, stark naked, with their Bow and Arrow. The nicer sort of Women are wont to hold their Fans before their faces." Odd as it may seem, even on the frontier, French ladies had to own fans, such was the obsession with fashion, but it was one of their countrymen who accused them of vanity and pride.

Lahontan went on to describe the dress of the Indians around Montréal: "The older and married men have a piece of stuff which cover them behind and reaches halfway down their Thighs before; whereas the Young Men are stark nak'd all over. They have likewise a sort of cloak or coat calculated for the season, when they go Hunting or upon Warlike Expeditions, in order to guard off Cold in Winter and the Flies in Summer. On such occasions they make use of a sort of Cap, made in the form of a Hat, and Shooes of Elk or Hart skins, which reach up to their mid-Leg."[19]

In 1705 Madame de Repentigny was licensed to be the first textile manufacturer in Canada, producing a rough cloth called druggets. By 1736 an anonymous government report noted that the colony was self-sufficient in the production of tools and goods: They make themselves the majority of their tools and utensils for work; build their houses and barns; several are weavers and make rough fabrics and stuffs which they call druggets, which they use to clothe themselves and their families.[20] Thus, many French Canadians could clothe themselves roughly on their farms, where, of course, they did not attempt to follow the fashions of Québec but retained their seventeenth-century peasant wardrobe into the nineteenth century, with the hip-length jacket and short skirt for women, and the doublets and breeches or trousers for men.

A long-standing problem was the Indian smuggling of English cloth. A critical report of October 1756 complained that the Company shipped only 1,200 pieces of cloth a year, which it obtained from England. The Indians brought in English cloth, muslin, English-Indian cottons, and callemandoes, and were

35 • French School, *A Rustic Meal*, c. 1740. This gouache brilliantly shows the time gap between the peasantry and their noble employers. The highly fashionable diners have all the latest styles of wig, the man's coat is full of pleats in the skirt, and the lady has a hoop and long skirt trailing on the ground. The peasant women have the look of 1640 rather than 1740 with neckpieces on their caps; their jackets, skirts, and aprons; and the absence of hoops. None of the men have full-skirted coats, and all are in short coats or waistcoats, which had sleeves. Their knee-breeches are much more bulky than the gentleman's, and the flutist still wears his breeches above the knee, as in the previous century. Only in their long hair do the men approximate to the fashionable look. Such social distinctions would have existed on estates in French Canada. (*Musée des Beaux Arts, Cholet, Maine et Loire*)

themselves dressing exclusively in English products: "The Savages in Canada use English scarlets to make the mantles which serve them as clothing and adornment. These cloths are dyed partly in red, and partly in blue-black, and the consumption of these last is the greatest, because the women and the men use them equally. Those who wish to please or are well off, add to the bottom of these mantles bands of ribbons of different colours."[21] In questioning why this state of affairs was allowed to continue, an anonymous official was told that officials turned a blind eye or themselves had a finger in the business. Matters in Canada needed reforming, the official insisted, noting that even some of the messenger boats on the St. Lawrence belonging to the colonial government were made in England! However, the French had modified Louis XIV's ban on printed cottons to allow French textile firms to start printing cotton and producing

oriental-type silks. In 1744 Wetter opened a manufactory in Marseilles, in 1752 the Danton brothers set up a works at Angers, Abraham Frey opened at Rouen in 1756, and the brothers Petitpierre started a works at Nantes in 1760. They all produced printed cottons known as *indiennes*, and silks called *siamoises*, which were inspired by the silks brought to Louis XIV by the Siamese embassy in 1686. Consequently, a supply of French "Eastern" fabrics was now available, also in Canada, but it was too late to affect the flood of Indian cottons that England was shipping into North America. Such cottons were most welcome in Louisiana, the most southern part of New France.

After exploring the Great Lakes, the French discovered the source of the Mississippi, which the Indians said flowed south. In 1683 Sieur Robert Cavalier de la Salle, then stationed at Fort Frontenac on the lakes where he was trying to control the illegal fur trade between the Iroquois and the English, set out to explore the river. His historian was the Franciscan Louis Hennepin, whose bare feet and sandals charmed the Indians. De Salle found downstream that large numbers of the Indians were dressed in European styles, so they obviously had been trading with the English. Some still wore skins, but most wore shirts, with cloaks and capes. A cloth piece around the middle was tied by a belt, and they wore footless stockings or gaiters, with shoes in natural skin. In the spring when they had beaver or otter skins to sell, they traded them for coats, stockings, shoes, and hats. Sometimes they donned mantles, but now they had a wider choice of clothing. Hennepin observed that the Louisiana Indians blacked the face only as high as the ears, unlike the Canadian Indians who blacked the whole face, or else blacked half the face, vertically. His report was sent to Louis XIV and published in 1683, and translations into Dutch, Spanish, and English followed before the decade was out. France was trying to create an empire from Canada to the Gulf of Mexico.[22]

In 1744 an officer stationed at New Orleans, which had been founded in 1718, reported on the French colony. It traded timber with the American colonies in return for fabrics. France also sent fabrics and cloth, in exchange for cotton, indigo, and hides. The town supplied the Indians with woolen blankets, ribbons, shifts, shirts, and blue and red cloth, in return for beaver, otter, buck, and kid skins. Plantations with African slaves were set up, and a wealthy society began to develop, with a taste for display, extravagant pastimes, and women. As the officer recorded, "The Rich spend their Time in seeing their Slaves work to improve their Lands, and get Money, which they spend on Plays, Balls, and Feasts; but the most common Pastime of the highest as well as the lowest, and even some of the Slaves, is Women." The rich gatherings were a market for France's silks, the *siamoises,* for evenings, and cotton *indiennes* for day. Since the English revived the wearing of hoops in 1708, fashion had begun to use more material. As the art likes to take an idea to its ultimate extreme, the hoops expanded as far as the technology of canvas, bamboo, and wire would allow, and the mills were happy as demands for fabric soared.

There was corruption here, too. Baron Lahontan had found that in Québec the money for clothing the troops was siphoned off, and the same situation obtained in New Orleans. "The Forces are pretty well kept: they have a Compleat Clothing every two Years, and Part of Clothing every Year; but 'tis not very faithfully distributed, for out of three Cloathings the Commissaries make shift to get one."[23] In his report, the officer included a list of goods that the governor, M. de Vaudreuil, thought the colony needed: 4,000 ells* of Limbourg linen, 4,000 shirts, 2,000 girdles, 200 pieces of scarlet worsted ribbon, 200 pieces of worsted Lace in different colors to trim the clothes of the chiefs, and 50 plumes of feathers. This list seems to have referred only to the Indians, although the plumes of feathers were probably ostrich plumes that were still very fashionable for trimming men's hats and adorning four-poster beds. Perhaps such plumes were now also presented to the Indian chiefs as marks of special favor. However, the English were not going to allow the French to sprawl across the American continent, and they took countermeasures in Canada. In 1713, having beaten Louis XIV in Europe, by the treaty of Utrecht they obtained Newfoundland and Nova Scotia from France. France retained Cape Breton Island and in 1717 built the immense Louisbourg fortress to defend it. But New England saw the fortress as a threat, and in 1745 they took it with the help of the Royal Navy. The peace terms required them to hand it back to the French, but the British recaptured Louisbourg in 1758. Halifax on Nova

---

*One ell equals 45 inches.

Scotia was founded by Lord Cornwallis in 1749 as the British military and naval base for the conquest of French Canada, and the counter to Louisbourg.

During the period of increasing tension between England and France in Canada, Professor Pehr Kalm of Sweden visited Québec in 1750, and commented upon the dress of the inhabitants:

> All the women in the country without exception wear caps of some kind or other. Their jackets are short and so are their skirts, which scarcely reach down to the middle of their legs. Their shoes are often like those of Finnish women, but are sometimes provided with heels. They have a silver cross hanging down the breast. . . . When they go out of doors, they wear long cloaks, which cover all their clothes, and are either grey, brown, or blue. Men sometimes make use of them when they are obliged to walk in the rain. The women have the advantage of being in *déshabille* under these cloaks without anyone perceiving it.[24]

He found Québec city much more refined than Dutch or English settlements:

> On the street they raised their hat only to acquaintances and to those of the upper classes. Young men often kept their hats on inside when there were women, but most of them, especially the older ones, took them off. The English, on the other hand, do not idle their time away in dressing as the French do here. The ladies, especially, dress and powder their hair every day, and put their locks into papers every night. This idle custom had not been introduced in English settlements. The gentlemen generally wear their own hair, but some have wigs, and there are a few so distinguished that they had a queue. People of rank are accustomed to lace-trimmed clothes, and all the crown officers carry swords. All the gentlemen, even those of rank, the governor-general excepted, carry their cloaks on the left arm.[25]

French society was ever the center of correct etiquette and formality, and this was true also of Québec. The city considered itself superior in taste to Montréal, but the Swedish professor found it a fault that French Canadian women made so much fuss about fashion and hairstyles: "Their hair is always curled, even when they are at home in a dirty jacket and a short, coarse skirt that does not reach to the middle of their legs. On Sundays and visiting days they dress so gayly" they could be taken for aristocrats. There was too much attention paid to new fashion,

FACING PAGE

36 • Antoine Raspal, *A Couture Workroom in Arles*, s.d. 1760. Even inside fashion, the workers did not wear the latest creations. The seated seamstress on the left has the traditional jacket and skirt, but some of the others have plain dresses as townees. The mistress of the couture firm wears a fashionable dress of printed silk, but with no hoop. All the girls wear the *couquetto*, the Arles bonnet held on with a headscarf. Thanks to imports their neckerchiefs are in printed cotton. Their dresses have boned bodices, as was usual. The hems are much shorter than the fashion. The finished silken garments are hung on hooks on the wall. Although a servant could be given an old silk gown, the dressmaker was not. (*Archives photographiques des Musées d'Arles, Provence*)

cutting up expensive dresses as soon as they are out of style, which the professor thought a shocking waste. But the Canadians were a year behind the mode, in any case. The company sent only one fleet a year, so the newest fashions seized on in Québec were a year behind the styles in metropolitan France.[26] Scented powders in the hair had been fashionable since the 1660s, but by the 1690s powdering the hair or wig white or gray had become the principal mode, giving everyone a standardized hair color. The Age of Reason disliked signs of individuality, which is why the Romantics, with their cult of Nature, were to revolt against the neoclassical ideal from the 1760s onward.

Professor Kalm also observed and commented on the influence of French fashion on the Indians. The French traded with

the Indians, offering a coarse white cloth with blue or red stripe at the edge, a blue or red cloth that was offered in New Orleans, and which the Indian women liked in blue for their skirts. Shirts and shifts were also on offer, and the Indians would not remove these garments until they fell to pieces. Kalm found that Indian women were slower to copy European styles, and preferred the old-fashioned look rather than the most up-to-date look. Some of them wore caps of homespun or of a coarse blue broadcloth, probably both made in Canada. The Indians preferred strips of cloth to wrap around their legs, like Russians, for they did not care for trousers: "A great number of the natives, i.e., the confederates of the French, had already begun to dress like the French; the same kind of jacket and vest, while on journeys they wore the same red cap or hat. But one could not persuade them to use trousers, for they thought these were a great hindrance in walking. . . . When the French are travelling about in this country, they are generally dressed like the natives, they wear no trousers."[27] According to Kalm, therefore, it seems as if the French traders wore trousers themselves, but had to give them up for leg strips in Indian country. The professor does not identity the tribe he is describing, but it may have been the Ottawas who were common in the west of the province. In Montréal Professor Kalm saw the range of furs the Indians brought—roebuck, otter, marten, cat, wolf, lynx, fox, black squirrel, stag, elk, reindeer, muskrat, and beaver. He also observed the French missionaries. For example, the Jesuits wore long black coats to the ankle; the younger Jesuits wore hats, the middle-aged hoods, and the elders a cone-shaped cap with a tassel at the top. The Franciscan Recollects wore long black cassocks tied with rope round the waist, and generally went without stockings in wooden shoes, although they would don woolen stockings during the Canadian winter. The gnats in the country were a pest, and the Jesuits advised the professor to wear grease on his face as protection.

The English Conquest

The good professor, whose survey of North America touched on details from age to weather, went home before the storm broke. The intense competition between England and France in India and North America led to the Seven Years' War, as a result of which France would lose both empires. The Royal Navy defeated both the French Atlantic and Mediterranean fleets so she was unable to send reinforcements to Canada. France had tried to build a chain of forts from Louisbourg to New Orleans, and the British now took the lot—Louisbourg, Fort Frontenac on Lake Ontario, Fort Duquesne (Pittsburgh), Fort Niagara, and then Québec city on its heights. Several Englishmen had told Professor Kalm that they thought the American colonies were strong enough to be independent in about fifty years, by about 1800. But the threat from New France made the English colonies anxious for the continuation of British protection. Britain now removed that threat herself. In 1763 New France became British Canada, and thus was cut off from French clothing developments, particularly from the multiplicity of peasant styles that began to evolve by the end of the eighteenth century in France.

The Definitive Treaty of Peace and Friendship between his Britannic Majesty, the Most Christian King (France), and the King of Spain was concluded at Paris on 10 February 1763. Spain had been involved in the Seven Years' War as France's ally for she had been ruled by a French dynasty since 1700. Under Article IV, France ceded to Britain all Canada and her dependencies, with Nova Scotia, Cape Breton Island, and all other islands in the Gulf and River of St. Lawrence. Britain promised that the French Catholics in Canada would be able to continue to practice their faith, and also gave them the option to leave the country, which some of them did. French fishermen were allowed to continue fishing off the Newfoundland coast, and, under article VI, Britain returned the islands of St. Pierre and Miquelon to France as a base for these fishermen, providing they had a British garrison. Article XX of the treaty required Spain to hand over to Britain all Spanish territory east of the Mississippi, that is, Florida and the coastal area along the Gulf of Mexico. Spain was allowed to gain New Orleans providing British ships had free access to the port and river beyond. Thus, a huge area was now brought within reach of the British Navigation Laws, which obliged the inhabitants to buy only British goods.[28]

In 1766–68, Captain Jonathan Carver was sent to explore the region of Louisiana, where previously French fur traders or *voyageurs* had been the principal explorers. Carver reported on the appearance of the Indians he observed on this frontier:

Those who trade with the Europeans, these exchange their furs for blankets, shirts, and other apparel, which they wear as much for ornament as necessity. The latter fasten by a girdle around their waists about half a yard of broadcloth which covers the middle part of their bodies. Those who wear shirts never make them fast either at the wrist or collar, this would be almost uncomfortable confinement to them. They throw their blanket loose upon their shoulders.[29]

Carver found that the more showy males plucked their hair, except for a spot at the top of the head that they allowed to grow to a great length, and decked with feathers. This hairstyle was the chief means for distinguishing one Indian tribe from another, he noticed. Some Indian males also liked to slit the earlobe and bind it with brass wire, pulling it downward until it reached the shoulder. European men's shirts were worn by both sexes, and the squaws dressed in a shirt to the hip or thigh, and a knee-length skirt beneath in broadcloth. Their hair was usually in a plait down the back. Carver spent some time living with the Noudoweseis. As in New England and Canada proper, most of the Indians were dependent on British and French fabrics and shirts. Now with the fur trade coming under British control, the supply became mainly British. The French Empire from Canada to Louisiana had acquired a British master.

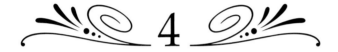

4

The English Colonies, 1689–1774

Information about colonial life at the turn of the seventeenth century and the start of the eighteenth century comes from government reports, visitors' diaries, and from the colonists and settlers themselves. For example, in 1699 the English journalist Ned Ward visited Boston, where he found that kissing in public would result in a fine, and adultery led to hanging; he also found horrible the habit of smoking copied from the Indians. And he commented on the appearance of the inhabitants, including their dress: "The Women here are not all inferiour in Beauty to the Ladies of *London,* having rather the advantage of a better Complexion, but as for the Men, they are generally *Meagre,* and have got that *Hypocritical* knack, like our *English Jews,* of screwing their faces into such *Puritanical* postures." Ward noted that the local Indians were using English terminology for their clothing: "Their Garments are *Mantles,* about the bigness of a *Cradle-Rug,* made of coarse *English Cloth,* which they call a coat. They also have a piece of the same cloth, about six Inches wide, between their Legs, tuck'd under a Deerskin Belt to hide their *Privities,* by them called *Breeches.* Adorning themselves with Beads of several Colours, of their own making. Their Heads, Breast, Legs and Thighs being bare.

Sometimes, for their Children, they weave Coates of *Turky Feathers*."[1] Thus despite wearing English cloth the Indians were still making some traditional turkey cloaks.

Effects of British Trade Laws

Writers also noted the scarcity of clothing in New England, the colonists having to import textiles and garments from England in exchange for fur and other raw materials. Thus it was reported in 1689 that "some Manufacturers there are amongst them, but not a Twentieth part of what the Country hath need of or is consumed there: most of their Cloathing, as to Woollen and Linnen, all sorts of Upholstery Wares, Haberdashers, and Silk Wares, Stuffs, Silks &c they have from *England,* and make returns in Plate, Pieces of Eight, Beaver, Moose, Deer Skins, Oyl, and Iron, all which but the Bullion the Country Offers."[2]

In Virginia, too, reports attest that clothing and other domestic necessities were scarce, requiring the colonists to produce raw materials in exchange for imported goods. Tobacco was the currency of exchange in Virginia, as noted in a report by three royal officials in Williamsburg, which replaced Jamestown as the capital of Virginia in 1699. "Their want of Cloaths and House-hold-Furniture, and all their other Necessaries instigates them to make as much Tobacco as they can."[3] Virginia with its plantations had a different economy than New England where the colonists had settled in towns, and officials said the absence of markets in Virginia hindered trade. For example, plantation labor was concentrated in the summer months, and the rest of the year the staff were idle. Lieutenant-Governor Nicholson of Virginia attempted to improve matters in 1691 when he passed acts to encourage linen manufacture and leather tanning, but the colony was still dependent on England for imported goods in 1720: "They have their Clothing of all sorts from England, as Linnen, Woollen, Silk, Hats and Leather. Yet Flax and Hemp grow nowhere in the world better than here. The Sheep yield good Increase, and bear good Fleeces, but they shave them only to cool them."[4] The anonymous author considered Virginians lazy since they sent skins to England to be tanned and used the hides only for servants' shoes. It was rare to see a Virginian who made himself a pair of deerskin breeches; most preferred to wait

FACING PAGE

37 • Matthijs Naiveu, *The Cloth Shop,* 1709. The lady holding a piece of brocade wears the manto, or mantua gown, pulled back in a duck's tail, over a pleated petticoat. Her commode headdress, supported by brass wires, dominated fashion on both sides of the Atlantic from 1686 to 1713. Her husband wears the long coat of a gentleman, but the tightly buttoned sleeves show him to be a sea captain. His fur hat was also nautical. One of his knee-breeches is undone, revealing his garter and striped drawers. The shopkeeper wears undress, an Indian nightgown, while his wife has a mantua and short *rayon* cap, which was common among the working women. Both boys wear short jackets, which was usual among farmers and laborers, but the kneeling boy has a vest too. He is playing with dice, which represent chance in life, the possibilities of poverty or wealth. *(Stedelijk Museum de Lakenhal [Drapers' Hall], Leiden, The Netherlands)*

for the ship from home. There were also many English ware-houses in the colony: "At the Stores in *Virginia* the Planters &c may be supplied with what English commodities they want."[5] As the Reverend Hugh Jones wrote of Virginia in 1724, "The *Habits, Life, Customs, Computations* &c of the Virginians are much the same as about London which they esteem their Home."

After South Carolina suffered an Indian assault in 1719, complaints about the Carolina Company were lodged in London, and in 1728 the crown bought the colony from the lords who had established it, offering European settlers 50 acres of land rent-free for ten years. In 1732, Charlestown in South Carolina had 500 to 600 houses as well as 5 churches, one

Presbyterian, one Anabaptist, one Quaker, one Church of England, and one French Huguenot. The economy was thriving, with 207 ships sailing to England between March 1730 and March 1731, loaded with rice, pitch, tar, turpentine, and 300 casks of deerskins, each cask containing 800 or 900 skins. Yet the colony still lacked tanners and shoemakers, as witnessed John Perry, James Richard, Abraham Meuron, and Henry Raymond at Charlestown in 1731: "Most of their shoes are bought from *England*, and generally sell for 40s per pair. I might say the same of Leather dressers, since they send every Year to *England* above 200,000 Deerskins undrest. Yet *Carolina* produces Oker naturally, and good Fish Oyl may be had from *New York* or *New England*, very cheap, so that they might be drest and made up into Breeches in the Country, for which these skins are very proper, being warm in Winter and cool in Summer."[6] The matter had not improved by 1761 when Carolina was still importing English shoes, boots, saddles, and bridles. In addition, the colony imported a wide range of English cloth and clothing:

> Druggets, drabs, duffles, duroys, serges and shalloons, camlets and grosgrams, cloth broad and narrow, from fine broadcloth to Negro cloth (obviously a rough cloth for slaves similar to the match cloth for Indians), Cloathes ready made an enormous importation, also blankets, flannels, hats in wool or beaver, stockings, shrouds, carpets, buttons and mohair. Linen from Cambrick to Onnabrig, sail cloth linen, ticking, chequered and printed Linens, haberdashery items, East Indian cottons, callico, white or printed, muslin, dimity and fustian. English silks, stockings, Indian's silks, handkerchiefs, gloves, ribbons, and Laces.[7]

Charlestown later exported some of these goods to the other colonies. In 1723 imports were £120,000, of which £100,000 was for English goods, and £20,000 for African slaves brought in British ships. At this time, the population consisted of 25,000 whites and 35,000 black slaves.

The large import of linen and silk was intended for lightweight clothing, which the southern colonies had to adopt for the very hot summers. The Spaniards had been the first to use large amounts of linen to clothe themselves in a hot climate, as is reflected in an order sent by the governor of Florida, Pedro Menéndez Marquez, to King Philip II in October 1577. The colony of Santa Elena needed 600 shirts, of which 300 should be

LAUDONNIERVS ET REX ATHORE ANTE COLVMNAM A PRÆFECTO PRIMA NAVIGATIONE LOCATAM QVAMQVE VENERANTVR FLORIDENSES
Jacobus Le Moyne dictus de Morgues ad vivum pinxit

I • Jacques Le Moyne, *René de Laudonnière and King Athore before the Column Erected to the First [French] Navigation, which the Florida Indians are Worshipping, at the Mouth of the St. Johns River*, 1564. The contact between European dress and native American styles became frequent on the American coast in the sixteenth century. The French explorer de Laudonnière wears a military buff doublet and trunk hose in yellow oiled leather, with a steel cuirass. The Florida Indians on the St. Johns River are almost naked, and they ornament the body with tattoos. The chief or king is distinguished by the number of beads he wears and by the two tails atop his mud cone of hair; none of his subjects wear such tails. The artist had made the Indians appear more fair-skinned than they could have been under the Florida sun. *(Print Collection, Miriam & Ira D. Wallach Division of Arts, Prints, and Photographs, The New York Public Library; Astor, Lenox, and Tilden Foundations)*

II • Pieter Angillis, *Covent Garden*, London, c. 1726. The painting is a valuable record of the difference between the colors worn by workers and the fashionable. Whereas the central ladies wear light-colored silks with their caps and straw hats, the porters and market women are all dressed in their traditional russet browns. Most of the working men wear jackets to the hips, unlike the long coats of the middle class. The market woman at the left wears a head-scarf and straw hat, not a cap like the ladies. Her plain dress has no hoop beneath, unlike the fashionable pair of women. This painting illustrates the range of clothes sent to the English colonies—fine silks for the few and russet cloths for the masses. *(Yale Center for British Art, Paul Mellon Collection)*

III • Anonymous, *Deborah Glen*, c. 1739. The rose and garland in
Deborah's hands represent love; and since she wears a wedding ring, it
shows that the portrait was painted about the date of her marriage to
John Sanders at Albany on 6 December 1739. She wears a very plain kind
of mantua gown in two tones of brown, with a pattern of white vines and
red flowers. Her high-heeled shoes in red match the floral pattern, but
the gown is lined with blue. The absence of a stomacher to conceal her
lacing is a provincial touch. Both the Glens and Sanderses were leading
families in New York State. Deborah's brother-in-law Robert is shown in
figure 40. (*Abby Aldrich Rockefeller Folk Art Center, Williamsburg, Virginia.
Photographed by Colonial Williamsburg*)

IV • Attributed to William Dering, *George Booth of Belleville, Virginia*,
c. 1748. Virginians regarded themselves as the most stylish British
Americans. George wears a fashionable coat with no collar, and with the
skirts flared out and wired to echo women's wide hoops. His head is
shaved and he wears a wig. The high forehead shows the effect of head
binding as a baby. Even when out shooting birds, he wears a red
waistcoat decked with gold lace. His stockings are tightly pulled into the
knee rolls, which had to be exact. The long waistcoat dominated from
1666 to the 1760s, when it began to shrink. The absence of ruffles shows
that this is an informal occasion. *(Colonial Williamsburg Foundation.
Photographed by Colonial Williamsburg.)*

V • William Williams, *Deborah Hall*, 1766. Deborah Hall lived only from 1751 to 1770. Since she tends a rose, this is probably a betrothal portrait. She wears a French rococo sackback gown, which is trimmed with ruching, but the amount of decoration is less extreme than in French originals and thereby shows some British restraint. The fine lace ruffles and Italianate garden suggest a wealthy family. The cap appears to be set with jewels. Girls of fifteen were still dressed like adults, but Deborah's youth is reflected in the squirrel pet. *(The Brooklyn Museum, Dick S. Ramsay Fund)*

VI • Ralph Earl, *Elijah Boardman,* 1789. The Connecticut merchant displays the range of fabrics he sells through an open door. He wears the slim line, with an English frock coat in skin tone. The white satin waistcoat and white silk stockings show that Boardman is dressed for evening. By now waistcoats had lost about two feet in length, and the legs are completely exposed. He still powders his hair, which is tied back in a bow, but that was becoming a conservative characteristic. The narrow sleeves reduce the size of ruffles, but knee buckles and shoe buckles add a touch of glitter. The whole body is now being revealed, whereas it had been concealed previously during the century. (*The Metropolitan Museum of Art, Bequest of Susan W. Tyler, 1979*)

VII • Gilbert Stuart, *George Washington*, c. 1797. For ceremonial occasions in New York and Philadelphia the first president of the United States chose black velvet in the narrow look with minimal ruffles and a discreet cravat. Washington probably felt that a Puritan-Quaker style was most appropriate for his new post. This was a pioneer step, since wearing all black for evening did not become general until after 1810. Being elderly, the president always powdered his hair and wigs. And as an old soldier he preferred a uniform dress rather than any attempt to set fashion. *(The National Portrait Gallery, Smithsonian Institution; on loan from Lord Rosebery)*

VIII • Anonymous, *Baby in a Red Chair,* c. 1800. This sleeping child illustrates the British liberation of children's dress, with swaddling abolished, and simple shifts that allowed the arms and legs to move freely. The baby chair with a protective bar in front is eighteenth-century in type, and probably had served earlier generations. (*Abby Aldrich Rockefeller Folk Art Center, Williamsburg, Virginia. Photographed by Colonial Williamsburg*)

in Rouen linen, and 300 in *Crea,* a coarse Spanish linen that was much worn in Spanish America, along with collars of fine Holland linen, 200 doublets of coarse linen and 50 of Holland linen. The governor also wanted 10 pieces of London cloth, fustian for lining, sewing thread in all colors, and buttons. Footwear was also required; and shoes were ordered, 500 in cowhide and 500 in Cordova leather with two soles. This order shows the Spaniards coping with the climate, with linen to be worn in summer and English cloth during the cool winters.[8] The settlers seem to have despised native deerskin for their wardrobe chest.

Professor Kalm studied the trade in Pennsylvania. Philadelphia sent wood, tar, iron, and skins to the West Indies in exchange for sugar, molasses, rum, and indigo, but most imports were from Britain:

> Ready money is likewise sent over to England whence in return they get all sorts of goods manufactured viz. fine and coarse cloth, linens, and iron ware and other wrought metals, and East India goods. For it is to be observed that England supplies Philadelphia with almost all stuffs and articles which are wanted here.[9]

From the custom-house records he worked out that between 1723 and 1747, British exports to Pennsylvania had totaled £1,312,838, of which £969,049 were paid for British goods made in Britain, and £343,789 for foreign goods, that is, imported from the East Indies and West Indies.

In 1773 the governor of Connecticut, Jonathan Trumbull, received a list of questions from London about the state of his colony. The population consisted of 191,392 whites and 6,464 blacks, the opposite of the situation in the Carolinas where the plantation slaves outnumbered the white settlers. The governor reported: "The Quantity of British Manufactures the Inhabitants do annually import hither from Great Britain are few, but including those taken from the merchants of Boston and New York, upon a Medium from the best Observation is £200,000 Sterling per annum." Connecticut exported to Britain timber and salted food to the value of £10,000, but her biggest customer was the West Indies with which she traded timber and farm animals for rum, sugar, cocoa, cotton, and sugar. There was also some manufacture in Connecticut: "The manufactures are coarse Linnens, and Woollens done in the Family-way, for the use of the poorer Sort, Labourers and Servants."[10] Thus, home-spun American materials were considered suitable only for workers, until the rebellion brought an attempt to wear only American products.

St. John de Crèvecoeur, a Norman from Caen, had been posted to French Canada, but when Canada was taken by the British, he moved south and bought a farm at Pine Hill in Orange County, New York. He observed in his letters of 1770–74 that American wool would never be equal to the European quality because there were no plains in New England, and the summers were too dry to grow lush grass for grazing sheep. In his opinion, the colonies' dependency on British goods would keep them permanently in debt to Britain:

> Another reason which keeps us in debt is the multiplicity of shops with English goods. These present irresistible temptations. It is so much easier to buy than it is to spin. The allurements of fineries is so powerful with our young girls that they must be philosophers indeed to abstain. Thus, one-fifth part of all our labours every year is laid out on English commodities. These are the taxes that we pay.
>
> Another is that most of the articles they send us from England are extremely bad. What is intended for exportation is good enough when there are no rival merchants. Their linen and their duffle and their wool cards are much worse now than they were ten years ago.[11]

The English colonies were a tied market, as were the French and Spanish colonies, bound to the mother country by navigation acts that designated them an exclusive market for British goods; and de Crèvecoeur expresses a dissatisfaction with the system. Living in the country among farmers, and observing their dress and customs at close hand, he noticed that many farmers' wives did their own dyeing:

> In that of dyeing you will be surprised to see what beautiful colours some families will have in their garments, which commonly are streaked gowns, skirts and petticoats of the same stuff. This we have borrowed from the Dutch, as well as the art of producing so many colours from the roots and barks of our woods, aided with indigo and alum, the only foreign products we use. I have often, while among the Indians, wished, but in vain, to find out how they dye their porcupine quills with that bright red and yellow, which you must remember to have seen on the moccassins I gave you. Nor is the art of the squaws to be despised, when you see it as it is

displayed in the embroidery of their belts, shoes, and pouches, knife cases, &c.[12]

Other observers of the colonial scene have also commented on the variety of customs, including some that were adapted from the Indians. For example, an anonymous gentleman of Connecticut reported that the colony had copied the Indian treatment of babies. "The greatest care is taken of the limbs and bodies of infants, which are kept strait by means of a board, a practice learnt of the Indian women, who abhor all crooked people, so that deformity is here a rarity." This was a major difference from the English treatment of babies, so Connecticut had gone Indian in this respect. How far the other colonies used boards, the author did not say. Some English customs certainly crossed the Atlantic, for in Connecticut, etiquette considered it "the greatest rudeness for a gentleman to speak before a lady of a garter, knee or leg, yet it is thought a piece of civility to ask to *Bundle*, a Custom as old as the first settlement in 1634."[13] Bundling refers to the practice for a couple to lie together in bed when fully dressed. Periodically, clergymen would fulminate about it, only to be informed that it was innocent. The practice was becoming less frequent in England by the end of the eighteenth century, although the Welsh continued bundling.

Kalm encountered a quaint wedding custom in Pennsylvania in 1750. If a man died in debt, his widow's wardrobe belonged to creditors; so if she should remarry she had to leave her clothes behind and go to church in her nightgown (dressing gown). Once she had remarried she now belonged to the new husband, and the wardrobe he provided was his property. Kalm did hear of a case where the new husband lent his bride her bridal clothes, and went around informing all creditors of the fact. At royal marriages in the seventeenth century, bridegrooms had worn respectable black and the brides cloth of silver. The middle classes could imitate this style of dress in black cloth and white linen, but the poor would marry in their usual browns, grays, and undyed.

The good professor noted that the storage of clothes was difficult because of the Pennsylvania moth: "I have seen cloth, worsted gloves, and other woollen stuffs, which had hung all summer locked up in a clothespress, and had not been taken care of, so damaged by these worms that whole pieces fell out.

Sometimes they are so spoiled that they could not be mended again. Furs which had been kept in the garret were frequently so ruined by moths that the hair came off by the handfuls."[14]

The Diversity of Dress

The increase in letters and diaries in the eighteenth century provides an impression of the wide range of garments and styles of dress worn in the colonies. The writers' observations include comments on dress and undress; fashion for women, men, and children's dress among the lower, middle, and upper classes; among whites, blacks, and Indians; and in the northern and southern colonies.

The diaries of William Byrd, plantation owner of Westover, Virginia, have been hailed as the American Pepys, but they lack the real Pepys's interest in fashion. Where Pepys was most observant, William Byrd was blind. Educated in England he returned to Virginia in 1705, and became a member of the Council of State and receiver general of royal revenues from 1706 to 1716. One diary entry notes that Byrd took his daughters to Williamsburg in 1720, and changed before going up to the capitol; since it was November he was probably wearing a greatcoat and riding suit, and changed into a town suit of fine cloth or velvet, with a silk waistcoat, but Byrd does not tell us that. He had a personal tailor, for he settled his accounts on 17 January 1741; but unlike Pepys, he does not record what he ordered. He returned to London in 1719 to find a second wife, and attended some masquerades "where I shall naturally look for some charming shepherdesses," he wrote on 2 April. At another masquerade he encountered "a Nun shap't like the Queen of Love." So Byrd was aware of women's dress, although he does not describe it. However, he does resemble Pepys in the number of affairs he conducted behind his official façade, and like Pepys, he sinned first before asking the Lord's forgiveness. "Rogering his mistress" was the way he put it. Byrd may have bought clothes in London, although he does not say so; and he had an English wife, so the style of his wardrobe was likely to have been completely English, with the exception that Virginians wore undress more often in the summer.[15]

For women, undress could simply be the usual attire of working women out on the farms, who in summer would wear their shift, corset with shoulder straps, a petticoat and an apron and no gown. Light thread stockings (or else bare feet) covered the lower limbs, while the white linen cap on the head was always covered by a straw hat out of doors. Middle-class ladies who wore the outfit could quickly don a little jacket in printed or embroidered linen if company should call. Around 1600 these jackets were termed "waistcoats," but in the eighteenth century the term "jacket" became more common. In construction they were exactly the same as the peasant woman's cloth jacket, but were made of lighter linen. By the middle of the eighteenth century the bedgown, a longer version of the jacket to the hips, appeared and was widely adopted among working women into the next century. The bedgown could be in cloth or linen, according to the season, and Colonial Williamsburg has examples of undress jackets and bedgowns in its costume collection. Full dress, when in town or visiting the governor, meant wearing a gown, with gloves and a fan, and a cap trimmed with lace. Other forms of undress for hot weather were the nightgown and the Indian gowns, which were so called because they were introduced by the East India Company. The Dutch more correctly called them Japanese coats, and they were in fact kimonos in origin, but in Europe were soon copied in silk or quilted cotton as undress, which became very modish in the 1660s, although a few examples had been worn before then.

Samuel Pepys, ever alive to the latest innovation, bought himself an Indian gown for 34/– [shillings] on 1 July 1661. Periwigs were now fashionable, but when they were taken off before bed, the man could wear either a turban to keep his scalp warm or else a Spanish montero, a fur-lined cap. Pepys described Sir Philip Howard undressed on 21 November 1666 when the knight had just risen: "I find him dressing himself in his night-gown and Turban like a Turk." Wearing a nightgown or Indian gown with a turban became the vogue. By 1725 the term "banyan" had begun to enter the language, from the term for the trade caste in Bengal. Gradually, the anglicized version of banyan was used for the trader, and then for the goods he sold, so a banyan became a nightgown in Indian silk or cotton. The British shipped banyans to America. Nightgowns were also worn by ladies as *déshabille,* and portrait painters were very pleased for they draped very classically, where the fashionable look was all stiff corsets and heavily embroidered clothes. Nightgowns were easier to depict in paint, so they rapidly became a standard uniform in portraiture. And since they were approved by the easygoing Charles II, court beauties were soon queueing up to be depicted by Sir Peter Lely in this new, casual, informal style. Pepys pressed his mistress Mrs. Penington to try the look on 4 December 1665: "did pray her to undress herself into her nightgown, that I might see how to have her picture drawn carelessly (for she is mighty proud of the conceit)."[16] Accordingly, nightgowns for ladies were transported to America to appear at home and in portraits.

In the winter of 1704 Mrs. Sarah Kemble Knight traveled from Boston to New York by horseback and canoe. On the way she lodged at the home of a merchant when a country tradesman arrived. He stood for a long time without speaking a word,

38 • Willem van Mieris, *Hurdy-Gurdy Player Asleep in a Tavern*, d. 1690. When Mrs. Kemble Knight of Boston visited Dutch New York in 1704 she found the women wearing French *muches*, caps like the one worn by the tavern maid in this painting. They were not the fashion, but were popular among the lower classes. Typically the maid's dress fastens with hooks and eyes, because lacing was too complicated for workers. The blind musician half wears an Indian gown over his jacket, one of his knee-breeches is undone, and he appears to have lost his garter since his stocking is falling down. *(Baron de Ferrière's Collection, Cheltenham Art Gallery and Museum, Gloucestershire)*

chewing and spitting tobacco, and the merchant commented that rural types were struck dumb on seeing his range of merchandise. The country tradesman's girlfriend, on the other hand, was full of "Law you" and "How Gent!" They purchased ribbon, hood silk, and sewing thread. Of the New Yorkers Mrs. Knight wrote that "They are generally very plain in their dress throughout yᵉ Colony, and follow one another in their modes: that you may know where they belong, especially the women, meet them where you will."[17] On 22 December 1704 she reached New Rochelle in New York:

> The English goe very fasheonable in their dress. But the Dutch, especially the middling sort, differ from our women, in their habit go loose, were French muches wᶜʰ are like a Cap and a head band in one, leaving their Ears bare, which are sett out wᵗʰ Jewells of a large size and many in number. And their finger's hoop't with Rings, some with large stones in them of many Coullers as were their pendants in their ears, which You should see very old women wear as well as young.

She noted that New Yorkers in winter liked to take sleigh rides out to the Bowery where some houses of entertainment were situated. Mrs. Knight returned to Boston safely. When Professor Kalm visited New York in 1750, he noticed that the Dutch and the Jewish settlers were entirely English in their dress, so the French muches may have died out (see figure 38). In any event, they were a subordinate fashion, for the mainstream style in 1704 was still the towering commode, which did not diminish until the Duchess of Shrewsbury took the one-tier English cap to Versailles in 1713, when all the French copied her at court.[18]

In 1710 the Reverend John Buckingham was appointed chaplain to the troops of Connecticut in the colonial expedition against the French ordered by Queen Anne in view of the frequent French attacks upon her colonies. He equipped himself at Hartford as follows: "A great coat, a new black broadcloth coat, a serge coat, a drugget jacket, a white waistcoat, a new pair of serge breeches, a pair of leather ones, two shirts, three bands, five handkerchiefs (three white and two Rumels), stockens, two pair of grey ones and one of black, a new pair of shoes, two pairs of gloves, a hat new in May last, and silver shoe buckles."[19] At Boston he bought other items: "a pair of stockings 4/6,

39 • Justus Kühn, *Eleanor Darnell*, c. 1710. Kühn liked to give his American customers elaborate gardens, as an aristocratic touch. Eleanor is dressed as a wealthy lady in a mantua gown pulled into a train. Her long lace apron and bib were common for children, but hers is edged with lace. Her hair is dressed up in a tower effect. Under her gown she wears the new hoop, which the British had just revived. Width was beginning to replace height. *(Maryland Historical Society, Baltimore)*

5 yards of black Russel cloth 9/6, 2 yards of Garlick cloth 4–, 1 yard of 3–4 saloone 4–, two dozen buttons at 8*d*. three bands 6/9, a silk handkerchief price not stated, to the taylor for mohair, silk and making a jacket 12/5, a knit waistcoat 10/11, a pair of black milled [thickened] stockings 7/-, a loose gown and a grey drugget coat (seperate bills), 3 silk handkerchiefs 9/7, a pair of gloves and a knitted cap given by Mr. Wadsworth."

The loose gown would have been an Indian gown, so he purchased 20 yards of damask at 2/8 the yard, total £2.13.4. Eight yards of gray drugget were for his coat, at 4/– the yard, £1.12.0. The tailoring, linings, and some linen shirts, came to £9.5.6. The chaplain accompanied the army on the next year's expedition in 1711, when he equipped himself with more black and gray coats, as befitted a clergyman, as well as knee-breeches and some jackets in black and white, which he bought at New Haven. He also availed himself of the sergeant tailor in the Army to make him a blue jacket for 8/–. However, the expedition was canceled when a storm wrecked eight transports loaded with troops, and Québec held out for a few more years.

The chaplain does not mention any periwigs, but the Church of England clergy wore them right into the nineteenth century, so possibly he wore what he owned already or else did not want to risk wearing them on a rough campaign. It was the army that ended the fashion for periwigs, since it had been tying wigs back out of the way since the 1670s. Tieback wigs gradually began to enter fashion around 1715, but the older generation retained full periwigs as did judges, the clergy, and the professions. This is shown in the Ridgely family letters, for example. Dr. Nicholas Ridgely of Dover, Kent County, Delaware, wrote to son Charles who was at the Academy in Philadelphia in 1752, enclosing 50/– "for a light gray wig. . . . It must not be a Short Bob, but as long as you can gett, full & big in the caul or head, full large to the Inclosed thread. . . . the wigg to be as light a gray as you can gett for that price, and as full of hair & good." Evidently Charles could not find such a wig ready-made, for on 16 December his father sent 15/– to have the wig made up and to buy a pair of black leather shoes. The doctor clearly thought a long wig still necessary for his professional image in 1752.[20]

Clothes were regularly dispatched by the family servants for the sons at school. Thus Dr. Nicholas Ridgely to Charles, on 20

40 • Anonymous, *Robert Sanders, Later Mayor of Albany, New York,* c. 1714. Painted when he was about nineteen or twenty, Robert wears a peach-colored suit, with the coat tails wired out to match women's hoops. Both sexes had to go through narrow doors sideways, for different fashions impose different movements. The absence of decoration on Robert's suit speaks of the sober American Puritan who kept fanciful display down to his decorated buttons. Despite his good background he still wears no periwig. *(Abby Aldrich Rockefeller Folk Art Center, Williamsburg, Virginia. Photographed by Colonial Williamsburg)*

November 1751, writes of "an Ozenbrig bag per Andrew Doz (the servant), Broadcloth and all Trimmings to make you a winter Jackett." with 41/– to cover the making up. Also "a pair of mittens, and some thread and worsted to mend your stockings and things." On 7 December 1751 the doctor sent his son "yarn stockings for cold weather" but ordered Charles not to come home for Christmas as travel was expensive and uncomfortable. On 16 July 1752 mother sent a bundle of clothes, and on September 29th send "4 new shirts, one pair of worsted and two pairs of Yarn stockings," but she wanted the boys' old clothes returned by the negro servants. Father sent two pieces of eight "to buy you Germantown Stockings, which are much better & cheaper than any I can gett in Maryland or with us" (in Delaware). As Charles was based in Philadelphia, he also received family commissions for their clothes. On 20 March 1753 the doctor sent £3.10s for cloth: "Mother wants 20 yards of best black Callimanco of a shiny clear black for herself & your sister Ruthy, and your sister Polly ten yards of scarlet Callimanco. Polly also wants black leather shoes with white rands in soft leather." Charles asked if he could use his dancing money to buy a jacket before he came home and his father agreed, but only if he brought his father two volumes of *Universal History.* When Andrew Doz, a black servant, failed to take a box to Charles, Negro Tom was sent instead, with an order for "fine soft leather and white rands or thin good pumps for Mother" on July 1753. On 21 June 1753 Charles had written to ask if he could have a "tunick" for hot weather costing about 45/–, "for it is full warm to wear a cloth coat, and it does not look very well to wear Jackets." Jackets were worn by the working class, and the doctor's son wished to look superior. The "tunick" was a longish jacket with long sleeves, which was in reality a waistcoat without the coat on top. It could be made in linen or cotton for hot weather.[21] As the elder son, Charles had been allowed the more adult, stylish clothes.

The quill pens of the period cannot have lasted well, for on 3 December 1753 the doctor sent 300 goose quill pens and wrote: "Mother's jumps to be sent down if boning has been done. . . . also three shirts and a pair of yarn stockings for you, and two shirts for James." Mother Mary Ridgely wrote the next day with "three ruffled shirts, and a pair of very fine yarn Stockins, for yourself and two shirts for James. The jumps will be useless if not sent down this trip, for I want them for the Cold Weather." The jump was a lightly boned bodice worn instead of stays. In 19 February 1754 Charles thinks he needs a spring wardrobe and suggests "Knit breeches in patterns cost about 30/–, in shagg about 50/–. but the latter wear exceptionally well." When it was November in 1754 Charles thought he needed a thick coat and jacket in green nap. There is a hiatus in the family letters until the 1790s, by which time Charles was the doctor in his family's practice.

The Virginians were known for their elegant dress. The Reverend Jonathan Boucher left Cumberland, England, to serve as a tutor in Virginia in 1759, where he was astonished at the finery. He wrote home to the Reverend Mr. James and his wife on 7 August from Port Royal.

> I assure Mrs. James, the common Planters' Daughters here go every Day in finer Cloaths than I have seen content you for a Summer's Sunday. You thought (homely Creatures as you are) my Sattin wastecoat was a fine best, Lord help you, I'm nothing amongst your Lace and Lac'd fellow that are here. Nay, so much does their Taste run after dress that they tell me I may see in Virginia more brilliant Assemblies than I ever c'd in the North of England, and except Royal Ones, p'rhaps in any Part of it.[22]

The Reverend Boucher was appointed rector at Annapolis in 1770 and became a close friend of George Washington; but he was horrified by the colonies' rebellion and returned to England.

Virginia was becoming more like Québec in its love of display, which made the settlers there very different from the plainly dressed New Englanders or even the English back home. The Swiss César de Saussure had visited London in 1725 and made the important observation that "Englishmen are usually very plainly dressed, they scarcely ever wear gold on their clothes; they wear little coats called 'frocks' without facings, and without pleats, with a short cape. Almost all wear small round wigs, plain hats, and carry canes in their hands but no swords."[23] The English had to dress up for court, but that was the only time when finery was compulsory. In the main they dressed down, with what I have dubbed the "Protestant Clothing Ethic." Like any child with a mother looming in the background, Virginia was shouting "Look at me, I am a big girl now" to her mother country, and trying to dress more grandly and dashingly than the parent.

Matters were very different in the newest colony, Georgia, which was established by the Trust of the philanthropist James Oglethorpe as an asylum for the poor and the persecuted. In 1741 the Trustees stated: "As the People in *Georgia* sent on the Charity were supported to enable them to raise their Provisions in the first place, on the Lands they should clear and to convert the Timber that they should cut down in clearing the Land into Lumber, which they might to their great Advantage export to the Sugar Colonies and further to raise Silk, Wine and Oil for which the Climate was very proper."[24] Under the rules for 1735 each male settler sent out under charity would receive a watch coat (greatcoat), tools, weapons, and provisions to start farming. Settlers could engage apprentices for whom the Trustees would supply bedding as well as "A Frock and Trowsers of Lintsey Wolsey, A Shirt, Frock and Trowsers of Osnabrig, A Pair of Shoes from England, And Two Pairs of Country Shoes." By giving trousers to the apprentices, the Trustees were treating them as farm workers and laborers, for the gentry wore knee-breeches. The settlers were given clothes suitable to the climate, as shown by the provision of linsey-woolsey, the mixed cloth of linen and wool, and a frock coat and trousers in Osnabrig linen, the coarse German linen made in Osnabrug.

The charity settlers were mostly English and Scottish, but they were joined by some Swiss and by Austrians from Salzburg, Lutherans who had been persecuted for their faith in Catholic Austria. The charity settlers were expected to repay for their provisions, transport, and clothes in three years, but on 9 December 1738 they wrote to the Trustees from Savannah that none of them could repay the loan so quickly. Struggling to be farmers meant that they could not start producing lumber or silk immediately. For example, in Carolina, slaves were used for farming, but the Trustees were opposed to introducing slaves in Georgia since the colony was intended to be a home for distressed white laborers as well as a refuge for those fleeing religious persecution. Writing to the Trustees, the Salzburg group said they had raised enough corn and rice to buy "Cloaths of which we were in want" and asked for more Salzburgers to be sent as settlers. A Swiss settler, M. Augspaugner, sent the Trustees some silk produced in Georgia that seemed equal to that grown in Carolina, but it took a long time to build up the industry. Yet despite the religious ideals, plantations from Carolina spread into the new colony, and with them the slave system.

An anonymous gentleman toured the area in 1735, and encountered some Scottish troops at Darien, the site of a British garrison. "The Highlanders were all under Arms on the sight of a Boat, and made a very manly appearance with their Plods, broad sword, Targets and Fire-Arms." Wearing full Highland plaids in Georgia does seem excessive, but if they were in the British army they had no choice. The separate kilt had not yet developed in 1735, so the soldiers must have been very hot.[25]

In 1734 a party of Georgia Indians was sent to London to be shown to the Trustees and to assure the latter that the natives were willing to sell land. There were six males, a boy, and a woman. The boy was dressed for the visit in a European suit with a knee-length coat and vest with knee-breeches, stockings, and buckled shoes. The woman was covered in English bodice and skirt to conceal her breasts and legs, but the men were allowed to wear their own mantles or else the piece of cloth around the middle, with moccasins. The braves plucked their scalps, leaving only a narrow crest of hair down the center, but this crest was kept short, and not formed into a cockscomb as

41 • Anonymous, *Henrietta Maria Tilgham, Mrs. William Goldsborough and Grandson Robins Chamberlain,* c. 1758. Mrs. Goldsborough's stomacher is so unusual that it must be homemade, and seems constructed out of many pieces of material. Her upright pose is caused by the corset that produced a rigid effect on women's posture. The mantua gown is worn over enormously wide hoops, which were flat in front in the English manner. The grandson's draped cloak gives him a classical touch. *(Maryland Historical Society, Baltimore)*

with other tribes further north. Some braves had the earlobe stretched down the neck and decorated with fluffy white feathers and beads. Two braves sported a spread of feathers at the shoulder. The women wore no decorations. They faced the Trustees who were all dressed in English suits with periwigs. Out of twenty-eight men, only one young man had a tieback wig; the rest, as respectable merchants, clergymen, and gentry, wore wigs down their backs, all uniformly powdered white. The Age of Reason did not like individuality; to have worn one's own hair color was considered too singular. Of course, farm workers and laborers wore their own hair, but they were not considered part of cultivated society.

Like the settlers in Georgia who wore linen outfits, so did the established gentry in Virginia. Although the wealthy in Virginia liked to sport finery, even they had to cope with the humid summers. Thus William Grove observed in 1732: "In Summertime even the gentry goe many in White Holland Wast Coat and drawers and a thin Cap on their heads and Thread stockings. The Ladyes Strait laced in thin Silk or Linnen. In Winter (they dress) mostly as in England and affect London Dress and wayes."[26] One cannot call this wearing of linen in summer a uniquely American development because it was common also in the Spanish colonies, and in Europe when there was a heat wave; but the regularity of hot summers in Virginia, Carolina, and Georgia, as well as hot spells in the other colonies, made linen a seasonal necessity.

The Mode

In fashion the biggest transformation in this period was from Late Baroque height to Rococo smallness. The towering person of the 1690s, with both sexes in high-heeled shoes, and the men in built-up periwigs and the women with their tiers of lace in the commode headdress, began to yield to a lower silhouette from around 1710. Flat-topped wigs and low-heeled shoes for men reduced the younger generation's scale, and by 1713 the English low cap with just a ruffle of lace around the cap had replaced *tours*. Width began to be the new ideal following slender height, and women in particular became more horizontal once the English revived hoops. *The Tatler* for 3–5 January

42 • John Wollaston, *Family Group,* c. 1750. This nursing mother wears no corset, and her bodice is laced very simply for ease of opening at feeding time. She wears a plain satin mantua gown and petticoat, which was typical of the good quality in simple taste favored by English and American middle-class people. The English cap is always wide at the sides. The husband wears a good-quality suit without any patterns or lace. His shirt sleeves protrude from his coat sleeves with no ruffles to conceal them, so he may be a minister of the Church. The daughter is dressed like mother in a mantua gown, petticoat, apron, and cap. *(The Newark Museum, New Jersey)*

1709 gave the first report of hoops in the press, which suggests that the first examples appeared in the autumn of 1708. From a modest cone shape the hoops rapidly spread out into a wide bell by 1720, and hoops became established wear at court—in France up to the revolution in 1789, and in England until 1820 when George IV abolished them. By the 1740s the English were wearing a squarer version of the hoops called the panier—two basket shapes on each side of the body—but by the late 1750s the French bell shape came to the fore. Hoops began to be reduced in size by the late 1770s, as fashion began to evolve toward the narrow classical figure of the 1790s, which left court hoops an isolated style (see figure 48).

As the *manto* or mantua gown had changed from being undress to constituting full dress for women, as often happens in fashion history, another form of undress was needed for at home and mornings. This was the *sacque* gown, which Mrs. Pepys had owned back in 1668 and which had been worn by pregnant women. In construction sacques differed from mantuas by being seamed or buttoned down the center front, where mantuas were always pulled back to display the petticoat. They were a round or closed gown, and enormous versions of their style appeared in the 1720s, when worn over hoops, with pleats falling from the shoulders, and a wide acreage of skirt, which encouraged fabrics to become meadows of flowers. J. de Troy painted several examples of sacques into the 1730s, when they began to be tamed by becoming more fitted in front, and retaining the pleats at the back. This was essentially a French style, and eventually the term *robe à la françoise* was used for dresses with pleats at the back (see figure 45). *Robes à l'angloise* were denoted by having a fitted back and front. (The suffix *aise* does not enter French until 1778.)

Confusingly, the word "nightgown" was used both for dressing gowns and for wrapover dresses in satin, which became very common in England and her colonies as a form of ordinary wear among the gentry and middle classes when just among themselves. It could not be worn for tea parties and receptions when mantua gowns were obligatory, but many examples appear in English and American portraits, so they were common on both sides of the Atlantic. They began to decline in the late 1750s, when the *robe à la françoise*, smothered with Rococo frills, appliquéd flowers, ribbons and bows, swept English restraint aside. The style was best seen in the dress of the royal mistress at Versailles, Madame de Pompadour (see figure 44); and many shoes, gloves, hats and such were named after her. Both the Americans and the English succumbed to this fashion, but the English were able to mount a counterattack, which took hold with French men, who began wearing English frock coats around the 1750s. By the 1770s and '80s, this English influence had become a flood, and the *Galérie des Modes* was full of garments that revealed their English origin by the anglicized

43 • George Knapton, *Lucy Ebberton,* c. 1755. The English shepherdess look was worn by high-class ladies from about the 1730s when playing at Arcadia. The straw hat and basket of flowers were *de rigueur,* but the resemblance to real shepherdesses ended in the printed silk gown and the pearls and jewel necklace. The gauze apron is too flimsy for outdoor work. Some American ladies would have copied the look, and so did Queen Marie Antoinette in France after 1770. *(By permission of the Governors of Dulwich Picture Gallery)*

names—*chapeau jockei* (jockey cap), *robes à la Marlborough* trimmed with braid, *chapeau á la Charlotte* (Queen), *robes à l'angloise* (see figure 60), and straw hats *à la Marlborough.* Since he had defeated Louis XIV several times, the Duke of Marlborough was one English general whom all French schoolchildren had heard about.

The first fashion influenced by the American colonies made its appearance in the 1780s on the international stage. The casual styles of Louisiana and New Orleans were reported to the French court, and illustrated in the *Galérie des Modes* in 1779 as *vêtement à la Créole* (see figure 58, p. 139). This was a muslin wrapover gown with narrow sleeves, which was worn open indoors, but when going out could be pinned together and held

44 • François Boucher, *Antoinette Poisson Marquise de Pompadour*, 1759. The epitome of French Rococo style, Mme de Pompadour's name was used for a whole range of fashionable items from shoes to gloves. She wears the French bell-shaped hoop, and her mantua is covered with bows, appliquéd scrolls, and flowers. She took the French love of display to its limit, and was just as well known among the English colonies as in England. (*The Wallace Collection, London*)

45 • John Singleton Copley, *Mary Mrs. Benjamin Pickman aged 19,* 1763. Her dress is an example of one French style in America. Mary wears a French sack-back gown, where the front is cut like a mantua, but the back is fuller. The satin is appliquéd with gold ruching and gold ribbon, but Mary has not added any bows, or fluffy ornaments. The American version of French style was less cluttered than the original. The parasol is to protect Mary's complexion from the sun, for a suntan was considered decidedly vulgar. *(Yale University Art Gallery, Bequest of Edith Malvina K. Wetmore)*

by a sash. Queen Marie Antoinette was very interested in this créole costume; and while she could not wear anything so untailored at court, she wanted to create an easier gown, for she was Austrian, not French, and had been brought up by her mother, the Empress Maria Theresia, with comparative simplicity. The stiff styles of the French court with the *grand habit* court dress and paniers bored her, and were heavy and restrictive. The English ladies had started a fashion for dressing as shepherdesses to evoke rural simplicity, and Marie Antoinette imitated that style, but she was looking for an even easier costume (see figure 43). The créole look was too undressed to copy outright, but one could echo it with a muslin shift or chemise, decked with frills to dress it up for public appearances. The queen launched her muslin chemise dress in 1783, which caused a scandal, but in its white simplicity it was prophesying the classical styles to come. She sent examples to friends in England, and the chemise was taken up. The dress was termed the *chemise à la reine* (see figure 59, p. 140), and caused a crisis in the silk industry, for the queen had chosen muslin.

Nothing so revolutionary disrupted male fashion, by requiring them to parade in just their shirt and drawers, the masculine equivalent of the shift or chemise. Now that men had their English three-piece suit as a uniform, they had only to worry about the cut. In the 1660s the first coats for suits (as distinct from traveling coats) were cut straight up and down. In the low-waisted 1670s a curve was introduced from the hip to make the skirt stand out a little. In the 1680s, when women started wearing trains around the clock, the men acquired a little back emphasis with three pleats inserted in the side seams to cause some swing in the skirt. Once women adopted bustles in about 1693, the men's pleats increased to about five on each side. And with the arrival of width in 1708, this volume increased even more, with the use of horsehair lining to hold the skirts out. By the 1720s it was said that men were wearing paniers, as this vogue for width was taken to its limit. Buckram lining and even wires were employed to hold the coat skirts out. Six pleats on each side of the coat skirt were common by 1722, so a man had to spread his skirts over the arms of a chair when sitting down (see figure 46). The style was at its most extreme in France, whereas the English and Americans had the alternative of the plain frock coat, with no pleats, which was much easier to wear for most daytime activities; the fashionable, extremely wide, coat could be reserved for assemblies. Frock coats always had a collar and fastened up to the throat, whereas the fashionable coat had no collar, and was increasingly held open by the weight of skirts and pleating; so this open front became a feature from the 1740s, which gave a new importance to the vest or waistcoat. The first suit vests in 1666 were as long as the coat. By 1730 they shrank to show the knee, and by the 1760s they were rising to the hip level. This, in turn, affected the style of knee-breeches, which had to be shapelier once more of them came into view; as a result, they gradually evolved by the 1770s into a slim, leg-revealing line, which accorded with the trend toward classical taste that favored the revelation of the human figure (see figure 47). Of course, conservative males stuck to full-skirted coats right down to the 1760s and '70s, but the younger generation followed the slimmer line, which did not suit those with middle-aged spread.

Large cuffs had become fashionable in the 1690s, and by 1715 they had reached up to the elbow, where they remained into the 1730s. A gradual retreat followed over the next thirty years, as cuffs shrank toward the emerging leaner look. Similarly wigs were reduced in scale, from the mane of 1700–1715, which reached down to the elbows, to the version bobbed to the shoulder that polite society retained with variations for court

46 • John Singleton Copley, *Isaac Smith*, 1759. Mr. Smith wears a plum-colored suit with gold buttons. The huge cuffs were fashionable from about 1707 to the 1760s. The weight of the coat skirts caused coats to hang open, so they were cut back and thereby displayed more of the waistcoat. The coat skirts are still as voluminous as a woman's hoop, and a man had to spread his skirts before sitting down. The fastening of the knee-breeches over the knee can be seen very clearly, with four buttons and a knee buckle. A professional man, Mr. Smith favors a full wig, which was probably more common in American towns than in the farming communities. *(Yale University Art Gallery, Gift of Maitland Fuller Griggs, 1869)*

appearances down to the Revolution. The military campaign wig, or Ramillies, which was tied back into a black purse and held with a black ribbon or stock, was being sported by the young by 1715–20, but it was excluded from formal occasions. It could appear when a peer was dressing at a levée, and it had to co-exist with full wigs on the elderly, on judges, and courtiers. It was not until the 1760s that examples appear at informal events at court, after which the campaign wig was accepted for most occasions, saving the most grand. All wigs needed a lot of maintenance, with regular heating and curling, and applications of perfumed pomatum. As most men drank a lot, red faces and noses were common; so the judicious usage of white lead

47 • Mason Chamberlin, *Portrait of Benjamin Franklin*, 1762. By the 1760s a reduction in width takes place. Benjamin Franklin's waistcoat is shorter than Mr. Smith's and shows more of his knee-breeches. His cuffs are a fraction smaller, and his coat is cut back further. The human figure was beginning to show, after being concealed in the Baroque era, as taste gradually turned to classical ideals. The eminent scientist and printer had just been granted an honorary degree by Oxford University for his experiments with electricity. As a professional man he still wears a wig, which he did not give up until 1775. The plain cloth reflects a man more interested in ideas than in show. *(Philadelphia Museum of Art, the Mr. and Mrs. Wharton Sinkler Collection)*

makeup was found on the most foppish male, with a hint of rouge on the cheeks, to conceal the florid features beneath. If worn heavily, lead makeup pitted the face.

Hats in the "mathematickal cock," with three equal sides shaped like a triangle, became a standard uniform from 1700. Up till then, a man could cock his hat in as many ways as he pleased, but the eighteenth century distrusted strong individuality, and the three-cornered hat became its symbolic form. There were some different hats about, but in town the *tricorne* dominated.

The seventeenth-century postillion's peaked cap was adopted by some of the peerage by 1730 for hunting and shooting, and it was also copied by ostlers, grooms, and Masters of the Hunt. Jockeys were another member of the equine sports to adopt the postillion's cap. Some ladies wore it for riding, and some children as a simple head protector. The queen's postillions still wear these peaked caps with the state coach, and they are the origin of many sporting caps. For undress, men already possessed their turbans and monteros. In the southern states of the American colonies it is possible the men wore straw hats like the ladies, for peasants certainly did, and it was a light and wide hat to protect the wearer against strong sunshine. The Quaker man's round hat was very exceptional for most of the century, but by the 1780s country men in England were wearing a felt round hat, with a higher crown than the Quakers, which would evolve into the universal top hat of the next century. Some hunting types adopted this round hat during the last two decades of the eighteenth century, and the three-cornered hat received its first challenge when the excessive formality and standardization of society imposed by the Age of Reason was attacked by the natural and Romantic movements. This also explains the fashion for masquerades, as a way of relief from the rules of etiquette and dress prescribed by the *savants*. The first hints of rebellion emerged in the 1760s when a few men stopped wearing wigs or powdering their hair; over the next two decades this gradually became a movement, but the conservatives still wore wigs into the 1820s and '30s. This natural trend also elevated humble cloth and peasant trousers; thus children who were put into trousers in the 1770s tended to favor trousers for usual wear when they were adult males. The English had always worn cloth even to court, but now it was given

48 • John Singleton Copley, *Mr. and Mrs. Thomas Mifflin*, c. 1768. Narrowness comes to the fore along with height. Mr. Mifflin has narrow sleeves and wears an English frock coat with a collar, and his cravat covers all his neck. He has abandoned wigs. Mrs. Mifflin, on the other hand, shows the artificial height that has started to affect hairstyles, with hair pads and eventually false hair being added. Her hair is dressed up over a pad, but the cap has not yet adjusted to the size of the head. She wears a mantua gown with a gauze apron, but wide hoops have been discarded as the leaner look establishes itself. The mantua or *manteau* (manto) gown was very adaptable since it could be worn with a variety of skirts. (*The Historical Society of Pennsylvania*)

higher status by growing acceptable for evenings, dinners, and receptions without being highly decorated. Plain dark color sufficed.

The English liberation of children following John Locke's criticism of baby swaddling took fifty years to become general, but by the 1750s and '60s both the ideas of swaddling babies and dressing children as miniature adults began to fade. By the 1770s foreign visitors were astonished by how well built the English younger generation was, and this approach was exported to the American colonies by the simple expedient of sending them simpler clothes for children. Boys had a tiny frilled collar in the 1750s that was now expanded into a wide collar edged with a frill, and was worn over a simple jacket and trousers. Girls were not liberated from corsets, but they were given simple white dresses instead of ornate adult full dress, which they had been expected to wear previously. In aristocratic houses the children had to be fully dressed before they could appear before the parents, even when the latter were in undress. This reflected the age's obsession with status; no inferior could be undressed before a superior, regardless of what the superior might or might not be wearing. By the 1780s both the Hapsburg and the Bourbon dynasties were copying English dress for children, but below that royal level the peasants continued conservative, and baby swaddling survived in rural communities.

After fifty years of horizontal styles, height began to stage a comeback in the middle of the 1760s, and reached its climax in the 1770s, when the wig swept up to a last outburst of extravagance and artificiality, as if defying the more natural trends emerging (see figure 51). Cartoonists mocked the extremes, but their engravings were eagerly awaited in the colonies to see just how far the newest styles had gone. Fashionable ladies stopped wearing hats, as the wig became a foot high or more, and was so smothered with feathers, jewels, chains, bows, garlands, and model ships or groves, that no hat could fit. Instead the calash hood was devised, a collapsible arrangement of hoops in cane that could be raised to cover the headpiece when going outdoors. The most extreme styles would have been worn in Williamsburg at the governor's court, given the Virginian fondness for dressing up. Fashionable men attempted to echo this vogue for height in their wigs, by having them built up in front, and the most extreme examples were sported by the Macaronis, London dandies whose wigs towered up two feet, with six side curls, and a huge tail half way down the back. Doubtless these exhibitionists determined more men to give up wigs altogether.

That the formality of the eighteenth century was breaking down became clear in the 1770s when the peasant woman's

jacket, also worn by servant girls, was promoted to polite society. It was no longer undress for country or summer, but
could be worn in town and for visiting. Both the fitted jacket,
already about 170 years old, and a loose-backed type, the *caraco,*
were now worn with matching skirts instead of mantua gowns.
The democratic element in the jacket was that the wearer could
put it on herself, which was why farmers wore it. It was not, as
with the hairstyle and the gown, a matter of needing a maidservant to assist the lady into her fashionable outfit. This was, of
course, another element in the back-to-nature movement,
which involved the wearing of peasant garments, translated
into silks and cottons with frills, by the upper classes. As the
custom was well-established in the American colonies of wearing undress in summer, it was a case of fashion recognizing an
established habit. Indeed, the American colonies would become
regarded as a natural society, where the simplicity of life outside
the cities typified the ideal that Rousseau and the poets were
writing about. By the 1770s America was itself becoming a
fashion.

Colonial Diaries

At the bottom of American society were the slaves, and how
they were clothed is shown in the diaries for 1752–78 of Colonel
Landon Carter, who lived at Sabine Hall, Virginia, and had
several plantations. The colonel's attitudes were typical of
wealthy slave owners.

Some cloth was woven on the estate, but in 1758 the colonel
considered his "weaving boy" far too slow. The dressmaking
also was done by the domestic slaves, for on 25 November 1763
the diary records: "Cut out by Betty. Boys suits—10, Men's suits
and women's suits—40." The allowance to the domestics—"6
yards of Oznaburg to Betty, Winney, Peg, each for a waistcoat
and pettycoat, 2½ yards waistcoat, and breeches for Joe, Tomm,
Nassau, 4 yards each of them"—shows that the women were
wearing jackets and skirts, and the men waistcoats and knee-
breeches. On 8 September 1770 the colonel explained his policy
on clothing: "I allowed them but one shirt and I allowed no
more up here. My people always made and raised things to sell,
and I obliged them to buy linnen to make their other shirt

49 • Augustin Brunais, *Free Natives of Dominica,* c. 1770. Dominica had Spanish, French, and British rulers, but the dress of the black residents was the same as in Louisiana. The women wear the *tignon,* or turban, which was imposed by the Spanish. Their loose dresses have wide sleeves for coolness, and they wear neckerchiefs as do the white women. The man wears the typical short coat of male servants, and his cane denotes that he may be an usher or junior chamberlain on an estate. He has no cravat and only tiny ruffles, to distinguish him from his employers. He holds a miniature *chapeau-bras,* to bow with, but it is too small to wear and would not fit on his turban. The large hat worn by the middle woman was fashionable in hot climates. (*Yale Center for British Art, Paul Mellon Collection*)

50 • Augustin Brunais, *A Planter and His Wife Attended by a Servant*, c. 1780. Linen and cotton trousers were adopted in the South to protect against mosquitoes. The planter wears a frock coat and short waistcoat that shows he was aware of fashion. His hair is unpowdered, probably because of the intense heat. His wife has on a straw hat and a head-scarf instead of a cap, which illustrates the casual plantation way of life. Her gown and petticoat are worn over hip pads and a bum roll. The servant has no such underpadding, and wears the simple jacket and skirt of working women from the West Indies to Canada. Her petticoat looks like rough slave cloth akin to sacking. Her plain head-scarf is not worn as a turban, so perhaps her employers would not allow it. *(Yale Center for British Art, Paul Mellon Collection)*

instead of buying liquor with their fowls." The colonel's son ran another plantation, which he apparently supplied with apparel; thus on 4 November 1764 "A note to Sykes for 70 pair of shoes for the Charles Carter estate. . . . Gave Sam, the Estate coachman 3/9 to pay his ferrayages in carrying up the above 70 shoes for the Estate negroes." The family buyer was his daughter Lucy, so on 3 July 1770: "My daughter Lucy yesterday went to Tom Blair's store on Nomony, and laid out for me in brown linnen and Cotton for my people." To his surprise, Colonel Carter observed on 25 September 1775 that the women domestics were making the best of his clothing system: "I always thought my house wenches made the Virginian cloth given them last two years, but it seems, they have every other Year as much cloth as will make them two suits, so just as all the other negroes, they have a suit every year."[27] The Virginia cloth was one of the homespun attempts forced on the colonies when Britain banned exports following the outbreak of hostilities. The colonel, who was a loyalist in sympathy, did not think much of the attempt to make an American cloth out of cow's hair and cotton, which had too many curls in it.

Colonel Carter's diary records that on 12 December 1763 he received a visit from the trade: "Mr. D. Campbell Merchant of London here: He was so kind as to offer to send me in anything I might want. I wrote him the following invoice: (tea and spices), 3 livery suits middling men, 3 silver laced hats for ditto, a Rocelo cloak for myself, 10 yards of Welsh flannel, 2 pair of gloves lined with furr, a warm muff for myself." The colonel liked flannel waistcoats for winter, as he explained in December 1774: "I used to wear my flannel waistcoat next to my skin to accommodate the very cold weather of winter. This however produced Vast itching. . . . This year I only wore a Prudance, a breastplate of flannel, which hardly produced an itching."

A critical view of England was emerging in the colonies in 1770, Colonel Carter observed. "I believe every body begins to laugh at English education," he writes. "The general importers of it nowadays bring back only a stiff priggishness with as little good manners as possible, especially when the particular cut of a waistcoat, the multi oval trim of a hat, or the cost of a buckle does not attract great admiration." Colonists educated in England who possessed an English wardrobe considered themselves superior to the natives, which would goad wealthy landowners like the colonel who had as much land as an earl. One finds his sons supplying some of his attire, perhaps to keep him up-to-date: "3 December 1770. My son Jack sent me down according to his promise 5 and near ¼ yard of 6/4 cloth with 3 dozen Coat, 4 dozen breast buttons, 6 yards Shaloon and mohair to make me clothes." He also wore a wig and paid the Williamsburg wigmaker Mr. Charleton £4 for one on 20 November 1770. The most fashionable member of the family was Lucy: "3 June 1771. Sent also Mr. Ronand's account against me for my daughter silks amounting to £17.8.0. . . . 5 June 1773 . . . an invoice of shoes, gloves and stays &c for my daughter Lucy," and in 1775, "Lucy as usual is in want of necessaries. . . . I gave her 7 dollars to lay out. Note, her necessaries were first white and coloured ribbons. . . . My daughter got back by dinner and had laid out £6 in necessaries, a fan, some ribbons and several prodigious nothings. . . . 25 September 1775 Lucy went to Blanes, Got a pair of white Lutestring and a few ribbons and cost £11.9.0." With the outbreak of war, prices for silks rocketed. On occasion the colonel ordered something for himself, as on 12 September 1770: "Also for a pair of Soft, doeskin breeches, with Polished steel breeches buckle and knee buckler to fit the knee bands." He also ordered two pairs of doeskin gloves. On the whole, he does seem to have felt that fashion did not apply to his rural way of life and was critical of one of his manager's wives, Mrs. Beale, for wearing the upswept wigs of the mode on a plantation. For in a diary entry of September 1772 Colonel Carter notes: "I was so sorry to see his wife act the part of a fine Lady in all her towering apparell."[28] As he grew elderly, the colonel's style of dress altered, and he spent a lot of time with his Indian gown over his clothes.

In 1771 Anne Green Winslow, from Nova Scotia in Canada, was sent to school in Boston where she had some aunts. She was the sixth generation in descent from the Winslows of New Plymouth, her ancestor Edward Winslow being the brother of the governor John Winslow. Anne was ten years old and had to learn to sew and make linenwear: "I have made two shirts for unkle since I finish'd mamma's shifts." Mother sent her clothes as gifts "November 28. I have your favour Hon^d Mamma, by Mr. Gonnel, & heartily thank you for the broadcloth, bags, ribbin and hat. The cloath and bags are both at work upon, & my aunt has bought me a beautifull ermin trimming for my cloak."[29] Anne, however, had to inform her mother that her ideas about dress were too antique for Boston. Anne wrote on November 29th that she had been borrowing other girls' hats. "I hope aunt won't let me wear the black hat with the red Dominie—for the people will ask me what I have got to sell along the street if I do, or, how the folk at New Guinea do? Dear mamma, you don't know the fation here,—I beg to look like other folk. You don't know what a stir would be made in Sudbury street were I make an appearance there in my red Dominie and black Hatt! But the old cloak & bonnett together will make me a decent bonnet for

51 • Anonymous, *Israel Israel*, c. 1775. During the 1770s there was a vogue for huge ornate buttons, started by Louis XVI's brother the Comte d'Artois. Israel, born in Pennsylvania, made his fortune in Barbados, so he could afford these silver buttons and a fine lace cravat, even though his suit is plain, reflecting the sobriety of Pennsylvania. Narrow sleeves greatly reduced the room for ruffles at the wrist, so the sitter wears none. *(Abby Aldrich Rockefeller Folk Art Center, Williamsburg, Virginia. Photographed by Colonial Williamsburg)*

common ocation." Anne does not say whether the black hat was a modified sugarloaf, the pointed cone shape that farmers' wives were still wearing in the 1770s, or a black bonnet, but clearly it was not stylish enough for Massachusetts.

On New Year's Day 1772 Anne went visiting aunts, and reported the events to mamma on January 4th:

> I was dress'd in my yellow coat, my black bib & apron, my pompadore shoes, the cap my aunt Storer sometime presented me with (blue ribbins in it), & a very handsome loket in the shape of a hart she gave me—the past pin Hon.[d] Papa presented me with in my

52 • Anonymous, *Hannah Erwin Mrs. Israel*, c. 1775. Hannah wears a Quaker cap with no frills, and no ruffles at the elbow. Her completely plain dress is a Quaker pattern. Hannah, from Delaware, married Mr. Israel about 1774. *(Abby Aldrich Rockefeller Folk Art Center, Williamsburg, Virginia. Photographed by Colonial Williamsburg)*

cap, My New Cloak & bonnet on, my pompadore gloves &c. And I would tell you that *for the first time they all liked my dress very much.* My cloak and bonnet are really very handsome & so they need be. For they cost an amasing sight of money, not quite £45, tho' Aunt Sukey said, that she suppos'd Aunt Deming would be frighted out of her Wits at the money it cost.

The black bib apron was a German tradition, and Boston may have adopted this style from the German settlers. English aprons for women were white, and blue were for butchers. The yellow coat would have meant a dress, and the shoes and gloves were named for Madame de Pompadour.

Anne moved in comfortable society since her diary records elegant fabrics and jewelry: "January 31, I was at Aunt Sukey's, with Mrs. Barrett dress'd in white brocade, & cousin Betsey dress'd in red lustring, both adorn'd with past, perls, marquessett &c." Even so she had to study good housewifery, and in February was taught flax spinning to make linen thread, and did knitting in the evenings. On March 9th she was industrious: "I sew'd on the bosom of unkle's shirt, mended two pair of gloves, mended for the wash two handkerchiefs (one cambrick), sewed on half a border of a lawn apron of aunt's." On August 18th she went to a wedding, and described the bride dressed in a nightgown as daywear: "The bride was dress'd in a white satin night gound." Earlier on May 25th Aunt Storer had decided that Anne should be more fashionable and don a wig: "I had my *Heddus* roll on. It makes my head itch, & ache & burn like anything Mamma. This famous roll is not made *wholly* of a red *Cow Tail,* but it is a mixture of that, & horsehair (very course) & a little human hair of a yellow hue, that I suppose was taken out of the back part of an old wig. But D- made it (over head) all carded together and twisted up. When it first came home, aunt put it on, & my new cap on it." Anne was then measured, and the wig and cap were found to be one inch longer than her face, which accorded with the latest ideal.

The use of dolls dressed in the fashion dates back to the Middle Ages, and Anne offered to make one for her mother in English attire: "It was taken from a print that came over in one of the last ships from London." The editor, Mrs. Earle, notes that there was a baby, i.e., doll agent in Boston, Mrs. Hannah Teatts Mantuamaker at the top of Summer Street, who imported fashion dolls. Such figures were fully dressed with the under-clothes, paniers, petticoats, and mantua, so one could see the whole ensemble, whereas a print only gave one view. On March 10 there was some argument among the aunts about Queen Charlotte: "Aunt Deming quite misunderstood the matter about the queen's night Cap. Mrs. Deming thought that it was black skull cap lin'd with red." Night caps were usually white trimmed with lace in royal circles. The queen was the ideal image to copy for respectable married ladies, who did not wish to imitate French royal mistresses such as Pompadour. It is a

53 • Antoine Raspal, *Madame de Privat and Her Daughters*, c. 1775. Height was taken to an extreme at the French court, and was copied in Canada and the American colonies. Madame's hair is dressed up over a huge pad, her cap has expanded in sympathy, and the structure needs a professional hairdresser to erect it. She wears the short *polonaise* jacket, which became very popular in this decade. The elder daughter imitates maman in having her hair up, but the baby lacks sufficient locks. She wears a vest and a bed. Although Marie Antoinette, like the English, gave up baby swaddling, in Provence and Canada, where life was very conservative it continued. (*Museon Arlaten, Musées d'Arles, Archives Photographiques, Provence*)

pity that Anne did not continue her lively observations into adulthood.

In 1773 Philip Fithian from Greenwich, Connecticut, in New England set out to ride to Virginia to become tutor to another member of the Carter dynasty, Robert Carter at Nomini Hall, who owned a plantation that produced and wove cotton, 500 slaves, an iron works, and some shipping. The tutor accordingly purchased a saddle, bridle, and spurs, and was measured for a surtout overcoat, before setting out in October. He was surprised at one Virginian custom: "Almost every Lady wears a red Cloak, and when they ride out they tye a white handkerchief over their Head and face so that when I first came into Virginia, I was distress'd whenever I saw a Lady, for I thought she had the Tooth-Ach!" His pupils were three boys and five girls: "The girls all dress in White & are remarkably genteel," having had some education already in Williamsburg. He was alarmed when Christmas was greeted by the firing of guns, and there were some signs of Misrule, the old custom of servants being masters for a day, when the boy Nelson who made the tutor's fire and blacked his shoes turned up "only in his shirt & Breeches." The slave who made the fire in the schoolroom always wore a green livery, and green liveries seem to have been common in Virginia households. The firm of Norton & Sons who imported cloth and clothes to the colony had on its account for 3 September 1770 ten yards of cheap green livery cloth, and Colonial Williamsburg has a servant's green livery frock coat, so green was fairly common as a livery color.[30]

On 18 January 1774 Fithian was required to escort Mrs. Carter to a ball. "The Ladies are Dressed Gay and splendid, & when dancing, their Silks and Brocades rustled and trailed behind them." He was also introduced to some of the local young ladies, like Miss Washington, aged 17: "Her dress is rich & well chosen, but not too tawdry, nor yet too plain. She appears to Day in a Chintz cotton Gown with an elegant blue Stamp, a Sky-Blue silk quilt [petticoat], spotted Apron. Her hair is light brown, it was crap'd up, with two Rolls at each side, & on the top a small cap of beautiful Gauze and rich Laces, with an artificial Flower interwoven." Quilted petticoats became fashionable in the 1730s, and Mr. Fithian encountered other examples in Virginia in 1774. There was Miss Hale, aged 14: "She is drest in a White Holland [linen] Gown, cotton Diaper quilt very fine, a Lawn apron, has her Hair crap'd up & on it a small Tuft of Ribbon for a Cap." Miss Betsy Lee, aged 13, is depicted as "drest in a neat shell Callico Gown, hair very light Hair done up with a Feather." But the tutor did not approve of Betsy Lee's attire when he met her again in July 1774: "She was pinched up rather too near in a long pair of new fashioned Stays, which I think are a Nuisance both to us & themselves—For the late importation of Stays which are said to be now most fashionable, are produced upwards so high that we can have scarce any view of all the Ladies Snowy Bosoms." He also disliked the length of the new corsets, but he approved of the remainder of the outfit: "She wore a light Chintz Gown, very fine, with a blue stamp, elegantly made, & which sat well upon her—She wore a blue silk Quilt—in one Word Her Dress was rich & fashionable." The fichu or neckerchief tucked into the top of the new high corsets concealed the bosoms even further, so men were deprived of even a glimpse. They did not have to moan for long, as low necklines returned in the 1780s.

An English governess arrived, Miss Sally Panton, who wore a very modest and old-fashioned style: "But her huge Stays, low Headdress, enormous long Waist a Dress entirely contrary to the liking of Virginia Ladies." Evidently Miss Panton felt that being only a step above a domestic servant, the governess should not ape the fashion of her employers; hence the very unmodish low cap instead of the towering new wigs. The Virginia ladies, however, seem to have wanted even their staff to look stylish, such was their preoccupation with fashion and display.

Philip Fithian did notice one male, Mr. Lane, whom he considered well dressed. "He was drest in a black superfine Broadcloth; a Gold Laced Hat; laced Ruffles, black Silk Stockings, & to his brooch on his Bosom he wore a Mason's Badge inscrib'd Virtute et Silentio cut in a Gold Medal."[31] As a New Englander, Fithian clearly admired this black suit touched with a little gold ornamentation. He did not describe the silk suits of his male employers. Although the fine ladies wore silk to balls, Fithian shows how general was the wearing of cotton chintz and linen by day.

54 • Ralph Earl, *Representative Roger Sherman*, c. 1770. Sherman began as
a shoemaker and studied law at home, eventually becoming a judge and
representative at the First Congress in 1787. This meant the plain
homespun suit appearing among well-tailored outfits in Washington. He
wears the short hip-length jacket of the working man, and the russet
brown is exactly the color ordered for laborers by Edward III in 1362,
which shows how unchanging were the color patterns of rural life. His
stockings are black knitted wool, but he has some sparkling shoe
buckles, in flashy contrast to the rest of his attire. *(Yale University Art
Gallery, Gift of Roger Sherman White)*

English Imports

One of the chief suppliers of clothes and fabrics to Virginia, as mentioned earlier, was the London firm Norton & Sons whose company representative was John Norton of Yorktown since 1742. He imported tea, books, and other goods, but the account for April 1768 includes "a consignement of linen, hose and cloaths for Mr. William Acton Jnr." and two pieces of Irish Linen for John Wills. A representative sample of items, sent out on 6 September 1768, included:

½ *Piece of best Jaquonot Muslin yard and a half wide, the best at 10/– yard*
6 yards handsome flowered Gauze E11 wide
2 pairs spotted Cambric Pocket Handkerchiefs, 1 purple and white, the other blue and white
1 pr. ditto white something coarser
3 prs. best and finest double mill'd rose large Bed Blankets
2 plain black satin Bonnets
2 prs fine large Men's gray worsted Hose
2 pairs white ditto, 1 pr. black ditto. 1 pr. strongest black silk ditto, 4 prs. finest thread brown ditto
2 pr. fine white worsted Hose for a small Woman
3 prs. fine thread ditto of the same size
4 prs. Cotton ditto, larger, 2 pr. string, 3 thread Hose for a girl of 11 years
2 pr. worsted ditto
18 prs. best unglazed Kid Mitts—6 pr. of 'em for a small Woman—12 pr. larger
6 prs. best French Purple ditto & 2 prs. for a small woman—4 pr. larger
6 prs. colour'd Lamb Mitts for girl of 11
2 pr. best Shammy Pumps for a very small woman, exactly 8 inches long, a pr. of Slippers of white and black Kid of same size, & a pr. of purple Satin ditto.
Exactly 9 inches long, 6 pr. best Calf skin do
6 prs. black callimanco Pumps.
2 pr. green Satin ditto
2 prs. Calfskins of the same size
6 pr. green calimanco Pumps & pr. of beaded ditto exactly eight Inches long with flat heels
28 yds. changeable Lustring pink and sky blue ¾ wide, at about 5/6 yd.
20 yds. of best blonde Lace that can be had for 2/6 yd.
1 piece of fine Calico, white ground and small blue running Vine, 1 pc. long Lawn white ground with small green running Vine very fine
6 ps. very narrow diaper tape, 4 oz. very fine Scotch thread at 2/2 ditto at 4/1
1 ps. yellow Quality binding
1 Man's Large best Beaver Hat, 1 fine black ditto. For a Boy of 12 years

2 black ditto. For a Boy or 9 or 10 years cheaper bound around with large Crowns, 2 ditto for a Boy of seven years, 1 ditto for a Child of 4 years, with narrow Silver binding, narrow Brim & large Crown

12 pr. Children's Pinchbeck Shoe Buckles

6 prs. knee ditto. 4 pr. of 'em for large Boys

As much superfine fashionable Broadcloth as will make a large Man a full suit, and two pr. of Breeches, garters and Trimmings of all sorts. As much black cotton Velvet with lining & Trimmings as will make a large Man a pr. of Breeches.

1 pr. superfine Dueroy with Trimmings [Breeches]

1 pr. finest brown Holland of yellowish dye [Breeches]

1 pr. strongest dark Colour'd Jean with Trimmings [Breeches]

As much blue bath coating as will make a large man a close bodied great Coat with Trimmings

6 pieces double milled blue Plains about 80 yds.

1 ps. coarse green Shalloon

6 yds. Coarse green Plush [used for servants' breeches]

1 ps. best German Oznabrig at 9½ or 10d. for House Servants

A green narrow striped Callimanco large Wrapping Gown for a large Man to be sent by the very first opportunity.

This shipment also included tea, ink, cheese, quill pens, and slop basins.[32]

In 1769 Thomas Everard wrote to John Norton to advise him that the Association scheme to boycott English goods except for cheap articles would soon become general in Maryland, since indignation with the British government was building up. This did not stop G. Wythe from putting in an order on 3 August 1769 for "2 ps. of sheeting linen, not exceeding 2s. yd., 2 ps. Irish linen for shirts 2s. yd.; 1 piece of green ditto. 1/3 yd; 1 piece of dark colour'd Russian drab." Mr. Norton was told that a William Gosley on a trip to England had spent £100 on a fine suit, but Martha Gosley in Yorktown wrote on 8 August 1770 to say that politics would ruin everything: "they will Put us under the necessity of wearing homespun altogether. I assure the Gentlemen wear nothing else all Summer, we have made great improvements." In December 1769 a ball at Williamsburg had seen American cloth as the dominant type: "To the number of near one hundred (ladies), appeared in homespun gowns" as a patriotic gesture, reported *The Virginia Gazette.* Despite this, another customer wrote to Norton on 17 April 1771: "Negroes Cloth we can't possibly do without, therefore hope you will send them by the first *Ship.*" Evidently he felt that American homespun would be insufficient to clothe slaves as well as white colonists. Norton & Sons continued trading in the period prior to the rebellion. An invoice for 15 February 1770 lists:

4 ps. coarse Scotch cloth
4 ps. white Dowles [coarse linen]
4 ps checks
6 dozen Monmouth caps [the knitted caps made in Monmouth]
10 prs. coloured stockings for Serrvants
10 plain hats for ditto
24 yds Duffle with Buttons and Mohair for Servants' Coats
8 ps. blanketing duffle
For a 21 year old, large hats, French kid gloves 4 prs, 1 pr. Buckskin, 3 prs.
   white Silk Stockings, 6 prs. Thread stockings, 8 yds of cloth with buttons
   & mohair & silk lining [for a suit], 1 pr. doeskin breeches[33]

The duffle, like the dueroy/duroy cloth earlier, was coarse cloth of rough wool, used for coats and blankets. The modern duffle coat with a hood was evolved by Normandy fishermen in the nineteenth century. The reference to jeans in these accounts means twilled cotton cloth, not trousers, although it was made into jackets, knee-breeches, and trousers, and even dresses.

The Earl of Dunmore had plantations in Virginia and was still ordering clothes for his servants and slaves on 12 June 1773. He wanted livery hats, and postillions' caps, 30 yards of blue cloth and 30 yards of brown cloth for his footmen, and 6 pieces of brown jeans also for footmen, plus one piece of green shag, a rough cloth. Thirty yards of striped flannel were required for the grooms' waistcoats. For the plantation his lordship ordered 100 pairs of strong, large shoes for negroes, 100 pairs of coarse, strong stockings for the same, and 50 coarse hats. In addition, for himself the earl required 18 new superfine cloth coats in brown, gray, scarlet, and black, to wear with his white silk stockings and gold laced hat.[34]

By 1773 colonists of English descent regarded themselves still as British subjects, but the population also included Dutch, Germans, and Swedes who had not lived under British rule before, and did not see why they should now. The ensuing revolution was not desired by many. Although Lord Chatham, Lord Camden, and Edmund Burke had all warned the British government against it, the government banned all trade with the colonial rebels in 1775. The French crown committed suicide over the American colonies. Already deeply in debt since the

Seven Years' War and the loss of India and Canada, assisting the colonies meant bankrupting the French crown, but the desire for revenge against the British overcame common sense. The French supported a republican rebellion overseas, only to fall prey to republican extremism at home in 1789. In 1778 the white population of the colonies was about 3 million. Some 80,000 loyalists moved to Lake Erie in Canada, and others to New Brunswick, which was set up as a home for them on the Canadian coast. Others returned to England. The supply of British garments and cloth stopped in 1775, although it continued in Canada and Florida-Louisiana.

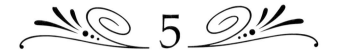

5

The United States and Canada, 1775–1800

The Revolutionary War

The homespun movement began in Boston in 1767, when the citizens voted to refrain from purchasing British hats and shoes, to buy colonial products, and to be frugal in mourning, thus avoiding the importation of huge amounts of English black cloth. (See Appendix II, "The Commencement of American Cloth Production.") Once Britain banned trade with the colonies in 1775, the wearing of homespun became compulsory; however, the future president Thomas Jefferson, who was governor of Virginia from 1774 to 1781, wrote in his report on the state that he did not believe that the homespun movement would outlast the conflict:

> During this time we have manufactured within our families the most necessary articles of cloathing. Those of cotton will bear some comparison with the same kinds of manufacture in Europe, but those of wool, flax, and hemp are very coarse, unsightly and unpleasant: and such is our attachment to agriculture and such our preference for foreign manufactures, that be it wise or unwise, our people will certainly return as soon as they can to the raising of raw materials and exchanging them for finer manufactures than they are able to execute themselves.[1]

Jefferson estimated Virginia's exports before the revolution to be at £850,000, with peltry in deerskin, beaver, otter, muskrat, raccoon, and fox still important, along with exports of tobacco, timber, shipping, farm produce, and some iron and coal.

General George Washington as a soldier obtained his uniforms from the regimental tailor, although he did have some trouble with Congress over payment for goods for their new army. It was one thing to object to British taxes, but now Americans had to tax themselves, and the revolutionary army was often short of uniforms and supplies. Washington's accounts for the headquarters saw the appointment of Giles Alexander as tailor to the servants on 17 August 1775. On 25 January 1776, the headquarters purchased cloth, linen, and furniture from Mathew Irwin, merchant of Cambridge, for £14.2.4. On 7 February 1776, slippers and mending shoes by Mr. Austin for Lady Washington came to £32.8.0. In April 1776 Richard Peacock of Cambridge did some tailoring work for the headquarters, and Elizabeth Hunt was appointed washerwoman. The cobbler Timothy Wood was paid £4.15.0. on 15 July 1776. On 2 October of that year the tailor Richard Peacock received £2.11s. for mending the servants' clothes and repairing breeches. There are no more references in Washington's accounts to clothing matters until 1781, when 5/2 was spent on washing at Williamsburg; and on 31 October the tailor charged 2/9 for mending the riding breeches of servant William. As the army passed through Philadelphia it purchased tea, so both Colonial and British forces in the conflict were drinking the same beverage.[2]

To the loyalists the colonial struggle was a civil war, a rebellion against the legal authority of the Crown, and they were outraged when the rebels dubbed them traitors and allowed them no democratic rights. For example, when the British garrison at Savannah defeated a Franco-American attack by land and sea, the loyalists felt safe, only to find that the act of 1 March 1778 passed at Augusta declared 286 loyalists sentenced to exile, and their estates and properties confiscated.[3] The loyalists' sad fate was repeated in other colonies; to the rebels, however, such harsh measures were necessary to ensure that their struggle would succeed.

The war caused inflation, and Mrs. Abigail Adams wrote on 15 October 1780 that "sheeps" wool was thirty dollars a pound, and flax twenty. The new country changed over to Spanish currency as a gesture against things British, but the elderly continued calculating in *lsd* (pounds, shillings, pence). The Reverend William Bentley described Mrs. Adams, a future first lady, as very conservative in her attire, "in the dress of the matrons who were in New England in my youth. The black bonnet, the short cloak, the gown open before, and quilted petticoat, and the high heeled shoes, as worn usually in that day. Everything the best but nothing different from our wealthy and modest citizens."[4] Mrs. Adams wrote in a similar vein about Mrs. Washington: "She is plain in her dress, but that plainness is the best of every article."[5]

William Smith wrote his history of New York in 1776, in the midst of the conflict, and observed:

> In Suffolk and Queen's County the first settlers of which were either natives of England, or the immediate descendants of such as began the plantations in the eastern colonies; their manners and customs are similar to those prevailing in the English counties, from whence they originally sprang. In the city of New-York, through our intercourse with the Europeans we follow the London fashions, though by the time we adopt them, they become diluted in England. Our affluence during the late war introduced a degree of luxury in table, dress, and furniture with which we were before unacquainted. But still we are not so gay a people as our neighbours in Boston and several of the eastern colonies. The Dutch colonies in some measure follow the example of New-York, but still retain many modes peculiar to the Hollanders.[6]

Trade was worth £100,000 for British dry goods, but duck, checkered linen, and oznabrigs were bought from Hamburg and Holland, and cotton from St. Thomas, Virgin Islands. Once peace was declared in 1783, the new state had to dispatch envoys and ambassadors to foreign courts. The Adamses were sent to Europe in 1778, but in 1786 Mrs. Adams paid a visit to the Netherlands and noticed the sort of Dutch traditional dress that could be found in New York's Dutch counties:

> The dress of the country people is precisely the same as it was two hundred years ago. . . . You recollect the short petticoats and long short-gowns [?bedgowns], round-eared caps with straight borders, and large straw hats the German women wore when they first settled in Germantown. Such is now the dress of all the lower-

class people who do not even attempt to imitate the gentry. I was pleased with the trig neatness of the women, many of them wear black tammy aprons, thick quilted coats [petticoats] or russet skirts, and small hoops, but only figure to yourself a child of three or four, dressed in the same way! Gold earings are usually worn by them, and bracelets upon holidays. The dress of the men is full and old fashioned; but the Court and genteel people dress part English and part French.[7]

The English and French influence was as expected in a small country influenced by two larger neighbors. But Mrs. Adams exaggerates the antiquity of the peasant clothes. Bedgowns and hoops were both eighteenth-century creations. Peasants did not

55 • The Beardsley Limner, *Harmony Mrs. Oliver Wight*, c. 1786. Caps expand into the mob cap to accommodate the increase in hair. This one is bound with olive ribbon with a black motif, which is picked out in Harmony's black shawl. Her dress is olive green with long narrow sleeves, which have completely replaced the elbow-length ruffle sleeve. The portrait was painted about the time of Harmony's marriage to Oliver Wight in 1786, and she lived until 1861, seeing a huge variety of fashions come and go by the time she died at 96. *(Abby Aldrich Rockefeller Folk Art Center, Williamsburg, Virginia. Photographed by Colonial Williamsburg)*

wear bedgowns or farthingales in the sixteenth century, although the straw hats and caps were older.

The English radical Tom Paine, who fought for the Americans, wrote in his letter, "To the Inhabitants of America," on 21 March 1778 that they ought to build up a huge army to defeat the British, predating Napoleon's application of the idea. He called on all colonial citizens to help the cause, noting that the elderly for "their portion of service, therefore, will be to furnish each man with a blanket, which will make a regimental coat, jacket and breeches, or clothes in lieu thereof, and another for a watch coat, and two pair of shoes."[8] However, outfitting the troops in this way required enormous organization beyond the

56 • The Beardsley Limner, *Mr. Oliver Wight*, c. 1786. Oliver was a cabinetmaker, but for his wedding is dressed as a fashionable gentleman, even down to the silver topped cane. He wears the English frock coat with the collar, and his waistcoat has gained a collar too, although it has shrunk to his waist at its other end. The tight line meant careful conduct, for clothes could split in violent action. The black riding hat from England still has a wide brim, but it is on the way to becoming a top hat. Oliver wears no hair powder, but he still ties his hair back in the conventional way. The two frills on his shirt and the bow cravat suggest Oliver had a touch of the dandy. (*Abby Aldrich Rockefeller Folk Art Center, Williamsburg, Virginia. Photographed by Colonial Williamsburg*)

powers of the infant state, and Paine's idea does not seem to have been put into practice.

The New Republic and the Courts of Europe

In 1778 Benjamin Franklin was appointed ambassador to Paris, and immediately found that homespun would not do at Versailles; thus he had to equip himself with a brown silk suit,

57 • Benjamin West, *Benjamin Franklin Drawing Electricity from the Sky.* The first American ambassador to France in 1778, Franklin's simple dress and abandonment of wigs struck the French as American national dress. He wears a plain dark suit, cut on the narrow line, with just a brief cravat. Having worked in Philadelphia, Franklin was probably influenced by Quaker simplicity in the town, where to look showy would have looked out of place. *(Philadelphia Museum of Art, the Mr. and Mrs. Wharton Sinkler Collection)*

which is now in the Massachusetts Historical Society. He had stopped wearing powdered wigs in 1775, so his white hair and simple tastes as a man of science from Quaker Pennsylvania made a great impact on the French court. The Adamses and Thomas Jefferson were also faced with European attitudes toward dress. Abigail Adams was in London in July 1784:

> I am not a little surprised to find dress, unless upon public occasions, so little regarded. The gentlemen are very plainly dressed, and the ladies much less so than with us. Tis true you must put a hoop on, and have your hair dressed, but a common straw hat, no cap, only a ribbon upon the crown is thought dress sufficient to go into company. Muslins are much in taste, but no silks but lutestrings. . . . They paint here nearly as much as in France, but with more art. The headdress disfigures them in the eye of Americans. I have seen many ladies but not one elegant one since I came, there is not to see that neatness in their appearance, which you see in our ladies.
>
> The American ladies are much admired here by the gentlemen, I am told, and in truth I wonder not at it. O my country, my country! preserve, preserve the little purity and simplicity of manners you yet possess. Believe me, they are jewels of inestimable value; the softness peculiarly characteristic of our sex, which is so pleasing to the gentlemen, is wholly laid aside here for the masculine attire and manners of Amazonians![9]

Abigail Adams was referring to the vogue for sports among the upper classes. Ladies started playing bowls, shooting arrows, and firing guns, in addition to hunting and riding, during the 1770s. Doubtless Mrs. Adams found such activities "unfeminine," but there was an air of independence for women that stemmed from the salons of Paris and the outdoor movement in England. The "Amazonian" habits were riding suits, which Mrs. Adams found too masculine, as they had exactly the same cut of jacket, shirt, and cravat as menswear. Clearly, she considered neatness, smartness, and softness the essence of the American female.

Thomas Jefferson expressed similar views when he wrote to his daughter Martha, aged 11, in Annapolis on 22 December 1783. His wife had died the previous year, and the father adopted the role of costume regulator.

> To advise you on the subject of dress, which I know you are a little apt to neglect. I do not wish you to be gaily clothed at this time of

life, but that your wear should be fine of its kind. But above all things and at all times, let your clothes be neat, whole, and properly put on. Do not fancy you must wear them till the dirt is visible to the eye. You will be the last one who is sensible of this. Some ladies think they may, under the privileges of the *déshabillée,* be loose and negligent of their dress in the morning. But be you from the moment you rise till you go to bed, as cleanly and properly dressed as at the hours of dinner or tea. A lady who is seen as a sloven or a slut in the morning, will never efface the impression she has made, with all the dress and pageantry she can afterwards involve herself in.[10]

How far a child of eleven would heed this advice is another matter.

Mr. Jefferson himself had to obey court dress regulations when in France. For example, Mrs. Adams writes of an incident where a prince of eight had died, an ally of the king: "Poor Mr. Jefferson had to hie away for a tailor to get a whole black silk suit made up in two days; and at the end of eleven days, should another death happen, he will be obliged to have a new suit of mourning of cloth, because that is the season when silk must be left off." She wrote on 5 September 1784, as the winter season was approaching. Of France Mrs. Adams wrote that "fashion is the deity which everyone worships in the country," an attitude the French brought to Canada. But she did not find French women very neat, as she described Madame Helvetius, the widow of the philosopher, who was wearing a blue lutestring dress covered by a tiffany chemise: "Her hair was frizzled, over it she had a small straw hat, with a dirty gauze half hand-kerchief round it, and a bit of dirtier gauze than ever my maids wore, was bowed on behind. She had a black gauze scarf thrown over her shoulders."[11]

Fashion had begun to alter. The vogue for high headdresses, from around 1767 to 1779, began to subside through a short fashion for rolls during the period 1779–1782, to a frizzled look, which Marie Antoinette launched in 1783. The hair was swept out at the sides and curled like a poodle, and it became the main style to about 1791. Since this was a wide fashion, caps increased in volume and hats made a comeback, with the Gainsborough style decked with feathers as the potent image. With it went a pigeon-breasted pout over the breast, which was achieved by gauze scarves, topped by a large kerchief that tied round at the back of the waist. Hoops were replaced by hip pads and bustles or rumps for that decade of the 1780s. The queen's advocacy of muslin was having a huge impact on the textile industry, and silk went into decline.

Mrs. Adams was not impressed when a French marquise called on her, and her letter is an excellent illustration of American versus French views on dress: "the lady's rank sets her above the little formalities of dress. She had on a brown Florence gown and petticoat, which is the only silk, excepting satins, which are worn here in winter—a plain double-gauze

58 • Le Clerc, *Creole Dress in Louisiana,* from *La Galérie des Modes, 1779.* This was the first American costume to influence Europe. Queen Marie Antoinette of France was most interested in this wrapover muslin dress, here worn with the new fashionable jacket, which peasants had been wearing for nearly two centuries. If the jacket had a straight hem it was termed a *caraco;* if it had looped-up hems it was a *polonaise.* The queen dearly wanted something like this informal outfit, but a wrapover dress was not suitable for court. This costume evolved to cope with the heat in New Orleans. A Creole was anyone born in that city.

handkerchief, a pretty cap, with a white ribbon on it, and looked very neat. The rouge, 'tis true was not so artfully laid on as upon the faces of the American ladies who were present." The Americans were dressed in evening dress with diamonds, watches, and girdle buckles all gleaming, and the marquise arrived in morning attire. Possibly the French aristocrat felt that republicans were not entitled to full dress on her part: it is still common for the aristocracy to dress down when receiving commoners, and to stand with their hands in their pockets. The

59 • Le Clerc, *The Queen's Chemise Dress,* from *La Galérie des Modes,* 1784. Queen Marie Antoinette's revolutionary white muslin chemise, which horrified the French silk industry. It was a closed dress, not wrapover, but like the Creole dress, it used muslin. Its first appearance in 1783 shocked French society, but it was a major step in moving fashion toward a more classical line. The English straw hat is a Marlborough model, for the informal English look was highly fashionable in France.

Americans had gone to the opposite extreme, and still do. The only person in a dinner suit at a private view of an art exhibition in London in 1987 was American. Being more correct than the occasion warrants has become an American characteristic.[12]

Mrs. Adams proclaimed of French fashion that "the dress of old women and young girls in this country is *détestable*, to speak in the French style, the latter at the age of seven being clothed exactly like a woman of twenty, and the former have such a fantastical appearance that I cannot endure it." She had just met

Watteau fil. del.   Le Beau sculp.

60 • Watteau fils, *Dress in the English Style*, from *La Galérie des Modes*, 1784. In contrast to French sackbacks and the queen's chemise, the English look had a fitted waistline, tailored from panels, which then opened out over the bum roll. There is a muslin apron in front and a muslin collar. The straw hat is English. The French magazine allowed clients to select an English or a French look according to taste. Given the close relations between France and the rebel American states, some Americans must have seen the magazine.

a French duchess of eighty who sported a chemise with enormous sleeves, which shocked Mrs. Adams's sense of propriety.[13] Her daughter Abigail wrote on 25 March 1785: "The beaux in this country aim very much at the English dress, as the English do the French; it is the particular aim of each to appear what they are not. When a Frenchman is in a great dishabille he says he is *à l'Anglais*." The young Abigail also records that her father went to Versailles on 1 January 1785, where the king's aunt Madame la Princesse Adelaide told M. le Compt de Mercy that he was too simply dressed for the occasion. He replied that his green velvet coat with diamond buttons had cost him 80,000 livres. "Then you should have pinned the price upon the back," snorted the dowager. At court, in the tradition laid down by Louis XIV, the height of luxury had to be sported.[14]

Her mother describes how in both the Netherlands and France, the English liberated style of clothing for children had not yet spread outside the courts, which adopted it first. Marie Antoinette did start dressing her son in a velvet trouser suit with a wide shirt collar, but it took time to percolate through the ranks of society. Mrs. Adams clearly disapproved of overdressing children, and the English reform had become generally accepted in the United States, although in Canada the French probably resisted until after 1800.

In 1785 the Adamses were posted to London, and Miss Adams asked her friend Eugenio about dress at the English court. "They tell me the queen appears always in silk, and very plain except on the king's birthday. The princesses too, generally appear in silk. The nobility dresses variously. The last year muslin was much wore, worked with gold sprigs, flowers &c, and may be worn this year also, 'tis worn over pink, lilac, and blue silk. The laces that are used are what the French term spring and summer laces, as I believe *point* is only worn in winter."[15] In London they found many American loyalist refugees, exiled by the law of the new republic. And by 1792 Miss Adams would be writing about the shiploads of French refugees fleeing their revolution. Her mother had to wear a hoop and go to court, and the information she sent back home was most valuable for the Washingtons, who were setting up their own republican version of court. In London, Abigail Adams wrote of her dress at court:

FACING PAGE

61 • Pine and Savage, *Congress Voting for Independence*. On 2 July 1776 Congress approved the motion for independence from Britain. Benjamin Franklin believed that a new empire had been born. The sobriety of the representatives would have looked odd to the French allies. A few are wearing wigs, most have powdered hair, while Franklin's open collar was considered unfit to be seen in a public place. The plainness of the suits is typical of British taste, and most of the men are wearing English-type frock coats with collars. The scene could be the English Parliament in session but for the absence of hats on the American members. The new republic did not introduce a new national dress, but continued to follow England and France. *(The Historical Society of Pennsylvania)*

I directed my mantuamaker to let my dress be elegant, but plain as I could possibly appear with decency, accordingly it is white lutestring, covered and full trimmed with white crepe, festooned with lilac ribbon and mock point lace, over a hoop of enormous extent: there is only a narrow train of about three yards in length, to the gown waist, which is put into a ribbon upon the left side, the Queen only having her train borne. Ruffle cuffs for married ladies, treble lace ruffles, and a very dress cap with long lace lappets, two white plumes, and a blonde lace handkerchief. This is my rigging.[16]

On 5 January 1790 Mrs. Adams described the courtlike atmosphere of a presidential reception in New York: "In the evening I attended the drawing Room, it being Mrs. Washington's publick day. It was just as crowded as a Birth Night at St. James's, with the company as brilliantly drest, diamonds and great hoops excepted." With her experience of the French and

British courts, Mrs. Adams would be regarded as an expert on what to wear at such formal occasions.

Isaac Weld visited the United States in 1795–97 and attended receptions at Philadelphia where President Washington held levees: "At these he always appears himself in a court dress, and it is expected that the foreign ministers should always attend in the same style: this they constantly do, excepting the French minister, who makes a point of going in dishabille, not to say worse of it."[17] France, of course, had had its revolution by this date, so the ambassador represented "La République," and wearing undress at a levee was a way of showing contempt for Washington's royalist style. Washington's black velvet suit was less gaudy than usual court dress, but to a French republican even this seemed too royal.

Foreign Views of American Dress

The dress that repeatedly impressed visitors to the States was that found on the Quakers of Pennsylvania, which the French thought was American national dress because Benjamin Franklin wore such clothes. Many foreign visitors commented on this fashion, starting with Pehr Kalm in 1750:

> The women have no clothing there differs from that of the other English (ladies) except that I do not remember having seen them wear cuffs, and although they censure all adornement I have seen them wear just as gaudy shoes as other English women. But the men's clothes differ somewhat from those of other gentlemen. For instance, they have no buttons on their hats, and these are neither turned up entirely nor turned down, but just a trifle folded up on one side and covered with black silk so that they look like the headgear of our Swedish clergymen.[18]

Kalm found it curious that the Quakers wore the most expensive silks and cloth, albeit in plain styles. Louis Philippe Comte de Ségur was sent to America with the Soissonais Regiment in 1782 to support the colonial army. Of the Quakers in Philadelphia he remarked: "Their apparel also, though neat, is apt to strike us as too plain and rustic, while that of the women, if it is black, resembles, with its stomachers, the dress of our Sisters of Charity." The count was much taken by Polly Leiton, a

Quaker girl: "Her gown was white, like herself, whilst her ample muslin neckerchief, the jealous cambric of her cap which scarcely allowed me to see her light-coloured hair, and the modest attire in short of a pious virgin." Polly lectured him for taking part in the civil war between the Americans and their government, which she thought did not concern France.[19]

Brissot de Warville visited Philadelphia in 1788 and commented on Quaker dress:

> I have seen James Pemberton, one of the most wealthy Quakers . . . wear a thread-bare coat, but it was neat. He likes better to clothe the poor. You know the dress of the Quakers—a round hat, generally white, cloth coat, or cotton or woollen stockings, no powder on their hair, which is cut short and hangs round. The white hat which they prefer, has become more common here, since Franklin has proved the advantages which it possesses over the inconveniences of the black. The Quakers in the country generally wear cloth made in their own houses. And at their general meeting here in September, the year 1788, which consisted of more than fifteen hundred, nine-tenths of the number were clothed in American cloth. This is an example to the other sects.
>
> There are some Quakers who dress more like other sects, who wear powder, silver buckles and ruffles. They are called *wet Quakers.*
>
> It is not more than fifteen years since it was a kind of crime in all sects in America to wear powder. In general, manners have changed since the war, by the intercourse of European armies. But to the honour of the Quakers theirs have not changed.[20]

Thus the Quakers were leaders of the homespun movement by their example. Their concern for neatness and modesty in dress influenced many Americans such as Abigail Adams; and while their dress was not the national dress of the country, their approach, combined with that of the Puritans, did place such concerns at the forefront of society. Brissot de Warville certainly took note of this influence:

> Neatness without luxury is a characteristic of their purity of manners, and this neatness is seen everywhere in Boston, in their dress, in their houses, and in their churches. Nothing is more charming than an inside view of the church on Sunday. The good cloath coat covers the man; callicoes and chintzes dress the women and children, without being spoiled by those gewgaws which whim and caprice have added to them among our women. Powder and pomatum never sully the heads of infants and children; I see them with pain, however, on the heads of men: they invoke the art

of the hair dresser, for, unhappily this art has already crossed the seas.

Warville quotes Penn's rule: "Modesty and mildness are the richest and finest ornaments of the soul. The more simple the dress, the more will beauty and these qualities appear." But he did not feel that New York was very observant of these principles. "If there is a town on the American continent where the English luxury displays its follies, it is New York. You will find here the English fashions. In the dress of the women, you will see the most brilliant silks, gauzes, hats and borrowed hair. . . . The men have more simplicity in their dress, they disdain gewgaws, but take their revenge in the luxury of the table."[21]

62 • Anonymous, *John Mix,* Connecticut, c. 1788. John Mix was an educated man who sat on the new school's foundation committee in New Britain. He wears the slim line that was now firmly established in the 1780s. The vogue for huge buttons continues, but Mix is restrained in his use of shirt frills and cravat bows. His hair is still tied back, but he followed the natural movement in giving up hair powder. The diamanté knee-buckle is the only ornament worn. Clothes are becoming skin-colored in grays, beige, and white, as part of the neoclassical naked look. (*Abby Aldrich Rockefeller Folk Art Center, Williamsburg, Virginia. Photographed by Colonial Williamsburg*)

Warville contradicts the New Yorker William Smith who thought that Boston was the gaudier of the two cities, but perhaps he was influenced by local pride. But the Frenchman also illustrates the need for balance and patience before judging. For example, on his arrival he cheered, "But to crown my happiness I saw none of those livid wretches, covered in rags," who were so common in Europe; but once outside the towns on a journey from Boston to New York he saw "children covered with rags." Thus, beyond the smart society of cities there was rural poverty.

The French Revolution caused a number of French émigrés to flee across the Atlantic. François-René de Chateaubriand

63 • Anonymous, *Ruth Stanley Mrs. Mix.*, c. 1788. The high headdresses of the 1770s yield to a wider style during the 1780s. The hair is built out at the sides with pads and false hair, and the mob cap had to widen to fit. As she is holding a needle and thread, Ruth probably embroidered the flowers on her cap and on her neckerchief herself. Her dress is old-fashioned in having ruffles and elbow-length sleeves. The ribbon round her neck is a provincial touch. The pair of paintings was created by more than one artist, since the faces are professional but the hands are very poor. *(Abby Aldrich Rockefeller Folk Art Center, Williamsburg, Virginia. Photographed by Colonial Williamsburg)*

landed at Chesapeake Bay in 1791. He was met by an almost naked black slave and made the devastating comment that "it was a slave who welcomed me to the soil of liberty." That glaring hypocrisy, which many visitors remarked on, would tear the new country apart during the next century. Chateaubriand, meanwhile, was particularly interested in meeting an Indian, so he crossed the mountains where he found the chief of the Onondagas who had large ear cuts, a pearl hanging at his nose, a face motley with diverse colors, a little tuft of hair at the top of his head, and tattooed arms. He wore a blue tunic, a skin mantle, a leather belt with his scalping knife and club, and moccasins on his feet. He was decked with beads and shells. In enormous contrast was a new American farmhouse right next door to a village of Iroquois huts, with a piano, carpets, and mirrors in the most bourgeois European style. Such contrasts would spread right across the continent.²³

Another French visitor was the Marquise de la Tour du Pin who took up residence on a farm in Albany in 1794. As soon as she reached Boston she realized that she had brought too much finery for a farmhouse, so she sold half of it—her piano, music, porcelain, lace, cloth, and clothing. She was most distressed at Lebanon Spa to find that the inn had no white bed-linen, but gradually she adapted to a simpler way of life than she had found at the French court. She even made use of Indian foot-wear: "We had acquired moccasins, a kind of foot-covering of buffalo skin, made and sold by the Indians. The price of these articles was sometimes quite high when they were embroidered with dyed bark or with porcupine quills." Like Chateaubriand, she had met some Onondaga Indians: "I was a little surprised," she wrote, "when I met for the first time a man and woman, practically nude, promenading tranquilly upon the highway, without anyone seeming to find this remarkable." The marquise also showed herself to be a good diplomat by going native in her appearance: "One thing had rendered me at once very popular with my neighbours. The day we took possession of our farm, I adopted the costume worn by the women of the neighbouring places, that is to say, a skirt of blue and black striped wool, a little camisole of light brown cotton cloth, a handkerchief of the same colour, with my hair parted, as it is worn now, and caught up with a comb. In winter, I wore grey or blue woollen stock-ings with moccasins or slippers of buffalo skin; in summer cotton stockings and shoes. I never put on a dress or a corset except to go into the city."[24] Brissot de Warville writes that September 15th was the date the Quakers changed from cotton to woolen stockings.

Madame la Marquise lived near a Shaker settlement, and one of the Shakers used to bring her produce "always perfectly dressed in a coat, vest and trousers of grey homespun cloth of their own manufacture." The Shaker sect had been founded by an Englishwoman, Ann Lee, in 1763, although the group did not arrive in America until 1774. "The children, boys and girls alike," wrote the marquise, "were clothed in a costume of the same form and the same colour. The women of all ages wore the same kind of garment of grey wool, well kept and very neat. Through the windows we could see the looms of the weavers, and the pieces of cloth which they were dyeing, also the work-shops of the tailors and dressmakers." Apart from the prayer meetings, most of the sect seems to have been involved in farming and making clothes. Their plainness contrasted greatly with the new vogue for stripes, which the marquise found in the skirts of her neighbors. Stripes were not the only pattern favored, for zebra-like zigzags became fashionable in 1787, but stripes were the principal pattern into the mid-1790s. Equally straight and tubular were men's trousers, which began to climb the ladder of respectability, to join the suit, in this decade. The English back-to-nature movement, one of the first stirrings of the Romantic urge, was one reason for adopting peasant trousers; the other was the democratic climate in the United States and France, which made working-dress the attire of gentlemen. Comte de Ségur detected this democratic element in the French wearing English styles: "While they were turning their formal gardens into English gardens, they did not remark that the plain clothing, replacing the ample and imposing dresses of the old court, betray'd an unconscious desire for equality."[25]

When François Duc de Rochefoucauld Liancourt visited the marquise on her farm, his dress was worse than democratic; she described him as looking like a shipwrecked sailor, for he had left his trunk at Albany. The duke was starting work on a study of America, which appeared in 1799. The marquise made him fetch a suit before she would take him visiting; she always wore her riding suits for such social calls. With the establishment of the Directoire in France in 1796 many aristocrats decided to return home. The marquise left for France that year, but still showed her adaptability. The only ship was one bound for Spain, and on arrival she donned mantillas and black skirts to harmonize with the inhabitants; she had passed the forty days of the voyage by making shirts and cravats for the passengers. She was a survivor.[26]

The Ridgely Family

Back at Dover, Kent County, Delaware, the pattern of parents sending clothes to children at school had not changed. Dr. Charles Ridgely now ran his father's practice, and his wife Ann sent the clothes, this time to their sons Henry and George in Newark, Delaware. Conveniently Mrs. Ridgely had a married niece in Philadelphia, Mrs. Wilhelmina Cadwalader. The latter wrote to Mrs. Ridgely on 20 June 1792 about stockings, to say she thought cotton stockings suitable and most genteel for boys all year round, so she had purchased ten pairs, large, medium, and small sizes, and estimated that four pairs a year should suit a boy. On 16 June 1794 Ann Ridgely wrote to her sons to say she was making them six new linen shirts each. She had also been to Philadelphia and bought nankeen and buckles, but whether they were knee or shoe buckles she did not specify. She wrote again to Henry and George on 13 March 1795 to say she was sending the servant Thomas Birch with material for coats and waistcoats and 4 dollars for each boy to pay the tailor: "The Blue Cloth is 7 quarters wd. superfine, there is 3 yds and three quarters of it. I beg you will have them made large, and tell your Taylor to face them with cloth as they should be done so as to cover the pockets." She sent the sewing silk, twist linen, buckram, thread, and four pairs of white cotton stockings. Buttons should be fabric, she stressed, since metal buttons were no longer fashionable in Philadelphia. This vogue for metal buttons of large size, set off in the 1770s by the Comte d'Artois, Louis XVI's brother, was twenty years old.

Later in 1795 Henry and George transferred to Dickinson College in Carlisle, Pennsylvania, and mother wrote on 1 November 1795 that there had been a lot of illness in the house "so no spinning, weaving or sewing, it was fortunate I had forty yards of Homemade Cloth beforehand for my people." Obviously the servants had to make their own clothes from cloth they wove themselves.

Mrs. Ridgely's niece Wilhelmina wrote from Philadelphia on 18 May 1796 to say that for boys' coats, pearl buttons were not the rage and English imported cloth was back in favor. She shows more evidence of the resumption of trade with Britain when she writes to her aunt on 21 January 1797 to offer two English bonnets and cloaks as well as a Dunstable bonnet, the last made from plaited straw. By 1797 Wilhelmina reports that the classical style had reached Philadelphia, for she wrote on 29 May that "Nothing is seen here on genteel People but white and

64 • The Beardsley Limner, *Young Boy in a Green Suit,* c. 1790. This young American wears the English liberated look for children. They were no longer dressed as miniature adults. The wide collar with no cravat became the mark of the Romantic rebel in the future. The hair was allowed to grow. Parents had to send clothes to sons at school, so this boy's mother has chosen a jacket and breeches instead of a frock coat for her son. The front flap of his flies is still worn on sailors' uniforms. *(Abby Aldrich Rockefeller Folk Art Center, Williamsburg, Virginia. Photographed by Colonial Williamsburg)*

certainly nothing is so pretty."[27] Thus the *chemise à la reine* (figure 57) had inspired a tremendous change from the colored silks and satins that had dominated the century until the 1783 launch of the chemise, which, in tune with the classical movement in art and architecture, made classical white and muslin the fashionable ideal. Men were less affected by this trend, except that they wore pale waistcoats and breeches in skin color, in semi-nude approximation to a classical statue.

By 1797 Henry and George Ridgely were old enough to have some evening dress, for mother sent brown cloth for coats, black silk for knee-breeches, silk stockings, and two waistcoats. The coats were in the newest style, a bit fuller and shorter. The letters cease here, although they continue during the next century.

Views of Trade and Manufacture

There were other indications that trade with England was resuming after the revolution. For example, John Norton & Sons had resumed trading with the new republic in 1789, when William Payne, on 22 September, ordered clothes for twenty-seven people on his plantation. A most valuable tour of the new United States and Canada was made by the English cloth manufacturer Henry Wansey in 1794, who kept his eye open for cloth production. The fare was 40 guineas, and he bought some trousers at Falmouth before he left, doubtless expecting the weather to be cold across the Atlantic in March. The ship called at Halifax Canada first, when Wansey observed that "the poor were very necessitous, ragged and without stockings and shoes; many negroes there: the poor are emigrating fast to the United States." The blacks were probably escaped slaves who during the fighting had fled to Canada. Wansey also noticed a Micmac Indian woman: "The dress of the young woman was remarkable, a cap made of rushes in the form of a sugar loaf, a blue serge petticoat, very short, a flannel cloke of a yellow ground embossed with red flowers, her hair was plaited into a long pigtail down her back." The "sugarloaf" tall, pointed hat of the 1660s was still being worn in Normandy at this date, and it seems as if it was still being worn in Canada for the Micmac Indian woman to try to copy it in rushes. Farther down the coast at Liverpool, a nursing mother, Mrs. Scott, whose husband hailed from Fifeshire, said she was "ashamed to be caught nursing . . . sitting by the fire without any cap on and hair uncombed."[28] For married Scottish women, caps remained important. Wansey would find a different attitude in New England.

Boston in 1790 had 18,038 inhabitants and 2,375 houses. At Newbury Port, Wansey found a clothier, Joseph Brown, who produced "a variety of woolen goods of the coarse kind," and a bonelace manufactory nearby. At Waltham Village, he wrote, "I was shown some homespun American cloth, it was kersey wool made very stout, and large spun, but serviceable; they could fix no price to it pr. yard." Wansey found Worcester similar to Lindhurst in the New Forest at home, but noticed the absence of caps on the women, which he did not like. "I observed the women in the county towns wore no caps; many had their hair plaited at full length down their backs like a queue; in this very unbecoming fashion could only have been adopted for oeconomy." Of course, that depends on where the women had come from. Plaits were widely worn in Switzerland, Germany, and Scandinavia, so emigrants would have brought plaits with them; or perhaps the women were copying high society where the ladies had stopped wearing caps for the moment. At Northford, Wansey was struck by the mulberry trees; and a woman told him that she and her sister had produced enough silk to make 18 yards of Florentine, and that the area sent 300 yards of silk a year to town. The Northford woman also wove flax for curtains, and a man on the coach said he had a pair of linen breeches that were stouter than European ones. At Hellgate, 5 miles from New York, Wansey found a cotton manufactory staffed by English women from Manchester. There was a huge waterwheel and two buildings: "In one shop I saw twenty-six looms at work, weaving fustians, calicoes, nankeens, nankenets, dimities &c—and there are other looms in the neighbourhood. They have the newly invented spring shuttle." A celebrated cotton manufactory at Beverley, Massachusetts, had been set up to weave corduroy, fustian, and jeans, but had failed hopes; a small cotton works in Brooklyn produced only yarn. On the journey to Philadelphia, Wansey found much rural industry: "Spinning of flax is the general employment in private families in the evenings when they are not in the fields, each family usually makes their own coarse linen, which they put out to the weaver, and afterwards bleach and finish at home." Wansey found, however, that the Americans needed to import hosiery, hats, ready-made shoes and boots, Irish linen, and English broadcloth. And he warned immigrants: "If to settle take plenty of wearing apparel. . . . articles are dear and bad if had in America."

On June 6 Wansey called on President Washington to discuss textiles, and afterward Mrs. Washington made tea and coffee. He described her as "short in stature, rather robust, plain in her dress, wearing a very plain cap, with her grey hair closely turned up under it. She holds routs or levees (whichever the people chuses to call them) every Wednesday and Saturday at Philadelphia during the sitting of Congress."[29] Since she was an elderly lady, Martha Washington retained caps.

In the evening, Wansey went to an English play, Mrs. Inchbald's *Everyone Has His Fault*, and observed:

> To judge from the dress and appearance of the company around me, and the actors and the scenery, I should have thought I had still been in England. The ladies wore the small bonnets of the same fashion as those I saw when I left England; some of chequered straw, &c some with their hair full dressed without caps, as with us, and very few in the French style. The younger ladies with their hair flowing in ringlets on their shoulders. The gentlemen with round hats, their coats with high collars, and cut quite in the English fashion; and many in silk striped coats.

Colonel Wadsworth, a member of Congress from Connecticut, showed Mr. Wansey his greatcoat, which had been woven in his works at Hartford: "It was an elastic cloth, very thick, large spun, and badly dressed, not near so good as the same sort from England, and much dearer." Wansey noted that £100 worth of clothes in England cost £140 in America. The colonel wanted Wansey to settle in the States and help its manufactures, but he declined.

At German Hagerstown, Wansey found two leather-breechmakers, six hatters, five tanyards, and three blue dyers, most of the families making homespun cloth, as in England before the Industrial Revolution liberated housewives from spinning and weaving at home. But to a manufacturer like Wansey, the developments in England were more exciting. There were still

65 • Edward Savage, *The Washington Family,* c. 1796. Martha Dandridge, in 1749, married first Daniel Custis, by whom she had Patsy and Jack Custis. After her husband's death in 1757, she wed George Washington in 1759. Being very conservative in her dress, she resembles the 1770s more than the 1790s, with her mob cap, mantua gown, and petticoat in satin, with her lace fichu. The most fashionable element in her attire is the absence of elbow ruffles. Patsy, however, is right up to date in a Marie Antoinette chemise, where the waist is higher and marked by a broad sash. Young Jack is dressed the same as the boy in figure 62. The first president of the United States wears military uniform but his black evening suit for receptions was advanced in taste, predating the general adoption of black for evening in about 1810. In the background is the valet William Lee whom Washington liberated in his will. *(National Gallery of Art, Washington; Andrew W. Mellon Collection)*

plenty of French émigrés in America in 1794, since they did not begin to return to France until 1796. Regardless of whether or not they supported the Revolution, Wansey observed, "At least one out of ten that I met in the streets was a French person, wearing the tri-coloured cockade, the men with them in their hats, the women on their breasts." Wansey looked with distaste at a French captain wearing gold earrings, although that was common among merchant seamen. Lastly, Henry Wansey visited Long Island, where he observed "a great deal of linen sheeting manufactured in the parish, it lay about on the ground to bleach." When a woman had spun eight or ten pounds of flax she took it to the weaver. In all his travels, however, Mr. Wansey found nothing in the United States that was likely to challenge Britain's preeminence in cloth production.[30]

Isaac Weld arrived during the winter of 1795, and shows us how Americans coped with the harsh weather. After downing an eggnog they would "fortify themselves against the severity of the weather with great coats and wrappers, over each other, woollen socks and trousers over their boots, woolen mittens over their gloves, and silk handkerchiefs tied over their ears and mouths &c so that nothing could be seen excepting their noses and eyes." The wrapper must have been a voluminous cloak, which according to the *Oxford English Dictionary* first appeared in the States in 1734. Weld traveled south to Virginia and observed that the cotton made a yellowish nankeen and "the slaves in general extremely well clothed." When he reached the College of William and Mary in Williamsburg, a sort of grammar school, he found that some parents were lax in supplying their offspring with garments: "Some are without shoes or stockings, others without coats." The residents of Philadelphia in summer "always walked with umbrellas to shade them from the sun; light white hats were universally worn, and the young men appeared in cotton or linen jackets and trousers," so trousers were becoming well established as an article of clothing in town.[31] In general, Wansey found that the United States was buying woolen cloth, figured cottons, hosiery and haberdashery from England, and coarse muslins and calicoes from the East Indies.

Travels in Canada

Weld next visited Canada. During summer in Québec the garrison band played before the chateau, which he described as "the resort of numbers of the most genteel people of the town and has a very gay appearance"; Québec was still the fashion center. The clothing supply now came from Britain, Weld writes: "Domestic manufactures are carried on in most parts of Canada, consisting of linen and of coarse woolen cloths but by far the greater part of these articles used in the country is imported from Great Britain." Since British merchants found it cost a third less to transport goods by way of the Saint Lawrence River and the Great Lakes than through New York, Weld forecast a great future for Montréal, which was already the center of the fur trade. From Québec Weld traveled to the Moravian or United Brethren at Bethlehem, in Canada, where he observed Brother Thomas "dress'd in a plain coat and waistcoat, & brown corduroy breeches, and a large round hat. . . . The dress of the

66 • François Beaucourt, *Eustache-Ignace Trottier,* Montréal, 1793. M. Trottier combines a sober suit with fine lace ruffles and cravat, and an embroidered short waistcoat. He is stylish enough to have a high collar on his suit, but it looks as if he still powdered his hair, for it has a stiff quality. The supply of clothes in Canada, apart from the homespun druggets, was now entirely British. *(Photograph the Musée du Québec)*

67 • François Beaucourt,
Marguerite Mailhot,
Montréal, 1793. Madame
is as conservative as
Martha Washington, with
her mob cap, fichu, and
caraco jacket. She wears
satin instead of muslin,
but she has the narrow
long sleeve as a gesture to
modernity. The ribbon
and miniature worn at her
neck could be either of
her husband or else a lost
relative guillotined in
France. On older women
the eighteenth-century
look survived into the
next century. *(Photograph
the Musée du Québec)*

sisterhood, though not quite uniform is nearly so. They wear
plain calico, linen or stuff gowns, with aprons, and close tight
linen caps made with a peak in front, and tied under the chin
with a piece of riband. Pink ribands are said to be worn as a
badge by those inclined to marry, however, I observed that all
the unmarried wore them." The group made its own linen and
cloth, hats, cotton and worsted caps, stockings, gloves, and
shoes. He does not mention garments, but they were probably
made as well since the Moravians wove their own cloth.

In Canada, Weld also visited Joseph Brant, the famous
Mohawk chief, who had received an English education after his
sister Molly became the Indian wife of the British Superintend-
ent of the Indians, Sir William Johnson. Brant had been ap-

pointed a captain in the British forces and visited England twice, in 1775–76 and 1785. He fought for the British with his Six Indian Nations, and after peace was given land at Lake Erie in Canada for his people. Weld noted that Brant "wears his hair in the Indian style, and also the Indian dress, instead of the wrapper or blanket he wears a short coat . . . similar to a hunting frock."[32] Weld observed that all Indians east of the Mississippi had given up deerskins for English blankets but that they retained moccasins.

Indians farther west were visited by Samuel Hearne of the Hudson's Bay Company, whose account appeared in 1795 although he explored up to the Arctic Ocean during his tour of the area from 1769 to 1772. He notes that deerskin was still worn in these parts, with some outlandish consequences: "Their clothing which chiefly consists of deerskin in the hair, makes them very subject to be lousy," he writes; but he also observes that the Indians considered the lice a delicacy and ate them.[33] Hearne himself was obliged to wear deerskin when unknown Indians stole his supplies and Chief Matonobbee ordered his squaws to make him a deerskin suit. Hearne writes that it took eight to eleven deerskins to make an adult suit for a European. He also describes the appearance of the Indians, the men plucking out their beards but growing the hair long enough to reach the ground, then binding it up. The northern Indians and the Copper tribe marked their cheeks with four lines scratched by a needle, and rubbed with charcoal. On the far west coast of Canada, Captain George Vancouver was reclaiming the coastline that Drake had first claimed as New Albion in 1580. Vancouver had served under Captain Cook when he had recovered the area in 1778–79, and so was chosen for the voyage in 1792. The Spanish had moved up into the region in 1789, but they were forced to abandon the territory when Captain Vancouver reclaimed it for Britain. Describing the appearance of the Pacific coastal Indians, Vancouver noted that they used less body paint, oil, and color than did the Indians further south. "In . . . dress they vary little; Their native woollen garment was most in fashion, next to it the skins of deer, bear &c, a few wore dresses manufactured from bark, which like their woollen ones, are very neatly wrought."[34] Vancouver gave the Indians blue cloth and trinkets. What the Indian wool was made of Vancouver does not say, but he mentions that the Spanish missionaries in San Diego, California, had taught the local Indians to make

68 • Benjamin West, *Colonel Guy Johnson with Joseph Brant*, 1776. The Superintendant of Affairs for the Six Nations, with the Mohawk chief Thayendanega, also called Joseph Brant, whose sister Molly was the Indian mistress to Guy Johnson's uncle. The partial adoption of Indian garments by British officers responsible for the Indians made for closeness between the Indians and the officers, and the Indian nations supported Britain against the American rebels. Colonel Johnson has an Indian blanket over his army uniform, with an Indian belt; some Indian beadwork decorates his straps; and he wears moccasins. He holds an Indian cap in his hand. While the wearing of moccasins was common among settlers, they did not go as "Indian" as British officers. *(National Gallery of Art, Washington; Andrew W. Mellon Collection)*

FACING PAGE

69 • William Berczy, *Portrait of Joseph Brant*. After the War of Independence, Britain resettled the Mohawks in Canada, for they refused to work with the American rebels. Like many Indians east of the Mississippi, Brant has adopted an English shirt and blanket, but his leggings and moccasins are traditional Indian dress. *(National Gallery of Canada, Ottawa)*

their own woolen garments; thus it is possible that woolen blankets from California had been introduced into Canada when the Spanish arrived in 1789. At that time, both Canada and Spanish America had a Pacific presence, although the infant United States did not.

When French Canada was invaded by the newly formed United States in September 1775, General Arnold took Washington's *Address to the Canadians* with him. But the last way to persuade a population is by means of an invading army. It was only twelve years since French Canada had been handed over to Britain, and the local settlers were not ready for yet another change. Moreover, they did not trust the Americans, for the Puritans would not allow the French to continue practicing their Catholic faith, as Britain had pledged to do. Consequently Canada refused to join the American revolt. When François Duc de La Rochefoucauld Liancourt visited Canada in about 1795, the British influence had increased: "The English fashions and manner prevail, even in some of the most opulent Canadian families connected with the administration. In other Canadian families of distinction the French customs have been preserved."[35] Obviously the degree of British character in dress varied from family to family, but the duke notes that thirty ships traded exclusively with Britain, so that apart from the homespun Canadian cloth made by the peasants, the supply of goods was now entirely British. The duke observed Indians using lampblack and red lead to paint their eyes, while the garrison British troops were plastering their hair and raking it with an iron comb. The army also retained head powder after fashion began to discard it. The Indians would laugh at a Turk's turban, but what could one say about women?

The Classical Ideal

The duke compared the dress of contemporary Greece, then under Turkish occupation, with the trend to imitate the dress of classical Greece, which was all the rage by 1795:

> . . . the women in the island of Melos, whose petticoats scarcely cover half their thighs, while their sleeves reach down to the ground, or . . . your *belles* who ten years ago confined their breasts

and waist in huge stays, with false hips, and strutted along on high heels, and who now screw up their waist to the middle of their bosoms, tied round with a girdle, which looks more like a rope than a sash, wear their arms naked up to the shoulders, and by means of transparent garments expose everything to view, which formerly they thought themselves obliged to conceal, and all this forsooth, to resemble Grecian ladies.[36]

Interestingly, since a Slavic population had overrun Greece during the seventh century, there was no direct transmission of traditional dress from antiquity. Classical dress, therefore, had to be studied from statues and tombs for the revival to be possible. Marie Antoinette's chemise dress was the first to encapsulate this classical trend in 1783. Gradually the slimmer line began to oust hip pads and rump bustles, until by 1790 the revolution had been achieved, and no stays or padding were worn at all, for the first time during the century, in the world of high fashion. As we have noticed before, corsets could be kept off on the farms or in hot weather, but now it was "official." A slimmer line meant lighter fabrics, and the white muslin and gauzes revealed the contours of the feminine figure. Abigail Adams did not approve of this exposure, when she viewed a Miss Mason from Boston dancing on 26 April 1800: "I could not lament that the uncovered bosom sh'd display what ought to have been veiled, or that the well turned and finely proportioned form should not have been less conspicuous in the dance from the thin drapery which covered it."[37] In her old age Mrs. Adams was a firm campaigner for flannel, as Colonel Carter had been: "I grow more and more in favour of the use of it, and advise you to wear it next to your skin. Make little waistcoats & put them on with the first coming of cold weather, & I had as much spair Room in my Stays as you have, I would not be without them."[38]

Warmth was a problem with the new classical dresses, so shawls and greatcoats became important items in the female wardrobe. Cashmere shawls were the most prized, and had to be draped in a classical manner in imitation of ancient *palla,* or stoles. Of course, ancient Greeks had worn their dresses in wool, not muslin, so they did not suffer so much as the ladies of the 1790s and early nineteenth century from colds, coughs, or worse. The vogue for consumptive heroines in Romantic literature may stem from this inadequacy of coverage. Outdoors, men's greatcoats and riding coats were the inspiration for women's overcoats, or the *redingote;* and cloaks and hoods were forsaken. The fit was tight and copied from men's coats the capes at the shoulder. The coat dominated women's clothing until dresses grew wider again in the late 1820s, when cloaks made a comeback. As the duke mentioned, waists grew higher to accord with the classical precedent; so to be in the fashion, waists had to be raised on all dresses and coats, and the whole wardrobe overhauled. The elderly, of course, resisted, and went on wearing corsets and lower waistlines to their dying day, but the younger generation now looked far more different from their elders than they would have forty years before. Youth was now in fashion, whereas the middle-aged look had dominated the century hitherto with its wigs, white hair, and mature styles.

For men the revolution in dress was less drastic. They wore skin color on their vest and breeches, but did not start wearing muslin or gauze see-through garments. Only women were expected to display their charms, and most men would argue that they did not possess any. So how has the human race survived if men cannot attract women? As illustrated in the novels of Jane Austen, who started writing in the 1790s, they do so by power, money, security of position, and status. What Austen termed the "vogue for the tremendous" referred to the multiple capes on the greatcoats, which young men copied from grooms and coachmen. What had clearly started as a practical protection for the shoulders in bad weather entered fashion when the number of capes worn exceeded necessity. Thus Jane Austen in 1797 described Henry Tilney in *Northanger Abbey*: "And then his hat sat so well, and the innumerable capes of his great coat looked so becomingly important."[39] It was all part of the natural or back-to-nature look and was accompanied by riding boots worn indoors, leather or buckskin knee-breeches, round hats instead of tricornes, huge cravats, and standing collars. It was the frock coat that had a collar, so it became the most fashionable garment, worn with the collar turned up. This vogue may have developed from the way the collar was worn in cold winds, and became a permanent feature in about 1786. Over the next decade the collar grew until it reached the ears, and waistcoat collars sprouted in sympathy. The huge collars meant that men had to adjust their movements, revolving the body since they could not turn the head. Every fashion imposed a different

FACING PAGE

70 • Ralph Earl, *Mrs. William Moseley and Her Son Charles,* 1791. As dresses grew thinner with neoclassical taste, overcoats for women replaced cloaks. The narrow line is sometimes called the Directoire look, but it started before the French Revolution. Mrs. Moseley has not dispensed with bum rolls completely, whereas girls like Patsy Custis Washington had abandoned them. The coat imitates the capes on a man's coat, and the tall hat and cravat are both masculine. A martial look for women was fashionable all through the wars with revolutionary France. Young Charles has gained trousers, doubtless before his father tried them. Putting sons in peasant trousers was part of the natural movement. Consequently Charles's generation would wear trousers as adults. (*Yale University Art Gallery; Bequest of Mrs. Katherine Rankin Wolcott Verplanck*)

71 • Benjamin Latrobe, *Billiards at a Country Tavern, Virginia,* 1796. This shows the marked contrast of the generations, with the elderly man on the right still wearing powdered hair and knee-breeches, while his younger opponent wears a sleeveless waistcoat and trousers with bare feet. Trousers had been worn since antiquity, but they rose in status by the end of the eighteenth century along with the rest of country style, which the British aristocracy adopted. Short, cropped hair without powder became the mark of youth. *(The British Library)*

body pattern, from the width of coat skirts in the 1740s to the tighter line that evolved from the 1770s, which required careful wearing lest it split.

The vogue for stripes lasted from the mid-1770s through to the mid-1790s, and Frenchmen would wear all stripes, including a mix of striped coats, waistcoats, knee-breeches, and stockings. The English and Americans would wear a striped waistcoat with a plain suit, or striped breeches with a plain coat and waistcoat, for they tried to avoid an extreme look. Striped silks were the French style for both sexes, but from the 1790s increasingly plain fabrics began to emerge under the influence of classical taste, which preferred monocolor textiles. This was evident particularly in the English country clothes, which were very plain and easily suited to classical taste. But as women started wearing plain whites and creams, Englishmen started to dress in a darker palette, which soon influenced the Americans. Black silk knee-breeches for evening were established in 1784, and could be worn with plain, dark cloth coats in brown or navy

72 • Benjamin Latrobe, *Travel on Horseback in Virginia*, 1796. Everyone is wearing hats wide enough to keep the sun off, but the lady is most concealed in her poke bonnet, whose long visor was still being worn by southern ladies in the next century to protect their complexions. The lady has a cloak with a hood, and the bulk of her attire suggests she is elderly. The men have become slimmer, but have not adopted trousers yet. (*The British Library*)

blue. The trend toward the all-black evening suit of 1810 had begun, which was why President Washington chose black for his court dress. The idea of sobriety, so common in Puritan and Quaker dress, was climbing up the ladder to high society. The French complained that the most famous men in British society dressed like farmers, which many of them indeed were in the sense that they owned estates and lived in the country. This rural image went down very well in the new American republic where agrarian roots were considered something to be proud of.

The French Revolution and After

A big problem for the United States was whether or not to support the French revolution. In a way, the Americans had a duty to do so because France had helped them in their revolution—but that had been the French crown, not the French republic, which even Tom Paine found too extreme. Britain was at war with the French republic, and banned trade with her. The Americans had been excluded from trading with the British Empire since 1783, and some argued that they should side with Britain to regain access to the trade. Others favored France, and the division was recognized by the appearance of two parties, the Federalists and the Republicans. A trade treaty with Britain eventually was signed in 1795, and the French destroyed their American support by attacking 300 American ships in 1797. This was the situation in 1797, when François Duc de la Rochefoucauld Liancourt compiled his report on American imports. There was a tax on imports, but it was lower for goods carried in American ships. Immigrants could bring their goods in free of tax.[40] The new republic needed to import items such as bonnets, hats and all kinds of headdresses, boots, buttons of all sorts, shoe buckles, cambric, stockings, chintz, calico, muslins, all merchandise of cotton and wool in color, tanned leather and all leather manufactures, laces and lawns, lace for edges, gold and silver lace, artificial flowers, feathers and ladies' items, furs, gauze, ready-made clothes, unwrought wool (which entered free), woolen yarn, merchandise of the mode, muslins dyed or plain, hair powder, satin and other silks, stuffs, shoes and pumps of silk for women and men, and velvet. The duke did not mention linen, so the homespun variety dressed most Americans. Despite independence the new republic was still dependent on foreign supplies, mostly British and East Indian, for her clothing. Imported silks and muslins had dominated the century, and the improvements in textile production made it impossible for American manufactures to compete. It would take an Englishman to bring the industrial revolution to the United States—Samuel Slater, who arrived in 1789. In 1795 he had his own factory at Pawtucket, Rhode Island, and would become the father of American cotton manufacture in the nineteenth century.

Of American society the duke wrote, "I have been severely exact as reporting excessive avidity of becoming rich, as the common characteristic of the American people, and especially the inhabitants of cities."[41] Some would say that still applies two hundred years later. It also helps to explain the vogue for imports. To own something from abroad was important as a status symbol in a society where competition began to be set before Christian charity and concern for the underdog. It could also explain the fixation with "smartness and neatness" in dress, which by the end of the eighteenth century Americans such as Abigail Adams were identifying as the national style. This concern with fashion reveals an anxiety about status, and a wish to be considered successful, which still affects American society. In contrast, the British peerage, who had no anxieties about their position in society, dressed as untidily as farmers.

These attitudes reflected urban society more than rural. For example, Isaac Weld, having cheered how well-dressed all Americans were in Philadelphia, was shocked to find uncouth Americans across the Blue Ridge Mountains. There one could find the likes of Colonel Daniel Boone, who first explored Kentucky in 1769 and was a prisoner of the Indians in 1778, which influenced him toward their way of life. Boone built his family a cabin in Tennessee and dressed in deerskin. He typifies the other major force in eighteenth-century American society—the pioneer settler. For those who could not conform to coastal attitudes, the interior of the continent called—on a larger, more primitive scale echoing the urban English nostalgia for the countryside. For both Britain and America shared the same dichotomy between the rural and the metropolitan ideal.

Apart from the early textile industries noted by Henry Wansey, Brissot de Warville observed a great deal of shoe manufacturing at Lynn, just outside Boston, which produced 100,000 pairs a year of women's shoes. Reading nearby manufactured men's shoes.[41] For both sexes, high heels had dominated in the seventeenth century, from the inch-high heel of 1620s to the three-inch block heel sported by Louis XIV's brother Philippe Duc d'Orléans in 1661. By 1710 young men began to favor a flat shoe, and this became the principal style for males in the eighteenth century; but women continued to wear high heels until the neoclassical movement made flat sandals the vogue. When undressed, of course, American ladies wore moccasins and pumps, and the latter became fashionable by the 1790s. Colonial Williamsburg has a nice collection of footwear, and women's fashionable shoes, as distinct from working ones, were made in damask, brocaded silk, satin, and taffeta. Whereas Lynn was producing women's shoes for the masses, the more stylish shoes at Williamsburg had English makers, such as John Hose, London, 1750s; Gresham, London, 1770s; Martin & M'Millan Ladies Shoe Warehouse, 111 Jermaine St., St. James's London, 1790. The early shoes in the collection are richly decorated, but simplicity of line came to the fore around

73 • Benjamin Latrobe, *Sketch of a Classic Group at Mount Vernon*, 1796. Patsy Custis goes Grecian, with a diadem, bare arms, and a high-waisted dress in slight muslin drapery. Her mother Martha Washington still has her mob cap and front lacing. The contrast between the generations becomes dramatic as the young pose in classical attitudes and the parents use the etiquette of thirty years ago. Master Lear has pantaloons, a wide collar, and long hair. *(The British Library)*

MISS CUSTIS.　　MRS. WASHINGTON.　　MASTER LEAR.

SKETCH OF A CLASSIC GROUP AT MOUNT VERNON.

74• Benjamin Latrobe, *Another Classic Group at Mount Vernon*, 1796. Patsy Custis poses as a Greek frieze and wears two Grecian tunics with a high waist. Flat sandals replace high-heeled shoes. The tutor is wearing boots indoors, with pantaloons, which would horrify the older generation. The tightness of the skin-colored garments left little to the imagination, for a man's thighs were now visible and waistcoats were reduced to half their original size. The large round hat is also a rejection of the three-cornered standard hat of the century. Mrs. Washington probably retains her mob cap, but she does look a bit slimmer in this sketch than in the last, so her daughter may have had an influence. *(The British Library)*

Sketch made at Mt. Vernon in July, 1796.

THE TUTOR.　　　MRS. WASHINGTON.　　　MISS CUSTIS.　　　YOUNG LAFAYETTE.

1790 under the influence of classical taste, and decoration was discarded in favor of plain pumps and sandals.

Thomas Jefferson was correct in forecasting that the homespun movement would not last and that Americans would soon return to European styles; only the Quakers and similar sects made a principle of homespun cloth. There were too many links with the Old World for a total break with European fashion to

75 • Anonymous, *Deborah Richmond*, c. 1797. Miss Richmond is right up to date in her dress, which is the high-waisted classical-type chemise, but her bulky hairstyle and hair powder belong to the 1780s. People are readier to wear a new dress than to alter their face and hair. Mrs. Adams detested these loose dresses, which she considered far too revealing, but the body was coming into fashion. (*Abby Aldrich Rockefeller Folk Art Center, Williamsburg, Virginia. Photographed by Colonial Williamsburg*)

be possible. Apart from ancestral ties, the education in the eighteenth century was classical and biblical. To many Americans the classical style of the ancient Greek and Roman republics was the perfect style for the new American republic, despite the American continent never having been under Roman rule. Since the new inhabitants thought like classical Europeans, classical architecture and classical fashion for women were considered ideal. However, American men preferred to sport the English country style. They enjoyed classical surroundings and classically dressed ladies, but wanted no revolution in their own attire; American senators did not don togas such as David designed for the French Senate. It was the same in Canada: the ideal in fashion for men was the casual British look, worn more smartly, while the women were expected to dress themselves in the manner of ancient Greeks. The men had their uniform and did not want to change it, but the women were expected to abandon their old uniform mantos for the classical line. The new republic was firmly under the influence of European ideals.

Glossary of Textiles

Basts • Packing material made from lime wood, also used for ropes

Bayes • A coarse russet cloth

Bonelace • Lace of linen thread knitted with bone bobbins

Borelaps • Coarse Holland linen

Brawles • A blue-and-white striped linen

Broadcloth • Finely dressed double-width black cloth, 24 yards long the piece

Callimanco • Woolen cloth with a gloss, either plain or striped and figured

Castor Hats • Originally beaver, by late seventeenth century made of rabbit fur

Dimity • Undyed stout cotton with raised stripes or figures

Dowles • Coarse linen

Dozen • Coarse Yorkshire broadcloth. Double dozen meant 2 yards wide.

Drabs • Cloth of linen or hemp, sometimes wool

Druggets • Cloth of either all wool or half-silk or half-linen

Duck • Expensive untwilled linen used for sails and sailors' clothes

Duffle • A coarse woolen cloth with a thick nap

Duroy • A coarse woolen cloth

Dutch Streaked Skirts • The Nederlands Kostuum Museum suggests skirts were striped, and says it has several late-eighteenth-century striped skirts in English glazed woolens. However, streaked in English implies irregularity, so home-dyed Dutch skirts in New York State would have had irregular stripes.

Friezes • A coarse woolen cloth usually with nap on one side

Fustian • A coarse cloth of cotton and flax

Garlic Cloth • Not in dictionaries; presumably garlic-colored cloth

---

NOTE: For glossary terms, Edward Phillips, *New World of Words* (1706); J. Powell, *New Classical English Dictionary* (1757); J. A. Murray, *Oxford English Dictionary on Historical Principles* (1912 seq.) have been consulted.

Jacquonot Muslin • Lightweight Indian cotton

Jeans • Twilled cotton cloth

Kersey • Coarse narrow cloth, usually ribbed, 18 yards long the piece

Linsey-Woolsey • Cloth of wool and flax

Long Cloth • Cotton cloth or calico, 36 yards long and 39 inches wide the piece; short cloth was 27 yards long.

Lutestring • Glossy silk fabric

Marquessat • Not in dictionaries; possibly a metal compound for brooches

Nap Cloth • A cloth with the nap of rough treads projecting

Oznabrig • Coarse linen from Osnabrück

Pennistones Friezed • Coarse woolen cloth with nap, used for linings

Perpetuanes • Durable woolen cloth favored by the Puritans

Rands • Strip of leather placed under the quarter of a shoe before the heel is fixed on

Rashes • A smooth textile of silk or worsted, from the French *rasé* (shaved)

Rocelo Cloaks • Knee-length cloak named for Duc de Roquelaure

Romell Cloth • Thin silk or cotton fabric

Ruggs • Coarse frieze cloth used for mantles, capes, and carpets

Russel Cloth • A coarse woolen cloth

Seletia • Fine cotton lawns, probably from India

Shagg • A worsted cloth with a velvet nap

Silk Thrown • Raw silk thread

Silk Wrought • Woven silk

Shalloon • Closely woven woolen cloth used for linings

Spanish Cloth • English-made two-color cloth, lighter than English cloths*

Stuff • Woolen fabric

Welsh Plains • Cotton cloth, undyed

---

*Spanish cloth weighed 16 ounces the square yard, whereas English cloth by law had to weigh 23½ ounces per square yard. See J. de L. Mann, *The Cloth Industry in the West of England, 1640–1880* (Oxford: Oxford University Press, 1971).

APPENDIX I

English Cloth and Clothing Exports to the American Colonies and Canada

The Exchequer Port Books

The archive of the Exchequer Port Books is enormous, amounting to thousands of registers. Exports to the colonies are not listed in volumes dedicated to America, but are scattered among England's other exports to Denmark, Russia, Germany, the Netherlands, France, Spain, Italy, Barbary, and the Levant. The registers for the Port of London are most useful as they list cloth as an export item, whereas for the ports outside London, such as Bristol, Plymouth, Southampton, and Liverpool, which certainly sent goods to the colonies, the catalogue list indicates only exports or imports, not goods. Consequently, in order to discover the variety and types of goods, and their range and distribution throughout the different colonies, this discussion will focus on cloth and clothing exported from the Port of London. Moreover, since the Exchequer Port Books consist of over 10,000 registers dating from the Middle Ages to 1700, the entries listed here are merely samples.

Virginia, for example, was the first colony to feature regularly in the registers, for on 1 August 1660 Richard Young for

Virginia exported a span and a half of kerseys, and camlett, and Thomas Muncaster shipped Gloster (cloth) all in the *Honour.* On August 6 the *Charles* sailed to Virginia with woolen hose for Richard Longman. In the same month the *Susan* carried dyed kerseys to Virginia. On September 29 the *Anne* conveyed kerseys to the same colony.[1]

Kersey cloth was the most common item in these registers. Named for the village in Suffolk, it appeared in the thirteenth century as *pannus cersegus.* Large amounts were also woven in Yorkshire, and Hampshire made a blue kersey. It was a narrow cloth, usually ribbed and coarse in texture. Other cloth centers were Devizes for broadcloth, Exeter for serges, Colchester for baizes, Gloucester for cottons, and Carlisle for linsey-woolseys. Silk centers were London and Canterbury. Regulations for cloths were laid down by Richard III in 1483 in his statute *Anno Primo Ricardi III caput viii:* broadcloth had to be two yards wide and 24 yards long the piece, and must be watered before sale. A half cloth must be 12 yards long. Streit cloth must be one yard wide and 12 yards long. Kersey cloth must be one yard wide and 18 yards long. These lengths apply in the registers, so that a merchant exporting two kerseys was sending 36 yards of the stuff.

The Port of London Registers, 1673–1696

When in January 1673 William Samson shipped goads to Virginia he was sending measures of cloth. By 1682 more merchants were involved in trading with the colonies. On 29 January Joseph Smart sent 64 lengths of woolen cloth to Jamaica. On 20 January Mr. Gower in (the part of) Elihu Robinson, 18 short cloths for Barbadoes. On 23 March George Bone in the *Wilde* for New England, four spans of cloth, and Ephraim Harnois for William Condy short cloth. On 26 March two kerseys were sent to Carolina. On 29 March, David Edwards for New England in the *James* sent 49 lengths of woolen cloth. On April 3 Edward Ellis sent 22 kerseys to New England. On 21 April David Edwards despatched in the *Glover* two Spanish cloths, probably made in England, to New England. On 23 April he sent 9 kerseys. On 25 May Joseph Wary in the *Maria* sent 34 kerseys and 4 short cloths to New York. On 4 July

Timothy Waldo sent Thomas Waldo 20 kerseys for New England.

Maryland appears on 7 July, when D. Whearley sent 24 kerseys and 3 short cloths. She occurs again on July 7 when F. Maldon in (part of) R. Cooper for Maryland, sent 16 kerseys and 4 short cloths. New England received another shipment from August 1 when George Cornish and Rudolph Cooper despatched 9 woolen cloths and 4 kerseys. On 29 August J. Foster sent in the *Quickly* woolen cloth remnants amounting to 30 pieces, and one kersey for New England. Thus the Americans were wearing mostly kersey cloth at this time, when the colonies were still new.[2]

This increased trade continued. In the registers, English merchants are listed on the left and American customers and merchants on the right. *In* is short for *in partis* (in.), literally "in part for," or "on behalf of." I have filled in abbreviations such as *spa* for "Spanish cloth" or *Caᵃ* for "Canada." Dates in the original are in Latin. Thus in 1683 on February 20, Richard Merriwether sent in the *Charles* to New England 16 kerseys, 2 Spanish cloths, and 7 friezes. On 27 February Captain East in the *Bellamy* conveyed 4 kerseys and 3 woolen cloths to Pennsylvania. On 3 March Samuel Klerbin despatched in (partis) John Wilde for New England, 9 kerseys. On 4 March Thomas Singleton sent in the *Philippe* for New England 2 long worsted cloths and 9 kerseys. On 19 March Thomas Serjeant in the *Samson* despatched 40 woolen cloths to New England. On April 16 John Doan in. W. Balston for New England sent 3 Spanish cloths, and 160 pounds of cloth remnants woolen, which would be useful for making clothing. On June 12 Thomas Shaw in. W. Orton for Carolina sent 6 kerseys. On 14 June, Christopher in the *Robuck* in. W. Orton for Carolina sent 2 perpetuanes, 2 friezes, 2 kerseys, and one long worsted cloth. On 1 July Henry Bernard in. W. Orton for Carolina despatched 27 kerseys. On 19 August Thomas Rudd in. J. Wasoy for Pennsylvania sent 1 frieze, 4 kerseys. The Orton family—Tom, William, and Captain Orton—seems to have been the leading importers for Carolina as they occur in the register for 1684 as well: On 25 June 1684 Tom Cox in. Captain Orton for Carolina 2 kerseys, and on July 1 Henry Bernard in. Tom Orton for Carolina, 27 kerseys.

Canada appears in 1684 with an entry on 30 May, Royall Highness in loo. Edgecombe at Hudson's Bay, 11 short cloths.

HRH, Prince Rupert, would have been the head of the Hudson Bay Company, so the order was placed on his behalf for a Mr. Edgecombe who was out there. Also in that register on 6 July John Broadnox in B. Hall for Virginia sent 1 Spanish cloth, and 1 and five halves of kerseys. On 29 July Tom Osbaldston sent 2 kerseys to Virginia, and on September 25 D. Ninch despatched for Virginia one kersey and one short cloth. On 17 October Robert Ashurst in. Z. Taylor for Virginia sent one kersey and one frieze cloth.[3]

<h2 style="text-align:center">1683–84</h2>

A register for 1683–84 shows the following activity. On 7 March 1683 G. Smith in. Thomas Singleton for New York sent three and a half short cloths. On 19 July 1684 in the *Potomach* in. W. Poole for Maryland 9 kerseys and 3¼ short cloths. On 21 July 1684 also in the *Potomach* for Maryland in. Thomas Elias 4 kerseys. On July 24 in the *Benedict* for Virginia in. John Wagstaff 6 kerseys, divers short cloths and 1 Spanish cloth were conveyed. The *Benedict* was also bound for Maryland, for on 29 July she shipped in. W. Osbaldson 2 kerseys. On 4 August 1684 in the *Adventure* P. Brown in. Arthur Bailey for Maryland sent 11 kerseys and 1¼ short cloths. On 26 April in the *Blossom* Richard Martin in. J. Sands for New York despatched 18 kerseys. On 7 September in the *Baltemer* John Conway sent in. Ian Hirrock for Virginia 3 kerseys. On 19 September in the *Augustine* Zacharias Pringle sent in. T. Pomfret for Virginia one kersey. On 19 September there is mention of commerce between two ladies, when in the *Constant* Mary E. Rhode sent for Virginia to Miranda Parry one short cloth, two kerseys, and 7 woolen cloths. On 9 October in the *Augustine* Zacariah Taylor in. Arthur North for Virginia sent 2 kerseys and 20 woolen cloths. Also on October 4 in the *Sam* Thomas Jones in. Richard Morris for New England sent 16 woolen cloths. On 11 November in the *Indian* Matt (illegible) in. Edwin Littsop for Virginia sent 30 woolen cloths. Gradually more choice of goods was becoming available, with woolen cloth, short cloth, and Spanish cloth joining the dominant kersey.[4]

There were more English exports to Bruges and Turkey than to the American colonies and Hudson's Bay Canada, but a supply of materials to North America was maintained, as is evident from the register for 1687–88. On 7 March Richard

Jenkinson in. Thomas Looch for New England dispatched 18 short cloths and 8 kerseys. On 10 April Norman Anselby in. John Wilde for New England sent two short cloths. On 30 June 1688 Sam (illegible) in. Humphrey Ayles for New England exported 14 kerseys. On 13 July Edward Carleton and Corry in. Z. Borman for Virginia sent 12 kerseys and woolen cloth. On 7 August Nicholas Cusson shipped in the *Jacob* for New York two kerseys. On 25 September F. Loss in. Nic. Goodridge for Virginia sent two kerseys. On 26 September Walter Ryan in. Sam Dodson for Carolina despatched 27 kerseys. On October 6 William Thornburgh in. Sam Dodson for Carolina despatched four kerseys, and on the same day Thomas Stark in. John Rudd for Virginia shipped 5 kerseys. On 8 October Sam Groome in. Robert Roberts for Carolina sent 4 long, 1 short cloth, and 15 kerseys. On 9 October John Bellamy in. Governor for Canada despatched 9 kerseys and 2 short cloths. On 12 October Richard Hudd in. the Captain for Canada sent 9 kerseys.[5]

1694–95

The next group of cloth exports falls in 1694–95, although some smaller items were probably sent in the years between. Kersey cloth continues as the principal clothing fabric also in this decade. On 11 May Matthew Estis in. Thomas Parker for New England supplied 4 kerseys and 14 woolen cloths. On 27 May Robert Myro in. Thomas White for New England sent 20 woolen cloths. On 31 May, Eliza Saunders in. Captain White for New England shipped 35 woolen cloth remnants. On 19 October Thomas Sands in. Henry Sutton for Virginia despatched 17 kerseys. On 23 October Richard Moad in. John Farmer for Canada sent 36 kerseys. On 21 November Richard Whittingham in. Guillam for New England sent 3 Spanish cloths, and a quantity of cloth remnants. The large order for Canada, 36 kerseys at 18 yards each, may have been for clothing the Indians near Hudson's Bay.[6]

An English member of the house of Washington appears in the register for 1694–95. Thomas Washington on 30 December 1694 in. J. Enos for Virginia sent one short cloth. Also on that date Sam Wilkins in. Thomas Martin for Virginia sent one pair of kerseys, John Reynolds in. Robert Ranson for Virginia sent 14 kerseys, and 1¼ short cloths. George Mason in. Etherington for Virginia sent two pairs of kerseys, John Lambert in. John Gaudy for Virginia sent 10 woolen cloth remnants, and Augustus Munford sent 2 long cloths and 4 kerseys to Virginia. On 31 December 1694 Daniel Lodge in. Captain Taylor for Carolina sent 4 long worsted cloths and 9 kerseys, and Nicholas Atholby in. Harbin for Virginia despatched 80 woolen cloths and one kersey. On 2 January 1695 John Taylor in. Sam Phillips for Virginia sent 5 kerseys, on which date Edmund Hildegard in. W. Norrington for Virginia sent one kersey. As might be expected, Virginia was the most regular destination for these shipments.[7]

THE LAST PORT OF LONDON REGISTER, 1696

The last cloth register for the Port of London in the Exchequer Port Books is for 1696, since the Customs and Excise ledgers commence in 1697. In 1696, trade continues with notice that on June 3 Jon Wolson in. Guillam for New England sent two kerseys. On 20 July John Bridge in. Guillam for New England despatched 15 kerseys; Guillam seems to be a leading merchant in the New England trade, since he also appears in the volume for 1694–95. On 17 August 1696 John Donoro in. F. Portman for Virginia sent 8 kerseys. On 20 August Robert Cuthbert in. Store for Carolina shipped 3 long cloths and 4 kerseys. On 8 November Sam Groome in. Thomas Salsie for Virginia despatched 16 kerseys and 45 woolen cloth remnants. On 22 November Arthur Wilde in. Nic. Smith for Virginia sent 5 kerseys. Also on that date Richard Haynes in. Michael Coht for Carolina exported 32 kerseys, 5 Spanish cloths and friezes, namely 6 by half long and 6 short cloths. On November 27 Moses Frince (?) in. J. Keehr for Carolina despatched 9 kerseys, and Joshua Weith sent Captain Wyatt for Virginia a north kersey. This probably means a Yorkshire kersey as distinct from a Hampshire blue in the south of England. On 3 December Tim Kaiser in. Edward Barock for Virginia exported 39 by ½ kerseys, and 51 lbs of cloth remnants. Also on that date, Richard Chambers in. Nic. Smith for Virginia supplied 6 north kerseys, and Arthur Bailey in. Thomas Graves for Virginia despatched 20 kerseys, 6 Spanish cloths, frieze, and one short cloth. On 6 December Robert Bristow in. Thomas Harvey for Virginia sent 6 kerseys and 16 woolen cloths. On 7 December Thomas Kersey, whose family perhaps originated in the village of Suffolk, in. Captain Whittaker for Virginia exported 4 north kerseys.[8]

During this period, kersey cloth was still the principal material for American clothing in the colonies, and would have been used by the Indians as well.

The Inspector General's Accounts, 1696–1702

The Customs archives are not so enormous as those of the Exchequer Port books but they are still too big for more than a sample to be included here. Firstly, they consist of the Inspector General's accounts in 10 volumes for 1696–1702, and, secondly, the ledgers of the Customs and Excise in 82 volumes for 1697–1780. The Inspector General's accounts are useful for they include more details of goods shipped, but they omit the names of English merchants and their American customers. They cover English manufactures exported through the Port of London, and the first volume is for Michaelmas 1696 to Michaelmas 1697. The following account for the year 1696–97 is arranged by colony.

NEWFOUNDLAND, 1696–97

Newfoundland ordered 150 suits at 10/- [shillings] each, £75.0.0; haberdashery worth £2.2.0.; two kinds of hats; castors 5½ dozen £30.5.0; and felts 34⅔ dozen £32.10.0.; linen, 15 pieces at £10.15.0.; shoes 710, £53.5.0.; fustian 22 pieces, £16.10.0.; silks, thrown at ½ lb for 10/- and wrought at 11 lbs for £22: Stockings were classified as children's woolen, 12 dozen at £2.10.0; men's ditto, 53½ dozen £32.2.0.; children's worsted stockings 1 dozen 9/6; men's ditto 5 dozen £5.5.10.; gold thread, 2¾ lbs. £9.19.9. Newfoundland also ordered a full range of cloth and linen, starting with bayes, single, 4 pieces £9.; cottons 40 goads £3.2.0.; flannel 71 yards £3.13.11½.; long cloth 6 pieces £90; kersies 9⅔ pieces £17.6.0.; serges 24 lbs £3.12.0.; worsted 100 lbs £17.10.9.; and millinery at £202.0.9. The large figure for millinery suggests some lace items were included for the towering caps or commodes. The linen consisted of basts, 30 pieces, £22.10.3.; brawles 11 pieces £3.17.0.; callico 2 pieces £1.10.0.; Flanders 31 pieces £46.10.0., and Germany broad linen 2 yards £9.15.0.[9]

CAROLINA, 1696–97

Carolina occurs next in the account for 1696–97. She imported 52 parcels of apparel at £52.10.0.; belts 2⅔ dozen £1.12.0.;

bodices, two dozen, £4.16.0.; hair buttons, 13 gross £2.5.6.; fustian 97 ends £32.12.6.; dimity, 60 yards £2.12.6.; girdles 1½ gross £1.16.0.; haberdashery £45.26.; hats—castors, 70⅔ dozen £300.13.4, felt 116½ dozen £110.13.6.; gloves plain at 9/- dozen £36.4.6.; wrought leather (given that the colonies were too lazy to make their own) 430 lbs £32.13.4.; linen 17 pieces £21.5.0; Irish ruggs 14 £5.12.0; shirts 5½ dozen £6.12.0.; silks, thrown 67½ lbs. £67.10.0.; and wrought silk 116½ lbs. £1,633.0.0.; silver lace ¼ lbs 12/6; stockings, children's woolen 74 dozen £16.13.0.; men's ditto 36 dozen £21.12.0.; children's worsted stockings 9⅓ dozen £4.0.0.; men's ditto 44⅙ dozen £46.7.6. Carolina also purchased cloth, bayes, small 96 pieces, £600; bayes single 7 pieces £15.15.0.; cottons 2401 goads £196.1.6.; flannel 1246 yards £64.17.11.; frieze 70 yards £16.12.6.; long Gloucester cloth 34 pieces £391.0.0.; short cloth 9 pieces £90.; Spanish cloth 43 pieces £419.5.0.; woolen 1½ lbs £1.1.0.; kersies 132 pieces £264.10.0; kersey northern double dozen £42.0.0.; Pennistones friezed one piece £3.5.0.; serges 309 lbs £50.7.0.; mixed cloth with silk 240 lbs £66.0.0.; worsted 267 lbs £460.13.0. Carolina also imported two lots of linen, Holland, 210 ells £36.15.0.; Holland duck 6 yards £57.0.0.; oznabrig linen 6,034 ells £213.11.3.; Russia linen 3 yards £3.10.0., Scotch 120 yards £3.2.6.; Seletia diaper and napking 70 yards £4.7.9.; Romall cloth 40 pieces £40. The second linen order was for Holland linen, 1,909½ ells £350.0.7½; Holland duck 3 yards £30.0.0.; Seletia lawns 64 pieces £50.0.0.; muslin 46 yards £9.4.0.; Scotch 1156 ells £30.6.4.; Seletia diapers and napking 27 yards £23.19.2½; silk Persian 20 yards £5; silk Bengal 4 yards 6/-; Romalls 30 pieces, £42.0.0; Scotch stockings 9 dozen £6.15.0.

This account indicates that Carolina had some rich inhabitants who wore silk and fine linens in the summer. For winter wear, flannel has replaced kersey as the major imported cloth. Since stockings wore out quickly, large orders for them are understandable, but the size of the hat orders, 186 dozen in two types, is surprising. However, below high fashion, women wore the same hats as men, and no doubt some of the Indians asked for hats in trade.[10]

HUDSON'S BAY, 1696–97

Hudson's Bay features next in accounts for 1696–97. It ordered 250 suits £125.0.0.; haberdashery £12.16.0.; tanned leather

£9.6.1.; stockings Men's woolen 10 dozen £6.0.0.; bayes cloth small 15 pieces £120; single bayes 4 pieces £9.0.0.; kerseys 5 pieces £10.10.0.; long Gloucester cloth 7 pieces £77; millinery £10; Holland duck one bolt £3.5.0. No silk was worn in north Canada.[11]

NEW YORK, 1696–97

New York starts with an order for 939 suits £419.0.0. and 126 bodices £25.4.0; fustian 134 pieces £100.10.0.; gloves plain £6.0.0.; haberdashery £30.0.0.; hats, castors 21$^{11}/_{12}$ dozen £120.10.10., felt 9$^2/_3$ dozen £17.14.9.; linen 99 pieces £111.5.0.; shirts 12 dozen £14.9.0.; silk thrown 10$^1/_4$ lbs £10.5.0.; wrought 137 lbs £274.; shoes 1,441 lbs £109.1.6.; stays women's 45 pairs £22.10.0.; stockings children's woolen 10$^1/_2$ dozen £2.7.9.; men's ditto 35 dozen £21; men's worsted stockings 20 dozen £21.; Irish hose 19$^2/_3$ dozen £9.9.0. The cloth was small bayes 24 pieces £192; Welsh cotton plain 1,429 goads, £110.14.11$^1/_4$.; flannel 262 yards £13.12.0.; friezes 210 yards £49.17.6.; long Gloucester cloth 1$^1/_2$ pieces £17.5.0.; remnants 20 lbs £2.0.0.; short cloths 10 pieces £112.10.0.; northern cloth double dozen 4 pieces £24.; kersies 115$^1/_4$ pieces £230.10.0.; Pennistones friezed 9 pieces £20; serges 435 lbs £65.5.0.; mixed stuff with silk 54 lbs £14.17.0.; worsted 352 lbs £61.12.0.

These registers tell us that less silk was worn by New Yorkers than in Carolina. The small number of women's stays ordered—45 for an entire town—may indicate that most settlers made their own or else went without.[12]

NEW ENGLAND, 1696–97

New England imported 97 parcels of apparel £97, hair buttons 59$^1/_2$ dozen £26.7.3.; dimity 162 yards £7.1.9.; dormix 226 lbs £11.6.0.; fustian 492 ends £209.2.0.; gloves plain 999 $^1/_3$ dozen £399.15.0.; gloves stitched decoration 11 dozen £6.12.0.; haberdashery £335.9.10; haircloth 14 pieces £9.6.10.; hats—castors 927$^3/_4$ dozen £4,552.12.0., felt 1,022$^1/_6$ dozen £971.1.2., straw hats 12 dozen 19/-; lace of gold and silver 53$^1/_4$ lbs £106.10.0.; leather tanned £6.15.4.; linen 469 pieces £596.5.0.; Irish rugg 1 9/-; shoes 1039 lbs £77.19.6.; silks thrown 1,291 lbs £1291.; wrought 2,505 lbs £5170.0.0.; stockings children's woolen 29$^1/_2$ dozen £6.12.9.; men's ditto 27 dozen £16.4.0.; children's worsted stockings 19$^1/_4$ dozen £9.11.7.; men's ditto 247$^1/_6$ dozen £259.10.6.;

gold and silver thread 96 lbs £312.; and wollen caps 3 dozen 6/-. The cloth for New England was bayes Barnstaple coarse 54 pieces £121.10.0.; bayes double 13 pieces £59.10.0.; bayes single 96 pieces £216.; and bayes minikin (small) 39 pieces £312.; cotton 3,092 goads £209.17.0½.; flannel 10,564 yards £550.4.2.; frieze 571 yards £135.12.3.; worsted crepe 100 lbs £7.10.0.; perpetuanes 2,345 lbs £359.16.0.; serges 9,944 lbs £1,491.12.0.; mixed stuff with silk 3,967 lbs £1,063.9.6.; worsted 34,711 lbs £6,074.9.6.; rashes 6 pieces £45.; long western cloth (Gloucester) 104 pieces £1,560, remnants 153 lbs £15.6.0.; short cloth 61 pieces £696.5.0.; Spanish cloth 142 pieces £1,394.16.0.; woolen cloth 593 lbs £47.13.3.; Devon cloth 3 pieces £7.10.0.; northern double dozen 114 pieces £694.; and kersies 467⅔ pieces £935.6.9. The registers tell us that flannel and worsted are more popular than kersey, and that for all its Puritan character New Englanders were wearing £5,000 of silks, some embroidered with gold and silver.

New England had imported English linen, but foreign linens are listed separately in the registers. Borelaps linen 2,690 ells cost £100.10.0.; callico 959 pieces cost £599.7.6.; cambrick two pieces £2.15.0.; Check 1232½ pieces £595.9.9.; East Country broad £126.5.1½.; Flanders 1,549 ells £154.19.0.; Germany broad linen £624.11.5½.; and narrow £5,093.1¾; Gingham 9 pieces £9.5.0.; Handkerchief muslin 22 pieces £20.7.0.; Holland 3,199½ ells £559.3.3.; Holland damask tabling 105 yards £22.19.4½.; Holland napking 940 yards £63.0.0.; Holland duck 190 goads £1,711.11.9.; Seletia lawns 1055 pieces £791.5.0; neckcloths 10 pieces £9.5.0.; Polonia linen narrow £26.6.0¼.; Oznabrig 6,160 ells £192.10.0.; Scotch 172 goads £699.16.0. New England clearly used lots of linen, for there is another order in the same year for callico 273 pieces £264.15.0.; cambrick 40 pieces £60.; checks 59½ pieces £29.5.0.; chintz 51 pieces £99.9.; damask napking 20 yards £1.11.9.; damask tabling 5 yards £1.2.6.; diaper 6 pieces £3.12.0.; Flanders 115 ells £12.19.9.; Germany broad £90.4.0., and narrow £330.7.6.; Holland 3024 ells £567.; East Country £31.10.0.; Irish 436 yards £27.5.0.; Seletia lawns 146 pieces £114.19.6.; muslin 33 pieces £99; neckcloths 6 pieces £7.13.0.; oznabrigs 2,492 ells £90.9.5.; Russia £3.9.9.; Scotch £42.9.7.

The linen was used for shifts, shirts, drawers, petticoats, nightshirts, caps, and neckerchiefs, and in summer for dresses and jackets.[13]

VIRGINIA AND MARYLAND, 1696–97

Virginia and Maryland were listed jointly in the accounts, and in 1696 they together ordered through the Port of London apparel, suits 237 £369.10.0.; dimity 70 yards £3.1.3.; fustian 51 pieces £39.5.0.; gloves plain 115 dozen £51.15.0., and stitched with silk 5½ dozen £3.6.0.; haberdashery £151.2.6.; hair cloth ½ piece 6/-; hats beaver 77½ dozen £1,960, castors 154 dozen £947, and felts 245⅙ dozen £232.19.2.; gold and silver lace 15½ lbs £31.; English linen 62 pieces £77.10.0.; Irish ruggs 16 £6.9.0.; silk thrown 409½ lbs £409.10.0.; and wrought 1,546 lbs £3,092.; stockings children's woolen 134 dozen £30.3.0.; men's ditto 109½ dozen £65.14.0.; children's worsted stockings 4½ dozen £2.0.4½.; men's ditto 176½ dozen £195.6.6.; Irish hose 1 dozen 9/-; mixed cloths with silks 1252 lbs £344.6.0.; cloth with hair mixture 79 lbs £3.19.0.; worsted 14,532 lbs £2,543.2.0.; serges 4,496 lbs £674.9.6.; bayes double 9 pieces £40.10.0.; single bayes 9½ pieces £19.2.6.; minikin (small) 145 pieces £1,160; cottons 6,362 goads £492.19.6½.; flannel 4,909 yards £250.9.4.; frieze 370 yards £97.17.6; long western cloth 32 pieces £490.; short cloth 7 pieces £79.15.0.; Spanish cloth 62 pieces £604.10.0.; woolen cloth 262 lbs £22.19.6.; double dozen cloth 112½ lbs £675.; double dozen single two pieces £6.; kersies 260 pieces £520.; Pennistone friezed 20 pieces £65; shoes 2,632 lbs £197.9.0.; and millinery £1,663.9.4. The foreign linen ordered in Maryland and Virginia included borelaps 2962 ells £107.6.6.; buckram 6 pieces £4.13.0.; callicoes 430¾ pieces £269.4.4½.; cambricks 1 piece £1.7.6.; checks 230 pieces £109.5.0.; Flanders 1233 ells £123.6.0.; Germany broad linen £120.6.2½., and narrow £1960.7.0.; Holland 561¼ ells £99.4.4½.; Holland duck £299.10.0.; Seletia lawns 419 pieces £313.10.0.; neckcloths 9 pieces £9.7.6.; muslin one piece £2.3.9.; oznabrig 9,926 ells £310.3.9.; Polonia linen £6.3.9.; Scotch £790.9.9.; Seletia diaper napking 449 yards £25.5.1½.; and Seletia tabling 92 yards £15.10.6.[14]

These accounts show that, as in other colonies, kersey was yielding to worsted and flannel. For the working class, oznabrig and Scottish linen were the chief fabrics worn.

THE ACCOUNTS FOR 1697–98

CAROLINA

The Inspector General's accounts on exports next covers the year 1697–98 Michaelmas to Michaelmas; as more details of exported goods are listed, the registers show that some luxurious items are beginning to be shipped across the Atlantic. The Port of London to Carolina sent apparel 247 suits £98.16.0.; bodices 91 pieces £15.18.6.; gloves plain leather 124¹⁰/₁₂ dozen £49.18.8.; gloves silk stitched 17 dozen £8.1.6.; haberdashery £49.26.; haircloth one piece 13/4; hats beaver 3 dozen £54.6.0.; Carolina hats 5 dozen £24., castor 100¹¹/₁₂ dozen £655.19.2., felt 91 dozen £191.9.0. The special Carolina hat may have been extra wide for working in the heat. Wrought leather at 661 lbs cost £74.7.3. and tanned leather £265.9.6.; English linen 19½ pieces £34.9.6.; silk thrown 13¾ lbs £22.13.9.; silk wrought 339½ lbs £594.2.6.; cloth was double bayes; 12 pieces £57.15.0.; single bayes 12 pieces £37; and minikin bayes 95½ pieces £907.5.0.; long western cloth (Gloucester) 44 pieces £462; short cloth 18½ pieces £231.5.0.; Spanish cloth 6 pieces £123.; cottons 2,438 goads £213.6.6.; flannel 2,000 yards £111.13.4.; frieze £23.3.9.; linsey-woolsey 521 lbs £78.3.0.; northern double dozen 3 pieces £36.; northern dozen single one piece £6.; kersies 171 pieces £384.15.0.; Pennistones friezed 5 pieces £30; ruggs 30 £12.; serges 988 lbs £185.5.0.; stockings men's worsted 85⁵/₁₂ dozen £149.9.7.; children's ditto 11½ dozen £6.6.6.; men's woolen stockings 177½ dozen £168.12.6.; children's ditto 75 dozen £4.10.0.; Irish hose 9 dozen £4.10.0.; worsted 4,222½ lbs £923.13.3¼; stuffs mixed with silk 237 lbs £68.2.9.; silver buttons £76.11.6.; headdresses £32.2.0.; millinery £6.15.3.

In this period everybody wore hats, which explains the large amounts ordered. The amount of silk worn in Carolina was much less than in Virginia, as might be expected, but the import of silver buttons is evidence that some wealthy planters lived there. The headdresses, now listed separately from millinery, were the lace and brass wire towers, or *commodes*, which were backed with ribbons *à la fontange* and *à la duchesse*.[15]

HUDSON'S BAY, 1697–98

No headdresses were ordered for Hudson's Bay, where there were probably very few women. The company received 550 parcels of apparel at £550, and 18 dozen plain gloves. Haberdashery came to only £11.; wrought leather was 168 lbs at £18.18.00., and 42 dressed sheepskins 19/3, with bayes minikin cloth 75 pieces £712.10.10.; long western cloth 42 pieces £440.; and stockings men's woolen 15 dozen £14.5.0.

This shipment shows that some of the company planned to make sheepskin coats to cope with the Arctic climate. Surprisingly, no linen was ordered, unless it arrived ready-made as shirts and drawers in the clothing parcels.[16]

NEW ENGLAND 1697–98

New England in 1697–98 imported from London apparel 425 suits £171.4.0.; bodices 18 £3.3.0.; breeches 15 pairs £1.10.0.; dimity 130 yards £7.6.3.; dornix hangings 490 lbs £24.10.0.; fustian 441 pieces £441; gloves plain leather 772 10/12 dozen £309.2.3.; gloves silk stitched 8 dozen £3.16.0.; haircloth 4 pieces £2.13.4.; hats, beaver 8½ dozen £153.17.0., Carolina 6 dozen £28.16.0., castor 387⅓ dozen £2,517.13.4., and felt 837 dozen £1,757.14.0.; straw hats 3½ dozen £1.; haberdashery £313.9.3.; gold and silver lace 22¼ lbs £66.15.0.; wrought leather 2,007 lbs £225.15.9.; English linen 243½ pieces, £426.11.3.; sheepskins drest 50 £1.7.6.; silk wrought 3,432½ lbs £6006.17.6.; silk thrown 816¾ lbs £1,347.12.9.; sewing silk 12 lbs £9.12.0.; gold and silver thread 7½ ells £22.10.0.; silver thread 114¼ lbs £31.12.6. New England also imported the same range of cloths as the other colonies, but also more luxurious articles such as caps 66 £5.18.0.; fans £14.5.0.; fringes, much used on petticoats in the 1690s, £121.10.0.; silver embroidered gloves £2.10.0.; headdresses £24.2.0.; millinery £600.13.7.; hair twist £16.; perukes and hair powder £203.; riband £144.0.3.; ruggs 136 £31.2.0.; and tippets fur £2.0.0.

Some signs of culture are evident in the import of paintings, unidentified, £110.10.0., and artists' colors £4. The first American portraitists depended heavily on engravings of British painters.[17]

NEW YORK, 1697–98

New York imported millinery £382.15.2.; women's pattens £8.00.; petticoats £1.4.0.; perukes £31.8.0.; ribands £31.8.0.; ruggs 162 £18.6.6.; laced shoes in the Quaker style, that is, without shoe buckles, £1.16.0.; and fur tippets £61.11.6.

Fur tippets had been made fashionable by Elizabeth Charlotte Duchess d'Orléans, an Anglo-German by descent, who was laughed at for wearing them when she arrived at Versailles in 1671. However, after Louis XIV made her a favorite court personality in 1676, the French court copied her fur tippets, and tippets enjoyed a vogue into the eighteenth century. By this time, both New England and New York had acquired perukes and hair powder, and luxurious silks worth a total of £7,374.10.5 were being worn in Puritan New England. It is surprising to see an article as simple to make as pattens being imported. This footwear, which served to keep the shoes out of mud, could be made in wood, and did not always have to be set on an iron ring.

PENNSYLVANIA, 1697–98

Pennsylvania appears in the accounts for 1697, ordering 120 parcels of apparel £120; bodices 8½ dozen £17.3.0; gloves kidd ½ dozen 4/6, gloves plain leather 3 dozen £1.4.0; haberdashery £43.3.12. and hats beaver 1⁵⁄₆ dozen £25.12.0., castor 57²⁄₃ dozen £374.16.8., felt 82¼ dozen £172.14.6, babies, the fashion dolls, £l., and perukes £3.15.0.

The same range of linens and cloths was imported as in the previous year, and the colony also acquired two coaches and one chariot. Signs of high society were now obvious in the colonies, as reflected in the import of some luxurious clothes, wigs, commode headdresses, lace trimmings, gloves, fans, fringes, and silks.

VIRGINIA AND MARYLAND, 1697–98

A joint order for Virginia and Maryland in 1697 well illustrates just how organized the English ready-to-wear industry was during the period, for the colonies imported 16,979 suits at 8/- each £6791.19.0., and bodices 537¹⁄₁₂ dozen £1,128.18.6.; caps plain Monmouth 100⅓ dozen £30.2.0.; caps trimmed 9⁵⁄₉, haberdashery £1,101.19.3½; and haircloth 48½ pieces £32.6.8. The hats were beaver 2⁷⁄₁₂ dozen £46.15.2.; Carolina 1¾ dozen £8.8.0., castor 723⁷⁄₁₂ dozen £1,778.5.10, felt 1,908⁷⁄₁₂ dozen £4,008.0.6., and straw 386⅔ dozen £154.13.4. Silver lace was only one lb £3., but wrought leather was 96,245 lbs £10,827.11.3., and English linen 433½ pieces £758.12.6.; silk thrown 416¾ lbs. £687.12.9.; and silk wrought 11,913½ lbs £3,348.12.6.; stays women's 10⅔ dozen £22.; breeches 348 pairs £38.8.0.; children's coats 104 £18.4.0. and woolen waistcoats 17 £1.14.0.

There was also a large order for foreign linen and cloth, but it is surprising to see Virginia and Maryland ordering less silk than did New England in this particular year. The beaver skins for hats were probably trapped in America, then sent across the Atlantic to be made into hats in England, and then re-exported back to America. Ready-made suits for men already were being imported, and women now also were beginning to have ready-made bodices available. Undergarments are not specified in the accounts, so they were still being homemade from linens. In general by the 1690s the range of goods had improved greatly from the secondhand clothing the Pilgrim Fathers had to buy in the 1620s.[19]

The Customs and Excise Ledgers

Beginning in 1697, accounts are registered in the 82 ledgers of the Customs and Excise, and clearly only a small sample can be quoted here. In 1707, starting with Carolina, only one bodice was ordered at 2/6. Linen was 161 pieces at 30/- to 40/- the piece. Silk, thrown 20 lbs was 26/- to 34/- a lb., and wrought silk was 249½ ells at 30/- to 40/- the ell. Minikin bayes was 74 pieces at £8.10. to £10.10. the piece. Cloth long was 10 ps. at £9 to £12 each and short cloth 17 pieces at £10 to £15 each; Spanish cloth was 14 pieces £19 to £21 each and remnants 60 lbs at 2/6 the lb. Cotton was 960 goads at £7.10. to £8.10 per goad and flannel 24 yards at 15/- to 21/-. Kersies were 100 pieces at 3/4 to 4/6 each. Northern double dozen, the coarse Yorkshire broadcloth dozen, was 3 pieces at £10 to £14 the piece. Worsted was 18½ dozen pieces at 28/- to 38/-. Grosgram was 50 ells at 4/- to 6/- the ell. Bonelace was 30 yards at 6/4.[20]

NEW YORK, 1707

New York in 1707 imported 29 garments, 7 clothes parcels, and one suit, which cost 5/- each, £1 per parcel, and 10/- for the suit. Dimity was 490 yards at 6/- to 12/- the yard. Hats, beaver and castor, were 303⅙ dozen £1061.18.0., and felt hats 242 dozen £184. Gold and silver lace was £5.3.1., laced shoes £26.10., linen 73 pieces £127.15.0. Silk thrown was 77½ lbs £116.5.0. and wrought silk 1,099 lbs £1,923.5.0.; long cloth was 188 pieces £1,239 and short cloth 26 pieces £325; Spanish cloth 22 pieces £440; and remnants 350 goads £42.15.0. Cotton was 2,300 goads £184. Flannel was 486 yards £364.19.0. and frieze was 81 yards

£14.3.4. Sixteen Irish rugs cost £6. Kersies were 219 pieces £438.; northern double dozen 37 pieces £444; and single dozen 3 pieces £18. Perpetuanes and serges were £135.2.0. Stockings were children's worsted 6 pairs 5/6, men's woolen 50 dozen £5.0.0., men's worsted 223 dozen £368.15.6. Stuffs at 14,462 pieces were £3,073.3.6. Millinery was £35 and mixed cloth with silk 473 pieces £118.5.0.; and gold and silver thread 1½ lbs at £3.4.0. New Yorkers also imported 10 periwigs £15.[21]

76 • William Hogarth, *Trade Card for His Sisters Mary and Ann Hogarth*, c. 1730. The Hogarth sisters had a ready-made clothes shop in Little Britain, Long Walk, London. They sold ready-made frock coats, fustian suits, flannel waistcoats, black and canvas smock frocks, the bluecoat school uniform, and linen dimity and Holland for underwear. Their stock was typical of the thousands of ready-made clothes that Britain sent to the American colonies during the seventeenth and eighteenth centuries. In the engraving the sisters are dressing a little boy in a ready-made suit. The ready-made clothing industry must have been bigger than economists have thought. *(The Trustees of the British Museum)*

PENNSYLVANIA, 1707

Pennsylvania imported a similar range of English goods, which had to be transported by English ships. Gloves leather 32½ dozen were £24.15.0. and haberdashery was £36.15.0. Hats beaver and castor were 26⅙ dozen at £74.1.8.; linen was 25 goads at £43.15.0.; silk thrown 13 lbs £19.10.0.; and wrought silk 124 lbs £217. Short cloth 7 pieces were £87.10.0. and remnants 7 goads cost 15/9. Kersies were 12 pieces £24, while perpetuanes and serges were 100 pieces at £17.10.0. Stockings worsted were 74 dozen £122.2.0. and gloves as pieces, 10 dozen, to be stitched up in the colony were £3. Signs of Quaker simplicity are evident in the haberdashery at only £1.10.0. Hats were beaver and castor, a second order, at 9½ dozen £32.18.0., and only three periwigs were ordered at £13.10.0. Thrown silk was 34 lbs £9.9.0. and wrought silk 30 lbs £52.10.0.

The ledgers show that although silk was worn, there was much less of it than in New England and Virginia.[22]

VIRGINIA AND MARYLAND

Virginia and Maryland are always listed as one account in the ledgers, and their joint order in 1707 was for 547 garments £136.15.0; 12 clothing parcels £12, and 766 suits £383, plus bodices 293 pairs £51.5.6. Fustian was 240½ pieces £240.10.0., gloves as pieces 187 dozen £56.2.0., and haberdashery was £122.7.6. The hats were beavers and castors 105⅚ dozen £370.8.4., felt hats 277⅚ dozen £555.13.4., and straw hats 11⅔ dozen £4.18.4. Linen English 129½ pieces cost £226.12.6., bayes double cloth 12 pieces £54, and minikin 180½ pieces £1714.15.0., with long cloth 19 pieces £199.10.0., short cloth 9 pieces £112.10.0., Spanish cloth 48 pieces £80, and remnants 288 lbs £32.8.0. Millinery was £23.4.1. and perukes £7.15.0.[23]

THE YEAR 1750

Moving on to 1750, the pattern of goods imported continues unchanged, with the exception that the amount of clothing ordered from England drops considerably. This can only mean that enough tailors and mantua makers were established in the colonies by 1750 to make the majority of clothes that Americans were wearing. To chart this drop in imports more precisely would involve going through all the ledgers between 1707 and

1750, which cannot be accommodated here. But, aside from less dependence upon British clothing, the types of goods imported continues to fall within the same range as before.

CAROLINA, GEORGIA, HUDSON'S BAY, 1750

The ledgers begin with Carolina in 1750. No clothes were ordered, but dimity was 350 yards £13.3.1 and fustian 43 pieces £43. Gloves plain leather were 2,100 dozen £630 and haberdashery £1,323. Hats beaver and castor were 427 dozen £1,705, felt 818 dozen £920, and straw 8 dozen £1.10.0. Gold and silver lace were 19 lbs. £54.9.5., silk thrown 19 lbs £411.9.4., and wrought silk 1478 lbs £2,556.16.6. Minikin bayes was 786 pieces £6,091.10.0. and single 70 pieces £138.5.0. Long cloth was 100 pieces £775, remnants 300 lbs £26.5.0., short cloth 22 pieces £253, and Spanish cloth 45 pieces £255. English cotton was 16,415 goads £968.9.8., flannel 8,540 yards £162.11.8., and perpetuanes and serges 900 pieces at £146.5.0. Stockings men's worsted were 2309 dozen £3,926.5.10. Stuffs were 15,940 pieces at £1,992.10.0. Mixed cloths, silk with cotton, were 1,258½ lbs £173.10.0., silk with hair 223½ lbs £30.14.7., and silk with grosgram 30 lbs £6.17.6. Cotton checks were 150 yards £150 and Irish linen 83 yards £228. Millinery was £30.[24]

The larger size of the orders reflects the larger population in 1750.

The new colony of Georgia ordered only 6 parcels of apparel £6. She imported 200 pieces of English linen at £350, bayes minikin 20 pieces £153, and cotton 2,000 goads £118, with 1000 pieces of stuffs for £125, which completed the little order.

Hudson's Bay was also a small settlement, and it ordered no clothes in 1750, but haberdashery £34; 8 dozen felt hats £9; long cloth 102 pieces £790.10.0.; white, undyed cloth 20 pieces £135; plus 200 yards of flannel £10.16.8. and two dozen men's woolen stockings £2.3.0.

NEW ENGLAND, 1750

New England still imported some clothing, garments 394 £98.10.0 and clothing parcels 66 £66. A large order for Monmouth caps was 1,190 dozen £1,487.10.0.; dimity was 2,340 yards £95.5.0.; fustian 326 pieces £326; and gloves plain leather 674 dozen £2,024.8.0. Haberdashery was £3,174.14.3. Hats were beaver and castor 654 dozen £2,617.; felt hats 791 dozen £889;

horsehair hats 23 dozen £55.4.0.; and straw hats 50 dozen £9.7.6. English linen was 9872 goads at £17,276. and silks were thrown 2,189⅛ lbs £3,284.8.9. and wrought silk 6,094½ lbs £10,664.18.9. Minikin bayes was 2,220 pieces £17,205. and single bayes 96 pieces £189.12.0. Long cloth was 157 pieces £1,216.15.0., remnants were 140 dozen £12.5.0, short cloth pieces 1,293 at £14,869.10.0., and Spanish cloth 749 pieces £3,745. Cotton was 2,124 goads £125.6.3.; flannel 3,297 yards £1,785.17.6.; frieze 7,000 yards £729.3.4.; and kersies 1,292 pieces at £2,261.3.4., with perpetuanes and serges at 9,608 lbs for £156. Men's woolen stockings were 26 dozen at £27.19.0., worsted stockings, 3,650½ dozen £6,205.17.0., and stuffs 211,113 lbs at £26,389.2.6. Mixed silks with worsted 11,164¾ lbs £1,535.3.0., with Indian cotton 1,045⅚ lbs £143.14.7. and grosgram 86 lbs £11.6.6. Bonelace was £220, caps woolen £170, Irish linen 169 yards £169, and gold and silver ribbons £193. New England clearly had an artist's colony by 1750 for she imported £260 of painter's colors.[25]

NEW YORK, 1750

New York ordered some clothing but less than before, with garments 107 £26.15.0. and clothing parcels 11 £11, along with 20 pairs of bodices £3.10.0. Monmouth caps 620 dozen were £850. Dimity was 590 yards £22.2.6 and fustian 404 pieces £404. Gloves leather plain 3,418 dozen were £1,025.8.0., haberdashery was £1,350.17.6., and haircloth 13 pieces £9.2.0. Hats were beaver and castor 711½ dozen £2,846, felt 787 dozen £885.7.6., and straws 5 dozen 18/9. Gold and silver lace was 5½ lbs £15.2.6. and bayes double 882 pieces £3,307.10.0., minikin 2,618 pieces £20,289.10.0., and single bayes 215 pieces £424.12.6. Long cloth was 677 pieces £5,246.15.0., remnants 740 lbs £64.15.0., short cloth 1065 pieces £12,247.10.0., and Spanish cloth 445 pieces £2,225. Cotton was 10,455 goads £615.13.3.; flannel 46,780 yards £2,531.4.2.; frieze 2,450 yards £255.4.2.; and kersies 264 pieces £462. Northern dozen cloth double were 30 pieces £225; pennistones friezed 40 pieces £90; perpetuanes and serges £382.13.9. Stockings were men's woolen 34 dozen £36.11.0. and men's worsted 2,762 dozen £4,695.8.0. Stuffs were 21,961 yards £27,451.5.0. Mixed silks with worsted were 10,523½ lbs £1,446.19.7., with Indian cotton 1,558⅝ lbs £214.6.2 and grosgram 96½ lbs £13.5.4. Grosgram yarn was 20 yards £50 and bonelace £210. Men's woolen caps were £175, Irish linen 13 pieces £34, Irish rugs 74 £38.17.0., and millinery £97.

NOVA SCOTIA, 1750

Nova Scotia in 1750 ordered no clothing, but haberdashery was £133.10.0. and gloves plain leather 30 dozen £9.0.0. Hats were beaver and castor 56½ dozen £226 and felt 62 dozen £69.15.0. English linen was 304 pieces £532; silk thrown 172 lbs £26.5.0. and wrought silk 33 lbs £57.13.0; Bayes double 30 pieces £112.10.0.; minikin bayes 68 pieces £527; remnants 30 dozen £2.12.6; short cloth 26 pieces £269; Spanish cloth 62 pieces £310; flannel 3171 yards £280.1.11.; kersies 6 pieces £10.10.0. Stockings were men's woolen 80 dozen £86 and men's worsted 700⅓ dozen £1,190.11.4. Stuffs were 3650 yards £456.5.0. and caps woolen 4 dozen £2.

In Nova Scotia only a few wore silk compared to those wearing flannel and stuffs.[26]

PENNSYLVANIA, 1750

Pennsylvania in 1750 did order some clothes—489 garments £122.5.0 and 18 parcels of clothing £18. Monmouth caps were 280 dozen £350. and gloves plain leather, 2,845 dozen £853.10.0. Haberdashery was £1,645.1.5. Hats were beaver and castor 557 dozen £2,228 and felt 2,239 dozen £2,518.17.6. English linen was 13,316 pieces £23,303; silk thrown 1379⅜ lbs £2,369.1.3.; and wrought silk 4,018½ lbs £7,031.18.9. Bayes cloth double was 1,263 pieces £4,511.5.0.; minikin 472 pieces £3,658; single bayes 551 pieces £1088.4.6.; long cloth 34 pieces £263.10.0.; remnants 500 lbs £43.15.0.; short cloth 245 pieces £6,267.10.0.; and Spanish cloth 157 pieces £785. Cotton was 20,900 goads £1,233.2.0.; flannel was 30,763 yards £1,666.6.7.; kersies 510 pieces £875; perpetuanes and serges 750 lbs £121.17.6. Irish rugs were 199 pieces £62.9.6. Stockings were men's woolen 20 dozen £21.16.0. and men's worsted 4093½ dozen £6,958.19.0. Stuffs were 136,664 yards £17,083. and mixed silk with worsted 7195⅞ lbs £989.8.7., with Indian cotton 256⅛ lbs £35.4.4. and grosgram 172 lbs £23.13.0. Grosgram yarn was 5 dozen £1.5.0., and caps woolen worsted £33. Irish linen was 317 yards £460. and millinery £50. Typically, gold and silver ribbons for the Quaker colony were only £4. There must have been a few artists living in Philadelphia, for painters' colors amounted to £143.18.0.

No colony could argue that it did not receive the same goods as the others. The ledgers at this time show that all colonies received exactly the same range of goods and wore the same range of clothing, although the amounts ordered varied.[27]

THE 1770 LEDGER, CANADA

Looking next at the ledger for 1770, Canada first appears as an entity. Canada ordered only 6 parcels of clothes £6, indicating that she was making most of her own. Fustian was 11 pieces £16, gloves plain leather were 753 dozen £225.18.0., and haberdashery £1,613.10.0., which shows a large purchase of ribbons, lace, and sewing threads. Hats beaver and castor were 259 dozen £1,036 and felt 404 dozen £454.10.0. Gold lace was 16 lbs £44.13.9. and silver lace 10 lbs £18.18.0. The linen was foreign 6,480 pieces £11,340., British 74,935 yards £3,746.15.0., and Irish 32,688 yards £1,634.6.0. Silk was supplied now in pieces at £2,531.3.9. Bayes double was 1,472 pieces £5,520., minikin bayes 141 pieces £1,092.15.0., and single bayes 1,344 pieces £2,567.10.0. Long cloth was 460 pieces £3,565; remnants 224 lbs £19.12.0.; short cloth 3,599 pieces £41,388.10.0.; Spanish cloth 555 pieces £2,775. Cotton was 11,700 goads £690.6.0., with Welsh plain 1,200 goads £66. Flannel was 24,430 yards £1,973.5.10.; frieze 71,300 yards £7,427.1.8.; and kersies 29 pieces £35.; once the chief fabric in the seventeenth century, kersey was still hanging on. Stockings were men's woolen 1030 dozen £1,107.5.0., worsted men's 3507 dozen £5,961.18.0., and yarn stockings 10 dozen £6. Stuffs were 70,790 lbs £8,848.15.0. and mixed cloth silk with worsted 59 lbs £2.4.5., with Indian cotton 108 lbs £14.17.4. and with grosgram 21 lbs £2.17.9.[28]

FLORIDA, 1770

In 1770, Florida was temporarily part of the English colonial empire. Florida ordered only 4 clothing parcels £4. Dimity was 90 yards £3. and gloves plain leather 30 dozen £9, with haberdashery £194. British linen was 32,737 goads £1,636.17.0., and Irish 10,573 goads £528.13.0. Bayes cloth double was 150 pieces £562.16.0., minikin 160 pieces £1,240., cloth remnants 150 lbs £13.2.6., short cloth 660 pieces £7,590., and Spanish cloth 20 pieces £100. Cottons were 300 goads £17.14.0., with Welsh plains 5,000 goads £275. Flannels were 1,700 yards £92.1.8. Stockings men's woolen were 30 dozen £32.5.0. and men's worsted 344 dozen £584.16.0. Stuffs were 25,000 lbs £3,125.0.0. and printed cotton and linens 666 yards £60.

Obviously Florida, with its hot climate, ordered less cloth than Canada.[29]

GEORGIA, 1770

Georgia ordered in 1770 only 8 parcels of clothing at £8, and no dimity. Haberdashery was £376, and gloves plain leather 170 dozen £51. Hats were beaver and castor 134 dozen £536, and felt 347 dozen £390.7.6. Foreign linen was 2,500 pieces £4,375; British linen 45,301 goads £2,265.1.0.; and Irish 33,124 goads £1,659. Silk in pieces was £484.19.4. Bayes cloth double 206 pieces was £750, minikin 555 pieces £4,301.5.0., and single 200 pieces £395. Long cloth 100 pieces was £775, remnants 2,700 lbs £236.5.0., short cloth 1,120 pieces £12,880, and Spanish cloth 100 £500. Cottons were 4,100 goads £241.18.0., with Welsh plains 51,150 goads at £2,813.5.0. Flannels were 5,400 yards £292.10.0. Stockings men's worsted were 650 dozen £935. Stuffs were 8,600 lbs £1,575. and mixed silk with worsted cloth 68 lbs £9.7.8, with Indian cotton 14 lbs £1.19.8., and grosgram 15 lbs £2.2.7. Printed cottons and linens were 725 square yards £50.

HUDSON'S BAY, 1770

Hudson's Bay still is listed separately but with its usual small orders. Haberdashery was £26, and felt hats 9 dozen £16.2.6. Bayes minikin were 47 pieces £364.15.0., long cloth 33 pieces £255.15.0., and white cloth 11 pieces £74.5.0. Flannel was 380 yards £20.11.8. and men's woolen stockings 19 dozen £20.8.6. Newfoundland ordered 5 clothes parcels £5. and gloves plain leather 66 dozen £18. Haberdashery was £456. Hats beaver and castor were 34 dozen £136. and felt hats 53 dozen £66.5.0. Foreign linen was 115 pieces £201.5.0., British linen 9,903 goads £495.3.6., and Irish 603 goads £30.3.0. Silk in pieces was 44 lbs £78.1.10. Bayes cloth double was 59 pieces £213.17.6.; single bayes 60 pieces £127.10.0.; and cottons 550 goads £30.18.9. Flannel was 3,000 yards £162.10.0.; frieze 500 yards £52.1.8.; stockings men's woolen 17 dozen £18.14.6. and men's worsted hose 300 dozen £532.10.0. Stuffs were 4,740 lbs £770.5.0., and silks mixed with Indian cotton 7½ lbs £1.11.10. Printed cottons and linens were 737 square yards £110.4.0.

NOVA SCOTIA, 1770

Nova Scotia ordered only 7 clothing parcels at £7. Gloves plain leather were 86 items £25.16.0. and haberdashery £142. Hats beaver and castor were 72 dozen £288, and felt 168 dozen £189. Foreign linen was 2,983 pieces £5,220.5.6.; British linen 21,026 goads £1,051.6.0.; and Irish 9,759 yards £487.10.0. Silk in pieces was 301 lbs £527.16.10. Bayes cloth double was 90 pieces £337.10.0.; long cloth 50 pieces £387.10.0.; short cloth 400 pieces £4,600; Spanish cloth 100 pieces £500; flannel 7,800 yards £422.10.0.; and frieze 200 yards £20.16.8. Stockings men's woolen were 360 dozen £387. and worsted 486 dozen £795.12.0. Stuffs were 25,830 lbs £3,228.15.0. Mixed silk with worsted was 211 lbs £29, and silk with Indian cotton £38.

VIRGINIA AND MARYLAND, 1770

The biggest clothing order in 1770 came from Virginia and Maryland. They imported 96 garments at £24 and 58 clothes parcels at £58, and bodices 70 pairs £12.5.0. Gloves plain leather were 3,665 dozen £1,099.10.0. and haberdashery £5,180.5.0. Hats were beaver and castor 3,616 dozen £12,657.15.0. and felt hats 7,446½ dozen £8,935.16.0. Foreign linen was 6,343 pieces £11,100.5.0.; British linen 124,491 goads £6,224.11.0; and Irish 644 yards £203.7.0., Silk in pieces 3,006 lbs £5,260.10.0. Bayes double was 2,131 pieces £7,991.5.0., minikin 1,149 pieces £8,955., and single bayes 1,082 pieces £1,785.6.0. Long cloth was 550 pieces £2,887.10.0., remnants 110 lbs £11.9.2., short cloth 648 pieces £5,184.; and Spanish cloth 40 pieces £140. Cottons were 300 goads £16,792.14.0.; Welsh plains 183 goads £9,189.14.0.; flannel 75,161 yards £5,011.1.4.; frieze 1,300 yards £135.8.4.; kersies 460 pieces £759. Perpetuanes and serges were 2,800 lbs £455. Stockings men's woolen were 741 dozen £815.2.0.; worsted stockings 4,426 dozen £7,745.10.0.; and yarn hose 120 dozen £72. Stuffs were 199,442 lbs £24,930.5.0.

As the leading colonial fashion center, Virginia placed the largest orders for imported goods until Britain imposed a trade embargo when the colonies rebelled.[30]

All the exports listed here were British manufactures exported officially through the Port of London. A lot of west-country cloth was sent to London for dyeing, but there was no need to send it back to Bristol for export to the colonies since the port of London was also convenient for shipping. Similarly, it was just as efficient to send Yorkshire cloth for export to London as it was to transport it overland to Liverpool, so London became the principal depot for exported cloth and clothes. Ready-made clothing in London was centered around Monmouth Street, which was active enough to turn out 16,000 suits when Virginia and Maryland required them. Little work has been done on the ready-made industry, but obviously it was quite big. This chapter has opened only a chink of an enormous archive but hopefully it should provide enough material to help in preparing comparative charts, which can be enlarged when more work is done with the Customs and Excise ledgers. Such charts can tell much to students of early American dress about the precise quantity and types of goods shipped to the colonies, their range and diversity, the variations in dress among colonies as reflected in imports, and the developments in trade, manufacture, and costume over time.

APPENDIX II

The Commencement of American Cloth Production

The wool historian John Smith collected a mass of material on the wool trade, including his own observations, pamphlets by contemporaries, and government reports, all of which he published in 1747. In volume II, Joshua Gee wrote a piece on English exports in 1728, and observed of the colonies:

> *Pennsylvania* within 40 Years, has made wonderful improvements, which has much enlarged their Demands upon us for broad Cloths, Druggets, Serges, Stuffs, and Manufactures of all Sorts. They supply the Sugar Plantations with Pipe-Staves, Lumber &- But all not sufficing for their Clothing, they are forced to make something by their own Labour and Industry to answer that end.
> *New Jersey, New York, New England,* like *Pennsylvania,* buy their Clothing from us, what they can afford; for the rest, they are their own Manufacturers."[1]

Thus there are some records that cloth production for making clothing was established in the American colonies around 1728, to supply those who could not afford imported English clothes.

Textile production seems to have started in New England, as the following report to the Lords Commissioners of Trade and Plantations in 1718 states:

We have a very considerable Manufactory already established in *New England,* begun in the great Scarcity and Dearness of Goods, about Nine Years ago, when the *English* Manufacture sold at 200 *per cent.* Advance to the Shop. . . . This put them upon making Buttons, *Stuffs, Kerseys, Linsey Woolseys,* Flannel &; which has decreased the Importation of those Provinces above £50,0001 *per Annum.* And for the Exportation increasing, that is only the Effect of the Peoples Increase, and has no more to it than that three Men require more clothing than two.[2]

This report implies that the commencement of American textile production goes back to 1709, when England was busy fighting France in the War of the Spanish Succession, which clearly affected transatlantic trade. Once imported materials became too expensive, New England had been forced to start weaving its own cloth for clothing.

When the Commissioners of Trade examined the Manufactures of the British colonies again in 1732, they learned that "in the Colonies of *New England, New York, Connecticut, Rhode Island,* Pensylvania and in the County of *Somerset* in *Maryland,* the People had fallen into the Manufacture of Woolen and Linen Cloth for the Use of their own Families; but we could not learn that they had made any for Sale in those Colonies, except in a small Indian Town in Pensylvania, where some Palatines had been lately settled." This report suggests that most production was homespun for domestic usage.

Colonel *Shute,* Governor of Massachusett's Bay, informed us, that in some Parts of this Province, the Inhabitants worked up their WOOL and FLAX and made an ordinary coarse Cloth for their own Use, but the Merchants could afford what was imported, cheaper than what was made in that Country.

Colonel *Hart,* formerly Governor of *Maryland,* who lived many Years in the Neighbourhood of this Government (Pensylvania) informs us that their chief trade lay in the Exportation of Provisions and Lumber; having no Manufactures established.

The Country People who used formerly to make most of their Cloathing out of their own WOOL, do not now make a third Part of what they wear.

Mr. *Belcher,* Governor of New Hampshire informs us, that the Woollen Manufacture of that Province was much less than formerly, the common Lands on which the Sheep used to feed, being now divided into particular properties; and their Exportation being naval Stores, Lumber and Fish &c.

> Mr. *Rip van Dam*, President of the Council of *New York*, acquaints us, there is yearly imported a very large Quantity of the Woollen Manufacture of this Kingdom, which they could not pay for, and should be reduced to the Necessity of making themselves, if they were prohibited from receiving from the foreign Sugar Colonies, in return for Provisions.
>
> *Major Gordon*, Deputy Governor of *Pensylvania*, informs us, that they do not export any Woolen or Linen Manufactures: all they make (which are of a coarse Sort) being for the Use of themselves and Families.[3]

Colonial representatives were of different opinions on the issue of whether to continue their heavy reliance on goods imported from Britain or to encourage the development of American production. For example, Rip Van Dam of New York, in the excerpt above, thought that New York should develop her own wool manufacture, but Governor Shute of Massachusetts Bay observed that imported cloth from Britain was cheaper than native homespun. This concern with British trade versus local manufacture was shared also by the British trade commissioners, who understood that colonial home production was not beneficial to British trade interests, which required that the colonies serve as a market for British goods. As the commissioners concluded in their 1732 report, "There are more Trades carried on, and Manufactures set up in the Provinces of the Continent of *America* to the Northward of *Virginia* prejudicial to the Trade and Manufactures of Great Britain," and they noted also that the climate and products in the northern colonies were roughly similar in kind, thus tempting the southern plantations to start producing their own cloth. The commissioners were also aware that the Charter governments of the colonies showed "the little Dependance they have upon their Mother Country," and foresaw the possibility of the colonies putting their own interests before Great Britain's.

Despite American hopes for a home-based cloth industry, however, it looks as if the variety of cloth produced in New England in 1709 may have diminished by 1732, once peace between England and France had been restored and British products had dropped in price. But for the middle classes to start wearing homespun one must wait until 1767 in Boston (see chapter 5, p. 131).

Notes

CHAPTER 1

The Discovery of the Indians

1. Christopher Columbus, *The Writings of Christopher Columbus*, ed. Paul Ford (New York: Charles Webster & Co., 1892), p. 33.
2. Christopher Columbus, *Journal of the First Voyage*, in *The Northmen, Columbus and Cabot: Original Narratives in Early American History*, ed. Julius Olsen and Edward Boure (New York: Charles Scribner's Sons, 1906).
3. Columbus, *Writings*, pp. 105, 117.
4. Richard Hakluyt, *Divers Voyages touching the Discoverie of America and the Islands adjacent* (London: Thomas Woodcocke, St. Paul's Churchyard, 1582), p. 17.
5. *The Journal of Christopher Columbus and Documents relating to the Voyages of John Cabot and Caspar Reale*, trans. R. Markham (London: Hakluyt Society, 1893), pp. 233–34.
6. Jacques Cartier, *First Relation of the New Land called New France* (1534), in J. Pinkerton, *General Collection of Voyages*, vol. 12 (London: Dent & Sons, 1808), p. 146.
7. William H. Prescott, *The Conquest of Mexico*, vol. 1 (London: Everyman, 1948), p. 33.
8. Ibid., p. 271.
9. Prescott, *The Conquest of Mexico*, vol. 2, p. 70.
10. Ibid., p. 116.
11. Albrecht Dürer, *Schriftlicher Nachlass*, vol.1, ed. H. Rupprich (Berlin, 1956), p. 155. An inventory of Indian artifacts sent to the kings was published by Torres de Mendoza in Madrid in 1869.
12. *Muster Roll and Equipment in the Expedition of Francisco Vasquez de Coronado*, trans. Arthur Aiton (William L. Clements Library,

1939); *Narrative of the Expedition of Francisco Vásquez de Coronado by P. Castanedo* in *Spanish Explorers of the Southern United States,* ed. F. Hodge (New York: Charles Scribner's Sons, 1907), p. 317.

13. *Narrative of the Expedition of Hernando de Soto by the Gentleman of Elvas,* ed. T. Hayes Lewis, in *Spanish Explorers;* Richard Hakluyt, *Worthye and Famous History of the Travailes. Discovery and Conquest of that great Continent of Terra Florida* (London: Matthew Lownes, at Sign of the Bishop's Head, 1611), p. 43.

14. Jean Ribault, *True and last Discoverie of Florida,* trans. Thomas Hackit (London, 1562), p. 80.

15. Richard Hakluyt, *True Pictures and Fashions of the People in that Parte of America now called Virginia discovered by Englishmen 1585–1588,* illustrated by John White (London: Theodore de Bry, 1590), captions to plates III, IV, V, IX, XI, XXIII.

16. Captain John Smith, *The Generall Historie of Virginia, New England, and the Summer Isles* (London: Michael Sparkes, 1624), p. 30.

17. William Bradford, *History of the Plymouth Plantation, 1620–1647,* vol. 1 (Boston: Massachusetts Historical Society, 1912), p. 180.

18. Edward Winslow, *A Relation or Iournal of the beginning & proceedings of the English plantation at Plimouth in New England* (London: John Bellamie, at the Two Greyhounds, Cornhill, 1622), pp. 32–34, 37.

19. Edward Winslow, *Good Newes from New England* (London: William Bladen and John Bellamie, at the Bible, Paul's Churchyard, and 3 Golden Lions, Cornhill, 1624), pp. 59–60.

20. Roger Williams, *A Key into the Language of America* (London: Gregory Dexter, 1643), pp. 110, 183.

21. John Winthrop, *Journal, 1630–1649,* vol. 1, ed. James Hosmer (New York: Charles Scribner's Sons, 1908), p. 62. For a study of Mexican dress, see Patricia Rieff Arewalt, *Indian Clothing Before Cortes* (Norman, Okla.: Oklahoma University Press, 1981).

1. Jonathan King, *The Mayflower Miracle* (Newton Abbott: David & Charles, 1987), p. 42.

2. Bradford, *History of Plymouth Plantation, 1620–1647,* vol. 1, p. 219.

3. Bradford, *History of Plymouth Plantation,* vol. 2, p. 67; vol. 1, p. 448.

4. John Winthrop, *Journal, 1630–1649,* ed. James Hosmer (New York: Charles Scribner's Sons, 1908), p. 120.

5. Celia Fiennes, *The Illustrated Journeys, c. 1682–1712,* ed. C. Morris (London: Macdonald, 1982), p. 196.

6. Winthrop, *Journal, 1630–1649,* vol. 1, p. 279; *History of New England from 1630–1649,* p. 143.

7. William Prynne, *The Unloveliness of Lovelocks* (London, 1628), p. 1.

8. Danby Pickering, ed., *The Statutes at Large* (1763), vol. 8: 1597–1660, pp. 452, 368–414.

CHAPTER 2

New England in the Seventeenth Century

9. Diana de Marly, *Louis XIV and Versailles* (London: Batsford, 1987; New York: Holmes & Meier, 1987).

10. George Fox, *Journal*, 2 vols., bicentenary edition (London: The Society of Friends, 1891), vol. 1, p. 220; vol. 2, pp. 412–13.

11. William Penn, *Account of the Lenni Lengs and Delaware Indians*, ed. Albert Myers (1683; rpt. Philadelphia, 1937), p. 29.

12. Louis B. Wright, *Cultural Life in the American Colonies, 1607–1763* (New York: Harper & Row, 1957), pp. 52, 58.

13. Diana de Marly, *Working Dress* (London: Batsford, 1986; New York: Holmes & Meier, 1987), pp. 96–97.

14. Bibliotheca Lindesiana, *A Bibliography of Royal Publications of the Tudor and Stuart Sovereigns 1485–1714*, vol. 5 (Oxford: Clarendon Press, 1910), p. 293.

15. Henry Black, ed., *Minutes of Town Courts 1652–1691* (Newton, New York: Historical Records Survey, 1940).

16. Samuel Wilson, *An Account of the Province of Carolina in America* (London: G. Larkin for F. Smith, Elephant & Castle, Cornhill, 1683), p. 305.

17. Pehr Kalm, *Travels in North America in 1750*, revised by Adolph Benson, vol. 1 (New York: Wilson-Erickson, 1937), p. 225.

18. Christopher Jeaffreson, *A Young Squire of the Seventeenth Century*, vol. 1 (London, 1878), p. 118; Lady Frances Verney, *Letters and Papers of the Verney Family* (London: Longmans, 1853), pp. 191–97.

CHAPTER 3

La Nouvelle France

1. Jacques Cartier, *First Account of J. Cartier of St. Malo of the New Land called New France*, in J. Pinkerton, *General Collection of Voyages*, vol. 12, p. 631.

2. Ibid., p. 637.

3. Ibid., p. 677.

4. [Anonymous] *Les Annales de l'Hôtel Dieu de Québec 1636–1716* (1939), p. 8.

5. *Canada: Edits, Ordonnances Royaux, Declarations et Arrets de Conseil du Roi* (1803), chronological lists.

6. Louis Armand de Lom d'Arce Baron Lahontan, *New Voyage to North America*, vol. 1 (London: H. Bonwicke, St. Paul's Churchyard, 1703), p. 9.

7. For the textile war and French sumptuary law, see de Marly, *Louis XIV and Versailles*.

8. Lahontan, *New Voyage to North America*, vol. 1, p. 9.

9. Charles Guillemeau, *De la Grossesse et accouchement des femmes* (Paris, 1620), p. 797.

10. Francois Mauriçeau, *The Accomplisht Midwife*, trans. H. Chamberlen (London, 1673), pp. 362, 382.

11. Reproduced in the catalogue *Costume Coutume* (Grand Palais, Paris: Ministère de la Culture et de la Communication, 1987), p. 174.

12. John Bulwer, *Anthropometamorphosis: Man Transform'd; or, The Artificial Changeling* (London, 1650), p. 186.

13. John Locke, *Some Thoughts concerning Education* (London, 1693), pp. 10–11.

14. Princesse des Ursins, *Lettres inédites de Madame de Maintenon et Madame la Princesse des Ursins,* vol. 1 (Paris, 1826), p. 114; my translation.

15. Lahontan, *New Voyage to North America,* vol. 2, p. 41.

16. Bulwer, *Anthropometamorphosis,* p. 61.

17. Madeleine Doyon, "Le Costume Traditionel Feminin," *Les Archives de Folklore* (Laval University, 1946), p. 112; Thomas Chapais, *The Great Intendant, 1665–1672* (Toronto, 1920), pp. 39, 123.

18. Lahontan, *New Voyage to North America,* vol. 1, p. 52.

19. Ibid., p. 50; vol. 2, p. 6.

20. [Anonymous] *Mémoire sur le Canada* (Québec: Literary and Historical Society of Quebec, Historical Documents, series 1, 1838–61), p. 1.

21. [Anonymous] *Considerations sur l'Etat de Canada,* Oct. 1758 (Québec: Literary and Historical Society of Quebec, Historical Documents, series 1, 1836–61), p. 16.

22. Louis Hennepin, *Description de la Louisiane nouvellement découverte* (Paris: Widow Sebastien, rue St. Jacques, 1683), p. 25.

23. [Anonymous officer] *The Present State of the Country, Inhabitants, European and Indian of Louisiana* (London, 1744), pp. 10, 12, 26.

24. Pehr Kalm, *Travels in North America in 1750,* vol. 2, p. 417.

25. Ibid., p. 446.

26. Ibid., p. 525.

27. Ibid., pp. 519, 560.

28. *The Definitive Treaty of Peace and Friendship* (London: T. Green, 1763).

29. Captain Jonathan Carver, *Travels through the Interior Parts of North America in 1766–68* (London: J. Walter at Charing Cross, 1778), pp. 226–27.

1. Ned Ward, *A Trip to New England with a Character of the Country and People both English and Indian* (London, 1699), pp. 6–7.

2. Abraham Kirck, *Brief Relation of the State of New England* (London: Richard Baldwin at the Black Bull, Old Bailey, 1689), p. 8.

3. Hartwell, Blair, and Chilton, *The Present State of Virginia in 1697* (Charlottesville: University Press of Virginia, 1940), p. 9.

4. [Anonymous] *The History of Virginia to 1720* (London: Fayram & Clark at Royal Exchange, 1720), p. 255.

5. Rev. Hugh Jones, *The Present State of Virginia* (London: J. Clarke at the Bible, Royal Exchange, 1720), p. 255.

6. [Anonymous] *A Description of the Province of South Carolina* (Charleston, 1732), pp. 129, 131.

7. [Anonymous] *A Description of South Carolina* (London: J. Dodsley, Pall Mall, 1761), pp. 218, 229, 261.

8. Jeanette Thurber Conner, ed. and trans., *Colonial Records of*

CHAPTER 4

The English Colonies 1689–1774

Spanish Florida from 1570, vol. 1 (Florida Historical Society, 1925), p. 275.

9. Pehr Kalm, *Travels in North America in 1750,* vol. 1., p. 198.

10. *Heads of Inquiry relative to the Present State and Condition of His Majesty's Colony of Connecticut,* signified by H.M.'s Secretary of State in a Letter of 5 July 1773 (New London: T. Green, 1775), pp. 6–7.

11. St. John de Crèvecoeur, *Sketches of Eighteenth-Century America,* ed. Bourdin, Gabriel, & Williams (New Haven: Yale University Press, 1925), p. 94.

12. Ibid., pp. 122–23.

13. [Anonymous] *General History of Connecticut* (London: J. Bew, Pater Noster Row, 1781), p. 323.

14. Kalm, *Travels in North America in 1750,* vol. 1, pp. 225, 214.

15. William Byrd of Westover, *The Secret Diary 1709–1712,* ed. L. Wright and M. Tinling (Richmond, Va.: Dietz Press, 1941); *Another Secret Diary,* ed. L. Wright and M. Tinling (Richmond, Va.: Dietz Press, 1942); *The London Diary 1717–1721,* ed. L. Wright and M. Tinling (Oxford: Oxford University Press, 1958).

16. Samuel Pepys, *The Diary,* ed. R. Latham and W. Matthews (London: Bell, 1970), vol. 2, 1/7/61; vol. 7, 21/11/66; vol. 6, 4/12/66.

17. Sarah Kemble Knight, *Private Journal of Madam Knight on a journey from Boston to New York in the year 1704* (New York: Wilder & Campbell, 1825), pp. 43, 45, 54–55.

18. Diana de Marly, *Louis XIV and Versailles,* p. 123.

19. Rev. John Buckingham, *The Private Journals of the Expedition against Canada in the years 1710 and 1711* (New York: Wilder & Campbell, 1825), pp. 79, 81, 105, 111.

20. *A Calendar of Ridgely Family Letters, 1742–1899,* ed. L. de Valinger and V. Shaw, vol. 1 (Dover, Delaware: The Ridgely Family for Public Archives Commission, 1948), p. 73.

21. Ibid., pp. 69, 72, 73, 76, 78.

22. Rev. Jonathan Boucher, "Letters," *Maryland Historical Magazine* 7 (March 1912): 5.

23. César de Saussure, *A Foreign View of England in the Reigns of George I and George II,* trans. Mme van Muyden (London: John Murray, 1902), pp. 112–15.

24. Trustees, *An Account shewing the Progress of the Colony of Georgia* (London, 1741), pp. 37, 43, 59, 66.

25. [Anonymous] *A Voyage to Georgia, in 1735* (London: J. Wilfrid at 3 Fleur de Luce, 1737), p. 45.

26. William Hugh Grove, *Virginia in 1732, Travel Journal,* ed. G. Stiverson and P. Butler II, *Virginia Magazine of History and Biography,* 85 (1977): 29.

27. *Diary of Colonel Landon Carter of Sabine Hall 1752–1778,* vol. 1, ed. Jack Greene (Charlottesville, Va.: University Press of Virginia, 1965), pp. 212, 242, 281, 299, 444, 484.

28. Ibid., pp. 754, 950–51, 769, 902.

29. *Diary of Anne Green Winslow a Boston Schoolgirl in 1771*, ed. Alice M. Earle (Boston: Houghton Mifflin, 1894), pp. 2, 4–5, 7, 31–34, 20, 40, 67, 71, 63.

30. Philip Vickers Fithian, *Journal and Letters, 1773–74*, ed. H. Farish (Colonial Williamsburg, 1957), pp. 29, 36, 39, 57; *John Norton & Sons Merchants of London and Virginia, Papers of their Counting House 1750–1795*, ed. Frances Mason (Richmond, Va.: Dietz Press, 1937), p. 146. The servant's green coat is illustrated in Linda Baumgarten's *Eighteenth–Century Clothing at Williamsburg* (Williamsburg: Wallace Gallery Decorative Arts Publication, 1986) p. 68.

31. Fithian, *Journal and Letters*, pp. 124–25, 130, 69, 90.

32. *John Norton & Sons*, pp. 47, 72–73.

33. Ibid., pp. 101, 143, 156, 124.

34. Ibid., p. 330.

1. Thomas Jefferson, *Notes on the State of Virginia* (London: John Stockdale, Piccadilly, 1797), p. 273.

2. George Washington, *Accounts of Expenses 1775–1783*, ed. J. Fitzpatrick (Boston: Houghton Mifflin, 1917), dates as cited.

3. *The Particular Case of the Georgia Loyalists* (London: G. Wilkie, 71 St. Paul's Churchyard, 1783), p. 12.

4. Abigail Adams, *Letters of Mrs. Adams the wife of John Adams*, ed. her grandson Wilkins Carter (Boston, 1853), p. 120; *New Letters of Abigail Adams, 1789–1801*, ed. Stewart Mitchell (Boston: Houghton Mifflin, 1947), p. xxxiii.

5. Abigail Adams, *New Letters*, p. 13.

6. William Smith, *The History of the Province of New York* (London: Alenson, Piccadilly, 1776), pp. 270–71, 276.

7. Abigail Adams, *Letters*, p. 303.

8. Tom Paine, *Political Writings during the American and French Revolutions*, ed. Hypatia Bonner (London: Watts & Co., 1909), p. 77.

9. Abigail Adams, *Letters*, pp. 174–75.

10. Sarah Randolph, *The Domestic Life of Thomas Jefferson*, 3rd ed. (1871; rpt. Cambridge, Mass.: Harvard University Press, 1939), p. 45.

11. Abigail Adams, *Letters*, pp. 193, 199.

12. Ibid., p. 215.

13. Ibid., pp. 250–51.

14. Miss Adams, *Journal and Correspondence*, ed. her daughter, vol. 1 (New York: Willeys & Putnam, 1841), pp. 63, 38–39.

15. Miss Adams, *Journal and Correspondence*, vol. 2, p. 35.

16. Abigail Adams, *Letters*, pp. 255–58; *New Letters*, p. 35.

17. Isaac Weld, *Travels through the States of America and the Provinces of Upper and Lower Canada 1795–97* (London: John Stockdale, Piccadilly, 1799).

CHAPTER 5

The United States and Canada 1775–1800

18. Pehr Kalm, *Travels in North America*, vol. 2, p. 651.
19. Louis Philippe Comte de Ségur, *Memoirs*, ed. Eveline Cruckshanks (London: Folio Society, 1960), p. 155.
20. J. P. Brissot de Warville, *New Travels in the United States of America in 1788* (Dublin: P. Byrne, A. Grubner, W. Mellaye, 1792), pp. 378–80.
21. Ibid., p. 156.
22. Ibid., pp. 97, 143.
23. François-René Vicomte de Chateaubriand, *Voyage en Amérique*, ed. Léon Delbos (London: Williams & Norgate, 1886), p. 24; my translation.
24. Marquise de la Tour du Pin, *Recollections of the Revolution and the Empire*, trans. and ed. Walter Geer (New York: Brentano, 1920), pp. 189–91, 219.
25. Ségur, *Mémoires*, p. 70.
26. Tour du Pin, *Recollections*, pp. 220, 240–43.
27. *A Calendar of Ridgely Family Letters*, vol. 1, pp. 115, 123, 136, 139, 148, 159, 166, 168.
28. Henry Wansey, *An Excursion to the United States of America in 1794* (London: J. Eaton, 1798), pp. 1–5, 11.
29. Ibid., pp. 30, 33, 48, 68, 70, 81, 87, 88.
30. Ibid., pp. 113, 115–16, 167, 175, 197–99.
31. Isaac Weld, *Travels*, pp. 56, 144.
32. Ibid., pp. 201, 217, 454, 409.
33. Samuel Hearne, *Journey from the Prince of Wales's Fort in Hudson Bay to the North Ocean, 1769–1777* (London: A. Strahan, T. Cadell, Strand, 1795), pp. 50, 305–6, 323.
34. Captain George Vancouver, *Voyage of Discovery to the North Pacific Ocean 1790–1795*, 2 vols. (London: G. & J. Robinson, Paternoster Row, 1798), vol. 1, pp. 253, 263; vol. 2, p. 197.
35. François Duc de La Rochefoucauld Liancourt, *Travels in the United States, the Country of the Iroquois, and Upper Canada* (London: R. Philip, 1799), p. 316.
36. Ibid., pp. 273–74.
37. Abigail Adams, *New Letters*, p. 248.
38. Ibid., p. 61.
39. Jane Austen, *Northanger Abbey* (London: John Murray, 1818), p. 157.
40. La Rochefoucauld Liancourt, *Travels*, p. 681.
41. B. de Warville, *New Travels*, p. 447.

APPENDIX I

English Cloth and Clothing Exports to the American Colonies and Canada

1. Public Record Office, Chancery Lane, London, Group E, Class 190, ms. 47/3. The majority of the registers are unfoliated.
2. Ibid., ms. 61/5; ms. 113/7.
3. Ibid., ms. 119/8.
4. Ibid., ms. 119/7.
5. Ibid., ms. 144/1.
6. Ibid., ms. 151/5.

7. Ibid., ms. 156/5.
8. Ibid., ms. 160/6.
9. Public Record Office, Kew, Cust. 2/2, 1696–97, f. 59.
10. Ibid., ff. 103–6.
11. Ibid., f. 107.
12. Ibid., f. 116.
13. Ibid., f. 123.
14. Ibid., f. 132.
15. Cust. 2/4, 1697–98, f. 39.
16. Ibid., f. 40.
17. Ibid., f. 45.
18. Ibid., f. 49.
19. Ibid., f. 50.
20. Public Record Office, Kew, Cust. 3/11–13, 1701–1710. This series is on microfilm and is mostly unfoliated.
21. Ibid.
22. Ibid.
23. Ibid.
24. Cust. 3/50, 1750.
25. Ibid.
26. Ibid.
27. Ibid.
28. Cust. 3/70, 1770.
29. Ibid.
30. Ibid.

1. John Smith, *Chronicon Rusticum Commercial; or Memoirs of Wool,* vol. 2 (London: Gray's Inn, 1747), pp. 227–28.
2. Ibid., p. 158.
3. Ibid., pp. 262–65. The volumes were reprinted by Augustus Kelley in New York in 1969.

APPENDIX II

The Commencement of American Cloth Production

Bibliography

Adams, Abigail. *Letters of Mrs. Adams the wife of John Adams.* 2 vols. Edited by Wilkins Carter. Boston, 1853.

———. *New Letters of Abigail Adams, 1788–1801.* Edited by Stewart Mitchell. Boston: Houghton Mifflin, 1947.

Adams, Miss. *Journal and Correspondence.* Edited by her daughter.

Les Annales de l'Hôtel Dieu de Quebec, 1636–1716. 1939.

Austen, Jane. *Northanger Abbey.* London: John Murray, 1818.

Baumgarten, Linda. *Eighteenth-Century Clothing at Williamsburg.* Williamsburg: Wallace Gallery Decorative Arts Publication, 1986.

Bibliotheca Lindesiana. *A Bibliography of Royal Publications of the Tudor and Stuart Sovereigns, 1485–1714.* 6 vols. Oxford: Clarendon Press, 1910.

Boucher, Rev. Jonathan. "Letters," *Maryland Historical Magazine,* 85 (1912).

Bradford, William. *History of the Plymouth Plantation.* Boston: Massachusetts Historical Society, 1912.

Buckingham, Rev. John. *The Private Journals of the Expedition against Canada in the years 1710 and 1711.* New York: Wilder & Campbell, 1825.

Bulwer, John. *Anthropometamorphosis: Man Transform'd, or the Artificial Changeling.* London: 1650.

Byrd, William of Westover. *The Secret Diary, 1709–1712.* Edited by L. Wright and M. Tinling. Richmond, Va.: Dietz Press, 1941.

———. *Another Secret Diary.* Edited by L. Wright and M. Tinling. Richmond, Va.: Dietz Press, 1942.

———. *The London Diary, 1717–1721.* Edited by L. Wright and

M. Tinling. Oxford: Oxford University Press, 1958.

Carter, Col. Landon of Sabine Hall. *Diary, 1752–1778.* Edited by Jack Greene. Charlottesville: University Press of Virginia, 1965.

Cartier, Jacques. *First Account of J. Cartier of St. Mâlo of the New Land called New France, 1534.* In J. Pinkerton, *General Collection of Voyages. 17 vols.* London, 1812.

Carver, Jonathan, Captain. *Travels through the Interior Parts of North America in 1766–68.* London: J. Walter, Charing Cross, 1778.

Chapais, Thomas. *The Great Intendant, 1655–1672.* Toronto, 1920.

Chateaubriand, François René Vicomte de. *Voyage en Amérique.* Edited by Leon Delbos. London: Williams & Norgate, 1886.

Columbus, Christopher. *The Writings of Christopher Columbus.* Edited by Paul Ford. New York: Charles Webster & Co., 1892.

———. *Journal of the First Voyage.* In *The Northmen, Columbus and Cabot: Original Narratives in Early American History.* Edited by Julius Olsen and Edward Boure. New York: Charles Scribner's Sons, 1906.

Conner, Jeannette Thurber. *Colonial Records of Spanish Florida from 1570.* Tallahassee: Florida Historical Society, 1925.

Considérations sur l'Etat de Canada, 1758. Québec: Literary and Historical Society of Québec, Historical Documents, series 1, 1836–1861.

Coronado, Francisco Vásquez de. *Muster Roll and Equipment in the Expedition of Francisco Vásquez de Coronado.* Translated by Artur Aiton. William Clements Library, 1939.

———. *Narrative of the Expedition of Francisco Vásquez de Coronado by P. Castanedo.* Edited by F. Hodge. In *Spanish Explorers of the Southern United States.* New York: Charles Scribner's Sons, 1907.

Crèvecoeur, St. John de. *Sketches of Eighteenth-Century America.* Edited by Bourdin, Gabriel, and Williams. New Haven: Yale University Press, 1925.

de Marly, Diana. *Louis XIV and Versailles.* London: Batsford, 1987; New York: Holmes & Meier, 1987.

———. *Working Dress.* London: Batsford, 1986; New York: Holmes & Meier, 1987.

A Description of the Province of South Carolina. Charleston, 1732.

A Description of South Carolina. London: J. Dodsley, Pall Mall, 1761.

Doyon, Madeleine. "Le Costume Traditionel Feminin." *Les Archives de Folklore.* Laval University, 1946.

Dürer, Albrecht. *Schriftlicher Nachlass.* Edited by H. Rupprich. Berlin, 1956.

Edits, Ordonnances Royaux, Declarations et Arrets de Conseil du Roi. Canada, 1803.

Elvas, Gentleman of. *Narrative of the Expedition of Hernando de Soto.* Edited by T. Hayes Lewis. In *Spanish Explorers of the Southern United States.* New York: Charles Scribner's Sons, 1907.

Fiennes, Celia. *The Illustrated Journeys, c. 1682–1712.* Edited by C. Morris. London: Macdonald, Webb & Bower, 1982.

Fithian, Philip Vickers. Journal and Letters, 1773–74. Edited by H. Farish. Colonial Williamsburg, 1957.

Fox, George. *Journal.* London: The Society of Friends, 1891.

General History of Connecticut. London: J. Bew, Pater Noster Row, 1781.

Grove, Hugh William. *Virginia in 1732, Travel Journal.* Edited by G. Stiverson and P. Butler II. *Virginia Magazine of History and Biography,* 85 (1977).

Guillemeau, Charles. *De la Grossesse et accouchement des femmes.* Paris, 1620.

Hakluyt, Richard. *Divers Voyages touching the Discoverie of America and the Islands Adjacent.* London: Thomas Wodocke, St. Paul's Churchyard, 1582.

———. *True Pictures and Fashions of the People in that Parte of America now called Virginia discovered by Englishmen, 1585–88.* Illustrated by John White. London: Theodore de Bry, 1590.

———. *Worthy and Famous History of the Travailes, Discovery and Conquest of that Good Continent of Terra Florida.* London: Matthew Lownes at Sign of the Bishop's Head, 1611.

Hartwell, Blair, and Chilton. *The Present State of Virginia in 1697.* Charlottesville: University Press of Virginia, 1940.

Heads of Inquiry relative to the Present State and Condition of His Majesty's Colony of Connecticut. London: T. Green, 1775.

Hearne, Samuel. *Journey from the Prince of Wales's Fort in Hudson's Bay to the North Ocean, 1769–1772.* London: A. Strahan, T. Cadell, Strand, 1795.

Hennepin, Louis. *Description de la Louisiana nouvellement decouverte.* Paris: Widow Sebastien, rue St. Jacques, 1683.

The History of Virginia to 1720. London: Fayram & Clarke, Royal Exchange, 1720.

Inspector General of Customs, Cust 2/2, 2/4; Cust 3/11–13, 3/50, 3/70.

Jeaffreson, Christopher. *A Young Squire of the Seventeenth Century.* Edited by J. C. Jeafferson. London, 1878.

Jefferson, Thomas. *Notes on the State of Virginia.* London: John Stockdale, Piccadilly, 1787.

Jones, Rev. Hugh. *The Present State of Virginia.* London: J. Clarke at the Bible, Royal Exchange, 1724.

Kalm, Pehr. *Travels in North America in 1750.* 2 vols. Revised by Adolph Benson. New York: Wilson-Erickson, 1937.

King, Jonathan. *The Mayflower Miracle.* London: David & Charles, 1987.

Kirck, Abraham. *Brief Relation of the State of New England.* London: Richard Baldwin at the Black Bull, Old Bailey, 1689.

Knight, Sarah Kemble. *Private Journal of Madam on a journey from Boston to New York in the year 1704.* New York: Wilder & Campbell, 1825.

Lahontan, Baron Louis Armand de Lom d'Arce. *New Voyages to North America.* 2 vols. London: H. Bonwicke, St. Paul's Churchyard, 1703.

Leroy, Alphonse, Dr. *Récherches sur les habillements des femmes et des enfants.* Paris: Le Boucher, Quai des Augustins, 1772.

Locke, John. *Some Thoughts Concerning Education.* London, 1693.

Mauriçeau, François. *The Accomplisht Midwife.* Translated by H. Chamberlen. London, 1693.

Mémoire sur le Canada. Québec: Literary and Historical Society of Québec, Historical Documents, series 1, 1838–1861.

Minutes of Town Courts 1652–1691 [Newton, New York]. Edited by Henry Black. New York Historical Records Survey, 1940.

Norton, John. *John Norton & Sons Merchants of London and Virginia: Papers of their counting house, 1750–1795.* Edited by Frances Mason. Richmond, Virginia: Dietz Press, 1937.

Paine, Tom. *Political Writings during the American and French Revolutions.* Edited by Hypatia Bonner. London: Watts & Co., 1909.

The Particular Case of the Georgia Loyalists. London: G. Wilkie, 71 St. Paul's Churchyard, 1783.

Penn, William. *Account of the Lenni Lengs and Delaware Indians.* Edited by Albert Myers. London, 1683; rpt. Philadelphia, 1937.

Pepys, Samuel. *The Diary.* Edited by Robert Latham and William Matthews. London: Bell, 1970–1980.

Pickering, Danby, ed. *Statutes at Large.* Cambridge, England, 1763.

du Pin, Marquise de la Tour. *Recollections of the Revolution and the Empire.* Translated by Walter Geer. New York: Brentano, 1920.

Prescott, William. *The Conquest of Mexico.* 2 vols. London: Everyman's Library, Dent, 1948.

The Present State of the Country, Inhabitants, European and Indian, of Louisiana. London, 1744.

Prynne, William. *The Unlovelinesse of Lovelocks.* London, 1628.

Public Record Office, London. Port of London ledgers E/190, ms. 47/s, 6/5, 113/7, 119/8, 119/7, 144/1, 151/5, 156/5, 160/6.

Randolph, Sarah. *The Domestic Life of Thomas Jefferson.* 3d. ed. Cambridge, Mass.: Harvard University Press, 1939.

Ribault, Jean. *True and Last Discoverie of Florida.* Translated by Thomas Hackit. London: 1562.

Ridgely Family. *A Calendar of Ridgely Family Letters, 1742–1899.* 3 vols. Edited by L. Valinger and V. Shaw. Dover, Delaware: The Ridgely Family for Public Archives Commission, Delaware State Archives, 1948.

La Rochefoucauld Liancourt, Duc François de. *Travels in the United States, the Country of the Iroquois, and Upper Canada.* London: R. Philip, 1799.

Saussure, César. *A Foreign View of England in the Reigns of George I and George II.* Translated by Mme. van Muyden. London: John Murray, 1902.

Ségur, Louis Philippe de, Comte. *Memoirs.* Edited by Eveline Cruckshanks. London: Folio Society, 1960.

Smith, Captain John. *The Generall Historie of Virginia, New England and the Summer Isles.* London: Michael Sparkes, 1624.

Smith, John. *Chronicon Rusticum Commercial; or Memoirs of Wool.* 2 vols. London: Gray's Inn, 1747.

Smith, William. *The History of the Province of New York.* London: Alenson, Picadilly, 1776.

Ursins, Princess des. *Lettres inédités de Madame Maintenon et Madame la Princesse des Ursins.* Paris, 1826.

Vancouver, Capt. George, RN. *Voyage of Discovery to the North Pacific Ocean, 1790–1795.* 2 vols. London: G. & J. Robinson, Paternoster Row, 1798.

Verney, Lady Frances, editor. *Letters and Papers of the Verney Family.* London: Longmans, 1853.

A Voyage to Georgia in 1735. London: J. Wilfrid, 3 Fleur de Luce, 1737.

Wansey, Henry. *An Excursion to the United States of America in 1794.* London: J. Eaton, 1798.

Ward, Ned. *A Trip to New England with a Character of the Country and People, both English and Indian.* London, 1699.

Warville, Brissot de. *New Travels in the United States of America in 1788.* Dublin: P. Byrne, A. Grubner, W. Mellaye, 1792.

Washington, George. *Accounts of Expenses, 1775–1783.* Edited by J. Fitzpatrick. Cambridge, Mass.: Houghton Mifflin, 1917.

Weld, Isaac. *Travels through the States of America and the Provinces of Upper and Lower Canada, 1795–1797.* London: John Stockdale, Picadilly, 1799.

Williams, Roger. *A Key into the Language of America.* London: Gregory Dexter, 1643.

Wilson, Samuel. *An Account of the Province of Carolina in America.* London: G. Larkin for F. Smith, Elephant Castle &, Cornhill, 1683.

Winslow, Anne Green. *Diary of a Boston Schoolgirl in 1771.* Edited by Alice Earle. Boston: Houghton & Mifflin, 1894.

Winslow, Edward. *A Relation or Journal of the beginnings & proceedings of the English plantation at Plimouth in New England.* London: John Bellamie, at the Two Greyhounds, Cornhill, 1622.

———. *Goode Newes from New England.* London: William Bladen & John Bellamie, at the Bible, St. Paul's Churchyard, & 3 Golden Lions, 1624.

Winthrop, John. *Journal, 1630–1649.* 2 vols. Edited by James Hosner. New York: Charles Scribner's Sons, 1908.

———. *History of New England from 1630–1649.* 2 vols. New York: Franklin's Original Narrators of Early American History, 1908.

Wright, Louis. *Cultural Life in the American Colonies, 1607–1763.* New York: Harper Brothers, 1957.

Index

Page numbers in italic type refer to illustrations.

Adams, Abigail, 132–34, 137–44, 145, 163, 168, *171*
Age of Reason, fashion and, 81, 103, 112
Allerton, Isaac, 30
American Revolution, 13, 129–30, 131–36
Austen, Jane, 164
Aztecs, dress of, 5–11

Barbadoes, imports to, 176. *See also* West Indies
Baroque style, vs. classical, 103
Bavolet, 65, 69, 70, 116
Bavolettes, 68–69
Beaucourt, François, *157, 158*
Bedgown, 93, 133–38. *See also* Undress
Berczy, William, *160*
Boone, Daniel, frontier dress, 169
Boston, 32–35, 37, 54, 85–86, 119–23. *See also* Massachusetts Bay
Boucher, François, *107*
Boucher, Reverend Jonathan, 99–100
Bradford, William, 28, 30
Brant, Joseph, 158–59, *160, 161*
Britain. *See* England; English dress
Brunais, Augustin, *116, 117*
Buckingham, Reverend John, 96, 97
Bulwer, John, 72–73
Bundling, 91

Burke, Edmund, 129
Burrough, Edward, 46
Byrd, William, 92

Cabot, John, 3–4, 22, 61–62
Canada: baby swaddling in, 47, 71–73, 123; British dress in, 3, 162; French dress in, 62–76, *68,* 79–80, 82, 156–58; fur trade in, 63–64; imports to, 66–67, 157, 181, 194, 195, 197; Indian dress in, 3–4, 61–62, 76, 158–61, *160, 161*; and Seven Years' War, 82–83; textile production in, 74–78, 156–62. *See also* Hudson's Bay
Caraco, 115, *139*
Carolina, 87–88; dress in, 57, 101, 103; imports to, 88, 176, 177, 179, 180, 181–82, 185–86, 192. *See also* South Carolina
Carter, Colonel Landow, 115–19
Carter, Robert, 124
Cartier, Jacques, 4–5, 61–65
Carver, Jonathan, 83–84
Catholics, Canadian, 56, 65, 83
Chamberlen, Hugh, 71–72. *See also* Head binding; Swaddling
Chamberlin, Mason, *111*
Champlain, Samuel, 63–64
Chapeau à la Charlotte, 106
Chapeau-bras, 117
Chapeau jockei (jockey), 106
Charles V, 9, 11
Charles I, 33, 55
Charles II, 46, 52, 55–56, 57, 92, 94
Charlestown, Mass., 32. *See also* Massachusetts Bay

Charlestown, S.C., 87–88. *See also* Carolina; South Carolina

Charlestown, Va., 50–51. *See also* Virginia

Chateaubriand, François René de, 147–48

Chemise, *59*, 109, 152, *155*, 163, *171*

Chemise à la reine, 109, *140*, 152. *See also* Chemise

Chickatabot (Chief), 26

Children's dress, 47, 72–74, 113–14, *123*, 142, 151. *See also* Swaddling

Chomedy, Paul de, 64

Classical style, 81, 110, *140*, 146, 152, 162–67, 170–72, *170*, *171*. *See also* Naturalist movement; Neoclassical look

Clergy, dress of, *44*, 97

Codex Mendoza, 6–10. *See also* Indian dress

Colonial dress: in Europe, 136–44; French style in, 105, 147–50; influence on French, 106–9; and Indian dress, 21, 29, 91; Pilgrim, 29–35; Puritan, 28, 31–38, 42, 46, 98; Quaker, 45, *55*, 112, *121*, 137, 144–45, *171*. *See also* English dress; French dress; *specific colony*

Columbus, Christopher, 1–3

Connecticut: dress in, 95; imports to, 89; Indian customs in, 91; manufacturing in, 89–90, 154; textile production in, 200

Copley, John Singleton, *108*, *110*, *113*

Cortés, Hernando, 5–9, 11

Court dress, English, 108, 142

Court dress, French, 52–53, 75, 106, 108, *123*, 136–44, *139*, *140*, 148–50

Creole dress, 106–9, *139*

Crèvecoeur, St. John de, 90–91

Customs and Excise Ledgers, 189–198. *See also* Imports

Dare, Virginia, 15

Decoration. *See* Ornament

Directoire look, *164*

Drake, Sir Francis, 14

Dürer, Albrecht, 9–10

Dutch dress, 26, 42, 51, 133–34

Earl, Ralph, *126*, *165*

Edict of Nantes (1685), 50

Edward III, 23, 35, *126*

England: baby swaddling in, 72–73; clothing exports from, 60, 86–91, 127–30, 151–52, 157, 175–198; defeat of French by, 83. *See also* English dress

English dress, 105; court fashions and, 108, 142; fashion extremes in, 114; versus French fashion, 105; and Indians, 76–77, 85. *See also* Colonial dress

Eskimo dress, *11*, *12*

Exchequer Port Books, 175–76. *See also* Imports

Fabric. *See specific fabric*; Textile industry

Fabric, dyed, 28, *34*, 35, 90, *91*, *146*, 152

Featherwork, 6–10, *8*, *14*, 20–21. *See also* Indian dress; Mexico

Ferdinand of Aragon (King of Spain), 1–3

Fithian, Philip, 124–25

Florida: exploration of, 11; French Huguenots in, 63; imports to, 88–89, 195–96; Indian dress in, 11–14, *12*, *13*; Spanish in, 48

Fox, George, 45–46, 49

France: and American Revolution, 129–30; in Canada, 62–76, 79–80; in New Orleans, 78–79; and trade with colonies, 78. *See also* French court; French dress

François I, 61–62

Franklin, Benjamin, *111*, 136–37 *136*, *143*, *144*, *145*

French court, 45, 49, 63, 65–66, 73, 75, 77, 79, *108*, *123*, *139*, 142; in America, 148–50; colonists in, 136–44; fashion imports and, 106–9, *139*; influence of, 45, 52–53, 75; traditions of, 142. *See also specific member*

French dress, 4, 45, 50–51, 105; baby swaddling and, 72–73; clothing laws and, 66; peasant styles in 68–71, 83, *116*; Rococo style in, 103–7; as social comment, 144. *See also* Court dress, French; French court

French East India Company, 66

French Huguenots, 50, 63
French Revolution, 147–50, 167
Fur trade, 82–83

Galérie des Modes, 105–6, *139*, *140*, *141*
General History of Virginia (Smith), 32
George IV, 104
Georgia: dress in, 100–3; imports to, 192, 196; Indian dress in, 102–3; textile production in, 101
German Quakers, 50
Gold, as decoration, 2–3, 6, 9–10, 45, 74–75
Grenville, Sir Richard, 14
Grisettes, 68. *See also* Canada, French dress in; French dress
Grand habit, 108. *See also* Court dress
Guillemeau, Charles, 71–72. *See also* Swaddling

Hair styles, 122–23, 138, 153, 166; commode headdress, 95, 103; and height, *113*, 122–25, 138; horizontal fashion, 103, 138; Indian, 4–5, 102–3; powdered, 146, 162; wigs, 93, 97, *98*, 107, 110, 125, *142*, *157*. *See also* Headcoverings
Head binding, *68*, 71–73. *See also* Swaddling
Headcoverings, 38, 40, 44, 95, 106, 114, *116*, 120–23, 125, 134, *147*, 151–52, 153–54, *158*. *See also* Hair styles
Headdress, 122–23, 138–39, *147*. *See also* Hair styles; Headcoverings
Hearne, Samuel, 159
Heddus roll, 122. *See also* Hair styles
Hennepin, Louis, 78
Henry VII, 3
Heraldry, in Mexico, 6–8
Hogarth, William, *190*
Hollar, Wenceslaus, *42*
Homespun cloth, 150–51, 168, 200–1
Homespun movement, 118, 131, 145, 168, 171
Hoops, 79, *98*, 103–5, 134, 138
Hudson, Sir Henry, 30, 64

Hudson's Bay, imports to, 177–78, 179, 182–83, 186–87, 192, 196. *See also* Canada
Hudson's Bay Company, 64, 159
Huguenots, French, 50, 63

Imports, 60, 66–67, 86–89, 154, 157, 175–98; necessity of, 29, 60, 86–90, 129–32, 201; as status symbol, 168; and tariffs, 129–32. *See also* Textile industry; Trade laws; *specific colony*
Indian dress, 11–26, 148, 152; baby swaddling, 73; of the Bahamas, 2; in Boston, 85–86; and British soldiers, *160*; in Canada, 3–4, 61–62, 63, 76–77, 158–61, *161*; clothing exchanges and, 29, 47, 71; and English clothing, 76–77, 84, 85; European influence on, 26, 71, 78, 81–82; in Florida, 11–14, *12*, *13*; in Georgia, 102–3; in Jamaica, 3; in Louisiana, 78, 83–84; in Mexico, 5–11, *6*, *8*; in New England, 21–26; in Newfoundland, 3–4, 62; social rank and, 9; in Virginia, 15–21, *15*, *16*, *17*, *18*, *20*
Indiennes, 78
Inspector General's Accounts, 181–89. *See also* Imports
Isabella of Castile (Queen of Spain), 1–3

Jacket, 93
Jamaica, imports to, 176; Indians in, 3. *See also* West Indies
James II, 56
Jamestown, 19–21, 86. *See also* Virginia
Jeaffreson, Christopher, 58
Jefferson, Thomas, 131–32, 136–37, 171
Johnson, Colonel Guy, *160*
Johnson, Sir William, 158

Kalm, Pehr, 58, 80–83, 89, 91–92, 95, 144
Kirk, Captain David, 63
Knapton, George, *106*
Knight, Sarah Kemble, *94*, 94–95
Kuhn, Justus, 96

Laborers' dress. *See* Working-class dress

Lahontan, Baron, 73–76, 79
Latrobe, Benjamin, *166, 167, 170, 174*
Laudonnière, René de la, 63, Plate I. *See also* Florida
Lee, William, *155*
Lely, Sir Peter, 94
le Nain, Louis, *68, 116*
Leroy, Dr. Alphonse, 73. *See also* Swaddling
Linen, 88, 91, 101, 103, 119, 154, 156, 158
Linsey-woolsey, 101
Locke, John, 56, 72–73, 113
Louis XIV, 45, 49, 52, 63, 65, 66, 73, 75, 77, 79, 142
Louisiana: dress in, 106–9, 117; Indian dress in, 78, 83–84. *See also* New Orleans

Macaronis, 114
Makeup, 2, 6, 11, 24, 111–12
Mantua gown (*manto, manteau*), 53, 86, 96, *102, 104, 105, 108, 113, 155*
Manufacturing. *See* Textile industry
Marie Antoinette, *106,* 108, 123, 138, *139, 140,* 142, 163
Marina, 9. *See also* Mexico, Indian dress in
Mary II, 56
Maryland, boycott of English goods, 128; imports to, 177, 178, 185, 188–89, 191, 197; textile production in, 200
Massachusetts Bay, 200; 201. *See also* Boston; Charlestown, Mass.
Matoaka, *32. See also* Pocahontas
Mauriçeau, François, 71
Mayflower, 28
Menendez Marquez, Pedro, 88
Men's dress, 51, 62, *98,* 169, 172; decoration in, 40, 120, *146;* headcoverings, 38, 40, 95, 112, 153–54, *158,* 172; naturalist movement and, 164; three-piece suit, 52, 109; trousers, 112, 149; wigs, 93, 97, 110, 125, *142;* working-class, 99, *117*
Mexico, Indian dress in, 5–11
Michelin, Jean, *70*
Montezuma, 5–6, 8–9
Montréal, 64, 67, 75–76, 82, 157
Moravians, dress of, 157–58

Morton, Thomas, 38
Muche, 94, 95
Muslin, 59, 60, 108–9, 137, *140,* 142, *163,* 168
Mytens, Daniel, *33*

Naturalist movement, 106–15, 149, *164,* 166. *See also* Classical style; Neoclassical look
Navigation Acts, 58, 83. *See also* Trade laws
Neoclassical look, *81, 146,* 152, 164, *165,* 169, 170–72, *170, 171*
New Amsterdam, 30. *See also* New York
New England: imports to, 86, 176, 177, 178, 179, 180, 183–84, 187, 192–93; Indian dress in, 21–26; textile production in, 199–200. *See also specific colony; state*
Newfoundland, 79; imports to, 181; Indian dress in, 3–4, 61–62. *See also* Canada
New France, 47, 63–66, 83
New Hampshire, textile production in, 200
New Jersey, textile production in, 199
New Orleans: as first colony, 49; French colonists in, 78–79, 83; influence on French style of, 106–9. *See also* Louisiana
New Plymouth, 29–31, *37*
New York, 90; clothes production in, 90–91; dress in, 95, 133–34, 146; imports to, 90, 176, 178, 179, 183, 187–88, 189–90, 193–94; textile production in, 90, 199, 200, 201. *See also* New Amsterdam
Nightgown, as fashion, 91, 105, 122. *See also* Bedgown; Undress
Northanger Abbey (Austen), 164
Norton, John, 127, 128–29, 152
Nova Scotia, 64, 79, 83; imports to, 194, 197

Oglethorpe, James, 100
Ornament: body paint, 2, 6, *162;* feathers, 5, 6, 8–9; gold, 2–3, 6, 9–10, 45, 74–75; large buttons, 40, 51, 62, 120, *146,* 150; makeup, 2, 6, 11, 24, 111–12; tattoos, 12, *13,* 17

Paine, Tom, 135–36, 167
Palla, 163
Pasqualigo, Pietro, 4
Peasant dress. *See* Canada, French
    dress in; Working-class dress
Penn, William, 47, 146
Pennsylvania, 47, 89, 91, 120, 144–
    45; imports to, 89, 177, 188,
    191, 194; textile production in,
    199, 200, 201. *See also* Quaker
    dress.
Pepys, Samuel, 52, 92–94
Petite Académie, 52
Phipps, Sir William, 66
Pilgrim dress, 29–35
Pilgrim Hall, 31
Pioneer settlers, 169
Plantation dress, 58, 115–119, *116,*
    117, 124–5, 129. *See also* Slave
    dress
Plymouth plantation, 21–23, 28
Pocahontas, 18, *20, 32,* 50. *See also*
    Matoaka
Polonaise jacket, *123, 139*
Pompadour, Madame de, 105–7,
    107, 122, 123
Port of London Registers, 176–81
Pring, Martin, 38
Prynne, William, 38
Puritan dress, 28, 31–38, *42, 44, 46,*
    98. *See also* Colonial dress;
    English dress; Pilgrim dress
Puritans, 45–46, 162. *See also*
    Puritan dress

Quaker dress, 45, *55,* 112, 121, 137,
    144–45, 171
Quakers: influence on fashion, 58;
    German, 50; homespun
    movement and, 145; and
    Puritans, 45–46. *See also* Quaker
    dress
Québec, dress in, 63–64, 74–75,
    80–81, 156–57. *See also* Canada
Québec City, 80. *See also* Canada;
    Québec
Queen Anne, 95
Queen Charlotte, 123
Queen Isabella, 1–3

Raleigh, Sir Walter, 14
Ramillies, 111. *See also* Wigs
Raspal, Antoine, *81, 123*
Rayon, 86

Ready-made clothing, 57, 60, 190.
    See also Textile industry
*Récherches sur les habillements des
    femmes et des enfans* (Leroy), 73.
    See also Swaddling
Redingote, 164, *165*
Repentigny, Madame de, first
    Canadian textile manufacturer,
    76
Rhode Island, textile production
    in, 200
Ridgely family, 97–99, 150–52
Riley, John, 58
Robe à la françoise, 105
Robe à la Marlborough, 106, *141*
Robe à l'angloise, 105, 106, *141*
Roche, Jean François de la, 62, 64,
    65
Rochefoucauld Liancourt, Duc
    François de la, 149, 162–63,
    164, 168
Rococo style, 103–4, *106, 107*
Romantic movement, and dress,
    81, 112, 149, *151,* 163
Rousseau, Jean Jacques, 73, 115
ruffs, 31–32, 42

Sacque gown (sackback), 105, *141*
Samoset, 22, 29
Savage, Edward, *155*
Seven Years' War, 82–83
Shaker dress, 149
Sherman, Roger, 126
Shoe styles, 43, 103, 148, 160, 169–
    71
Siamoises, 78–79
Silk, 50, 57, 75, 78, 86, 88, 101, 125,
    168
Slater, Samuel, 168
Slave dress, 56, 88–89, 101, 115–
    19, 124, 129. *See also* Plantation
    dress
Smith, Captain John, 19–21, *20*
Smith, John, 199
Smith, William, 133
Social rank, and dress, 9, 28, 31,
    34, 35–38, 42–44, 52, 53–54, 76,
    101, 112–15, 126, 128, 144. *See
    also* Sumptuary laws
Soto, Hernando de, 11
South Carolina, 50, 87. *See also*
    Carolina; Charlestown
Spain: explorations in New World,
    1–3, 5, 48; contact with Indians,
    11–14; in the Seven Years' War, 83

Speedwell, 28
Squanto, 29
Standish, Captain Myles, 30, 38
Style, American national, 144–50, 168
Sugarloaf hat, 55, 121, 152
Sumptuary laws, 35–38, 54–56, 66–67
Swaddling, 47, *68*, 71–73, 113–14, *123*. *See also* French dress; Head binding

Talon, Jean, 66, 74
Teuhtile, 5
Textile industry, 60, 74–79, 86, 89–90, 118, 131, 145, 152–56, 168, 171, 199–201
Tignon, 116
Toleration Act (1690), 56
Tour du Pin, Marquise de la, 148–50
Trade laws, 38–41, 66–68, 83, 86–92, 167–68
Traité des Maladies des Femmes (Mauriçeau), 71. *See also* Swaddling
Tricorne, 112
Trousers, 101, 112, 149, 164, *166*
Trumbull, Jonathan, 89

Undress, 92–94, 106, 112, 144. *See also* Bedgown; Nightgown
United States: formation of, 162; presidential reception, 143; shoe manufacturing, 169–71; style in, 162–67, 171–72; textile production in, 152–56; trade with Britain, 151. *See also specific colony, state*

Van Dam, Rip, 201
van der Helst, Bartholomeus, *39*
van Mieris, Willem, *94*
Vancouver, Captain George, 159
Vàsquez de Coronado, Francisco, 11
Vaughan, Robert, *14*, 20
Verney, Thomas, 58, 60
Vêtement à la Créole, 106, 108, *139*. *See also* Creole dress
Virginia: dress in, 50–51, 92, 99–100, 103, 114, 124; economy of, 86; imports to, 86–87, 127–30, 175–76, 178, 179, 180, 185, 188–89, 191, 197; Indian dress in,

15–21, *15–18, 20*; shoe manufacturing in, 169–71; slave dress in, 156; textile production in, 86, 118, 131, 201

Wade, Robert, 46
Wansey, Henry, 152–56
Warville, Brissot de, 145–47, 149, 169
Washington, George, 132, 142–44, 154, *155*, 167
Washington, Martha Dandridge, 133, 142–43, 154, *155, 170*
Washington, Patsy Custis, 74, *164, 170*
Weenix, Jan, 49
Weiditz, Christophe, *8, 9, 10*
Weld, Isaac, 156–59, 169
West, Benjamin, *136, 160*
West India Company, 30
West Indies: English dress in, 58–60; imports to, 176; plantation dress in, 116–17
White, John, *12, 13, 14*–16, *15, 16, 17, 18*, 19, *24, 25*
Wigs, 93, 97, *98*, 110, 125, 142
William III, 56
Williams, Roger, 23–25
Williamsburg, 86. *See also* Virginia
Winslow, Anne Green, 119–24
Winslow, Edward, 22–23, 25, *37*, 38, 119
Winslow, John, 119
Winthrop, John, 26, 32, 46
Women's dress, 53; chemise, 59, 109, 152, *155*; for French Canadian working-class, 68, *69*; hoops, 79, 103–5, 138; mantua gown, 86, *96, 102, 104, 105*; naturalist movement and, 162–64; restrictions on, 32–36, 54–56, 66–68; undress, 92–94; for working-class, 42, 92–93. *See also* Hair styles; Headcoverings; Headdress; *specific costumes*
Working-class dress, 42, *48*, 53–54, 92–93, 99, 101, *126*, 133; dyed cloth and, 28, 34, 35, 90, 91, 146, 152; of French Canadians, 66–71, *116*; of French peasants, *81*, 83, 116; adapted by society, 114–115; sumptuary laws and, 54–56, 67
Wrapover dress, *139*